Learning Christ

A Contemporary Study of the Person and Work of Christ

LARRY HART

TruthAflame Press

Learning Christ

Copyright © 2017 by Larry Hart. All rights reserved worldwide.

All Scripture quotations, unless otherwise indicated, are taken from the Holy Bible, *New International Version*®, *NIV*®. Copyright © 1973, 1978, 1984, 2011 by Biblica, Inc.™ Used by permission of Zondervan. All rights reserved worldwide.

Copyrights of Other Bible Versions Used

ESV: *The Holy Bible: English Standard Version*, copyright © 2001 by Good News Publishers. Used by permission. All rights reserved.

NLT: *Holy Bible. New Living Translation* copyright © 1996, 2004, 2007 by Tyndale House Foundation. Used by permission of Tyndale House Publishers Inc., Carol Stream, Illinois 60188. All rights reserved.

HCSB: *Holman Christian Standard Bible*®, Copyright © 1999, 2000, 2002, 2003, 2009 by Holman Bible Publishers. Used by permission. All rights reserved.

NRSV: *New Revised Standard Version Bible*, copyright © 1989 the Division of Christian Education of the National Council of the Churches of Christ in the United States of America. Used by permission. All rights reserved.

CEV: *The Contemporary English Version*, copyright © 1995 by the American Bible Society. Used by permission. All rights reserved.

NJB: *New Jerusalem Bible*, copyright © 1985 by Darton, Longman & Todd Ltd. And Doubleday, a division of Bantam Doubleday Dell Publishing. Used by permission. All rights reserved.

NCV: *The Holy Bible, New Century Version*, copyright © 1987, 1988, 1991 by Word Publishing, Nashville, Tennessee. Used by permission. All rights reserved.

NAB: *The New American Bible*, copyright © 1986, 1991 by the Confraternity of Christian Doctrine, 3211 Fourth Street NE, Washington, D.C. Used by permission. All rights reserved.

CEB: *The Common English Bible,* copyright © 2011. Used by permission. All rights reserved.

Graphic Design by Kevin Hart

truthaflamepress.com

Table of Contents

Introduction 7

The Contemporary Christ:
*Knowing Christ in the Light of the Resurrection
and Christian Experience* 9

The Historical Quests for Jesus:
An Analysis of Historical Quests Past and Present 27

The Life and Ministry of Jesus:
A Brief Survey of the Life of Christ 51

The Witness of the New Testament:
New Testament Portraits of Jesus Christ 87

The Witness of the Church:
The Person of Christ in Historical Theology 133

A Contemporary Christology:
A Summary Christological Statement 145

The Work of Christ:
*The Doctrine of the Atonement in
Contemporary Perspective* 171

Christ and the Future:
Future Prospects in the Study of Christology 193

Conclusion 203

Introduction

It was nine o'clock in the morning when they crucified him. The inscription of the charge against him read, "The King of the Jews." And with him they crucified two bandits, one on his right and one on his left. Those who passed by derided him, shaking their heads and saying, "Aha! You who would destroy the temple and build it in three days, save yourself, and come down from the cross!" In the same way the chief priests, along with the scribes, were also mocking him among themselves and saying, "He saved others; he cannot save himself. Let the Messiah, the King of Israel, come down from the cross now, so that we may see and believe." Those who were crucified with him also taunted him.

When it was noon, darkness came over the whole land until three in the afternoon. At three o'clock Jesus cried out with a loud voice, "Eloi, Eloi, lema sabachthani?" which means, "My God, my God, why have you forsaken me?" (Mark 15:25–34 NRSV).

If Jesus' life ended here in utter failure and defeat, then all there is left to study is the "historical Jesus"—the story of a first-century Jewish man, long dead, comparable to Mohammed or Buddha in significance and influence. But Mark's gospel goes on to indicate mysterious subsequent events. As the messenger at the tomb reported to the women, "Do not be alarmed; you are looking for Jesus of Nazareth, who was crucified. He has been raised; he is not here. Look, there is the place they laid him" (Mark 16:6 NRSV).

Authentic Christianity begins here in its understanding of Christ. Followers of the risen Christ for two millennia have given testimony to a personal knowledge of him that is both historical and experiential in nature, engaging both the head and the heart. Furthermore,

Christians aver that Jesus' death was *not* a defeat, but rather provided a saving atonement for all mankind. In addition, the cross became the paradigm of discipleship. Jesus announced: "If any want to become my followers, let them deny themselves and take up their cross and follow me" (Mark 8:34 NRSV). According to the New Testament, true knowledge of Christ and discipleship are inseparable. The evidence of true discipleship of Jesus Christ is a changed life.

The apostle Paul depicted the moral depravity of the pagans and then reminded his readers: "That is not the way you learned Christ! For surely you heard about him and were taught in him, as the truth is in Jesus" (Eph. 4:20–21 NRSV). Notice the description of true discipleship as *learning Christ* and discovering the *truth that is in Jesus*. That is the essence of the Christian life, and that is the heart of any study of the person and work of Christ.

The purpose of this volume is to further aid followers of Jesus Christ in just that process. In other words, it is the working premise of this book that the study of Christology and personal discipleship go hand-in-hand. Only as true followers of the risen Christ can we as the church truly appreciate and declare the wonders of Christ and his benefits! It will be an exciting journey, which surely must begin with a consideration of the *contemporary Christ* who rules us, leads us by his Spirit, and brings us to the Father.

Lesson One

The Contemporary Christ

Knowing Christ in the Light of the Resurrection and Christian Experience

Luke Timothy Johnson is precisely correct when he asserts that it makes a great deal of difference whether we think Jesus is dead or alive.[1] In reality, this conclusion serves as the watershed of contemporary exploration into Jesus. Is Jesus Christ truly our contemporary or is this language simply the inflated rhetoric of an overly emotional and simplistic evangelicalism? Can we really "know Christ"? Jesus himself defined eternal life in terms of such knowledge. "Now this is eternal life: that they may know you, the only true God, and Jesus Christ, whom you have sent," said Jesus in his High Priestly Prayer (John 17:3).

> It makes a great deal of difference whether we think Jesus is dead or alive.

To be sure, there are both parallels and contrasts between the way we know Christ today and the way we know other contemporary persons. Jesus is not *physically* present now. We cannot simply look up his address and pay him a visit, call his cell phone, or contact him through the social media. Further, Jesus is more than a man, according to the classical Christian consensus. The Christian claim of his uniqueness sets him apart from a Confucius, a Buddha, or a Mohammed. Does anyone

---

[1] Luke Timothy Johnson, *Living Jesus: Learning the Heart of the Gospel* (San Francisco: HarperSanFrancisco, 1999), 3–6.

today claim to have a "personal relationship" with such figures? But if Jesus is truly divine then he becomes *the* revealer of the grace and power of God.[2] God sends his saving love to us in Jesus (John 3:16). "The love of God for the world takes public form in Jesus Christ. In him the glory of God blazes forth into the world. Risen from the dead, he is the proof of the truth and goodness of God. Through the Spirit he stands before every heart and asks to enter."[3] But how do we know and love someone who is invisible? How do we *learn Christ* in the twenty-first century?

THE JOY OF FAITH

Although all personal relationships involve faith—a commitment to trust and a vulnerability to hurt—the faith that is entailed in knowing the contemporary Christ goes further. The context is the divine/human encounter. All true knowledge of God requires a questing, persistent faith (Heb. 11:6). But this faith is a revelatory faith that brings joy! "You love him even though you have never seen him. Though you do not see him now, you trust in him; and you rejoice with a glorious, inexpressible joy. The reward for trusting him will be the salvation of yours souls" (1 Peter 1:8–9 NLT). C. S. Lewis discovered this truth in his journey out of atheism. Brought kicking and screaming like a child into God's sanctuary, he was "surprised by joy." But beyond that, he was captivated by God himself, and a whole new life ensued for Lewis.[4]

Thus, true knowledge of the contemporary Christ requires entrusting our lives to him in discipleship. We learn to walk by faith (Rom. 1:17; 2 Cor. 5:7). We develop a passion for Christ: "I want to know Christ—yes, to know the power of his resurrection and participation in his sufferings, becoming like him in his death, and so somehow, attaining to the resurrection from the dead"

---

2 Russell F. Aldwinckle, *More Than Man: A Study in Christology* (Grand Rapids: Eerdmans, 1976), 253.
3 Clark H. Pinnock and Robert C. Brow, *Unbounded Love: A Good News Theology for the 21st Century* (Downers Grove, IL: InterVarsity Press, 1994), 52.
4 C. S. Lewis, *Surprised by Joy* (New York: Harcourt Brace Jovanovich, 1955).

(Phil. 3:10–11). We are captivated by his Great Commandment (Mark 12:29–31) and his Great Commission (Matt. 28:18–20). His kingdom gospel becomes the purpose of our existence. The apostle Paul's passion is paradigmatic: "I don't care about my own life. The most important thing is that I complete my mission, the work that the Lord Jesus gave me—to tell people the Good News about God's grace (Acts 20:24 NCV). This authentic life of faith is foundational to learning Christ. Without this starting-point, all knowledge of Christ is only speculative and dispassionate. Such "knowledge" may satisfy some, but most will not settle for it. If Jesus is really there, we want to know him!

KNOWING CHRIST IN POSTMODERN CULTURE

This relational and experiential approach appeals to the postmodern mind. To learn Christ is to think relationally, communally. Our tripersonal God invites us to family and fellowship—to Christ and his church. The invitation to come and know Christ is a summons to the supernatural. People want authentic relationships, not sterile religious formalities. They want to *contact* the supernatural, not merely speculate about it. They are interested in the news about a "quest for the historical Jesus," but only as it applies ultimately to their personal experience of Christ, both personally and corporately.

> *To learn Christ is to think relationally, communally. Our tripersonal God invites us to family and fellowship—to Christ and his church.*

If Christianity were presented more as a movement, a Way (Acts 9:2; 16:17; 18:25–26; 19:9, 23; 22:4; 24:14, 22), and as a communal life (Acts 2:42–47), postmoderns would listen. They are already interested in Jesus, who *is* the way (John 14:6). As the book of Ephesians teaches us, true Christianity is about two things: (1) union with the person of Christ, and (2) fellowship with the body of Christ. So postmoderns are actually poised for discipleship. They easily become disciples these days, but in these perilous times there are numerous spurious paths they could take.

Leonard Sweet understands this tidal wave of change better than most. He writes:

> Say "I'm a Christian" to these [postmodern] pilgrims, and they flee for their lives. Say "I'm a disciple of Jesus," and they gather 'round to hear more. Postmoderns have stars in their eyes about Jesus and the stomach for a fight about Christianity. The "global boom" in books about Jesus, with an average of four new books coming out every single day, attests to the brightness of this one star in the postmodern firmament. Worldwide, more than sixty-six thousand books have been written about Jesus, claims missiologist David Barrett. The quest for the historical Jesus has never been more frenzied.[5]

The Incarnation was God's greatest incentive to think relationally. It shouts to present generations that Jesus means that we can have soul-satisfying relationships and community—with God at the center.

If God can just get us to think the way he does—relationally—then our message and ministry as Christ's body would know no bounds. Creative church leader Daniel Vestal says it well:

> To think relationally is to think incarnationally. Scripture doesn't say, "the Word became a computer chip." Rather it says, "the Word became flesh." Jesus was a real person. He was a living, loving, giving, forgiving, suffering and relating human being. We must do the same and be the same.
>
> To think relationally is to think communally. We don't relate simply as isolated individuals. We don't pray only in the first person singular. We're not alone in mission and ministry. Rather, we are radically interdependent beings, far more than we realize or understand.
>
> To think relationally is to think missiologically. The mission of the church is to incarnate the life and ministry of

---

[5] Leonard Sweet, *AquaChurch* (Loveland, CO: Group Publishing, 1999), 41.

Jesus and thus extend the mission of God in the world.

This is a blessed privilege, even in the postmodern world—especially in the postmodern world.[6]

Experience and relationships are at the heart of vital Christianity, but the question of truth must also be faced.

Postmoderns have largely abandoned the idea of ultimate truth. Truth is whatever works for you and your communal relations. Thus, any mythology can provide perspective and meaning, and Christianity must simply get in line. Postmodernism and Christianity are in mortal conflict on this point. Pilate's "What is truth?"—whether in jest, cynicism, or seriousness—is inescapable in every generation. Therefore, the historical quests for Jesus have great significance for contemporary Christians. N. T. Wright has hammered this fact home in his voluminous writings. A part of our learning Christ, really knowing him, is historical study of his life and ministry. Such study is even *necessary* to our discipleship.[7] Christian faith is rooted in history. Our paradigm pronounces history as "his story." Jews and Christians alike largely agree on this point: We recite stories when we rehearse our faith. There is an integral relation between faith and history.

FAITH AND HISTORY

N. T. Wright and Luke Timothy Johnson, two of the leading scholarly voices on Jesus, defend contrasting positions on this issue. How much of our faith is dependent upon historical research? Do the historians then become the ecclesial authorities on Christian faith and life? We want our faith to be rooted in the real world and in intellectual integrity. What roles do historical study, biblical scholarship, and historical theology play in our learning Christ? Perhaps the most satisfying answer to these and other searching queries lies in a

---

6   Daniel Vestal, "Think Relationally" in *Fellowship! Newsletter of the Cooperative Baptist Fellowship*, July-August 1999, 24.
7   N. T. Wright, *The Challenge of Jesus: Rediscovering Who Jesus Was and Is* (Downers Grove, IL: InterVarsity Press, 1999), 14.

synthesis of insights from these two opposing camps. Such a prospect is singularly appealing to the paradoxical postmodern mind!

We will begin with the insights of Luke Timothy Johnson. Many became aware of the wisdom of Johnson, when voices of sanity were being pursued in relation to the published radical, so-called "scholarly results" of the Jesus Seminar. Most serious New Testament scholars saw these much-publicized findings as so much Swiss cheese—more holes than substance. But precisely because the Jesus Seminar aggressively popularizes its work in the media, the general public needed sage response. That Luke Timothy Johnson provided, beginning with *The Real Jesus: The Misguided Quest for the Historical Jesus and the Truth of the Traditional Gospels*.[8] Wright himself praised Johnson's efforts.[9] The issue was never whether historical research related to Jesus was legitimate. The problem was whether the Jesus Seminar advocates had themselves learned the lessons of history.[10]

The whole dismal chronicle of historical Jesus quests clearly revealed the limitations of history and of the historical and literary methods of critical study. Because the focus is more on external events, history often lacks the personal detail one would desire, for example, in deriving a full portrait of a person or event. Johnson would add that even the Bible itself has limits in the historical and biographical information it provides.[11] I personally would differ with Johnson at this point and point to the work of Darrell Bock, for example, who has shown that the biblical portraits of Jesus are significantly richer than some scholars would allow.[12] But Johnson's more important point is that grounding our faith in Jesus in historical reconstruction is a cul-de-sac. Our knowledge of Christ entails a more full-orbed approach involving Church, Canon, Creed, and Christology. It involves

---

8 HarperSanFrancisco, 1996.
9 See opening recommendations.
10 Luke Timothy Johnson, *The Real Jesus* (San Francisco: HarperSanFrancisco, 1996) ix–x (preface to the paperback edition).
11 Johnson, *The Real Jesus*, 167, 171.
12 Darrell L. Bock, *Jesus according to Scripture: Restoring the Portrait from the Gospels* (Grand Rapids: Baker Academic, 2002). And in defense of Johnson, his subsequent volume provides substantive treatment of the gospel portraits of Jesus: *Living Jesus: Learning the Heart of the Gospel* (HarperSanFrancisco, 1999).

LEARNING CHRIST   15

our worship and ministry as well. We encounter Jesus both in the worshiping community and in the "little ones" we serve.[13]

N. T. Wright, however, is much more optimistic about the contributions rigorous historical investigations can provide. Indeed, without these efforts, he warns, we are simply too susceptible to gnostic approaches to our faith. Johnson may not be impressed with the historiography employed by Wright,[14] but Wright continues his massive career project nonetheless. Wright is convinced that "the historical quest for Jesus is a necessary and nonnegotiable aspect of Christian discipleship and that we in our generation have a chance to be renewed in discipleship and mission precisely by means of this quest."[15] He is convinced that doing real history ("in all its complexity of hypothetical reconstruction") and having real faith ("in all its glory as the constant exploration of, and trust in, a god whom Christians believe to be, among other things, intimately and passionately involved in the historical process itself") are not contradictory.[16]

Both Johnson and Wright make important points. Johnson correctly demonstrates the limits of historical studies, given our human frailties, while Wright would balance this perspective by asserting that, given the nature of historical revelation, it is imperative that Jesus be rooted solidly in history through careful historical investigation. Each viewpoint has a potential weakness as well. Johnson's view could inadvertently leave the door open to relativistic postmodern, gnostic, docetic, even new age approaches, which would reject full biblical authority. Wright, on the other hand, could leave the impression that the average believer is dependent on the (often tentative) conclusions of historians and theologians, which, ironically, would also undermine biblical authority. The answer to this seeming impasse is surprisingly

---

13   Johnson, *The Real Jesus*, 167–177. Johnson's *Living Jesus* further develops these concepts.
14   Luke Timothy Johnson, "A Historiographical Response to Wright's Jesus" in *Jesus & the Restoration of Israel: A Critical Assessment of N. T. Wright's* Jesus and the Victory of God (Downers Grove, IL: InterVarsity Press, 1999), 206–224.
15   N. T. Wright, *The Challenge of Jesus: Rediscovering Who Jesus Was and Is* (Downers Grove, IL: InterVarsity Press, 1999), 14.
16   N. T. Wright, *Jesus and the Victory of God*, Christian Origins and the Question of God, Vol. 2 (Minneapolis: Fortress Press, 1996), 9.

self-evident: We must simply utilize the best historiographical methods available, while at the same time maintaining full biblical authority.[17]

I would suppose that both Johnson and Wright agree that prior to all our scholarly pursuits is our God-given faith itself. Dale C. Allison Jr. has devoted many years to the analysis of these issues in Jesus studies and has come to this humble conclusion:

> [W]hile I am proudly a historian, I must confess that history is not what matters most. If my deathbed finds me alert and not overly racked with pain, I will then be preoccupied with how I have witnessed and embodied faith, hope, and charity. I will not be fretting over the historicity of this or that part of the Bible.[18]

What has not yet been mentioned—and what will further clarify matters—is that it is this very *supernatural* nature of faith that has often prompted such debates.

THE SUPERNATURAL JESUS

The real dividing line in attaining true knowledge of Jesus is the miraculous! It is the watershed issue in all the scholarship and the touchstone of authentic faith. According to naturalistic historians and theologians, we must simply reject much (if not most) of the New Testament as historically reliable and attempt to reconstruct the "true" Jesus of history through a study of his historical context.[19] According to historians and theologians who accept biblical inspiration and miracles, we should affirm the trustworthiness of the Scriptures and utilize extra-biblical sources cautiously. In this second approach historical studies simply enhance the *background* for our

---

[17] A good example of this approach would be the following: Paul Barnett, *Jesus and the Rise of Early Christianity: A History of New Testament Times* (Downers Grove, IL: InterVarsity Press, 1999).

[18] Dale C. Allison Jr., *Constructing Jesus: Memory, Imagination, and History* (Grand Rapids: Baker Academic, 2010).

[19] See Leander Keck, *Who Is Jesus? History in Perfect Tense* (Columbia, S.C.: University of South Carolina Press, 2000), ch. 1.

understanding of Jesus, while the gospel portraits themselves give us the foundational *foreground*. So the Bible has priority.[20] There is also the perennial problem of presuppositions.

If one assumes that miracles are an impossibility, then one's whole approach to portraying the historical Jesus is altered. The Bible will be seen as simply one source among many—and perhaps not even the primary source for reliable information. Further, the Jesus one looks for will, of necessity, be different. He will be merely human with no transcendent overtones. The writings of the New Testament, for the most part, will be suspect precisely because of the obvious faith bias of the writers. James D. G. Dunn meets this challenge head-on. He maintains that developing a proper hermeneutic for deriving the "real Jesus" from the biblical sources entails a somewhat different approach from the traditional rubrics. Literary and historical analysis is still necessary. But the chaotic ferment of contemporary scholarship demands a humbler, subtler tack. We must simply admit, on the one hand, that a "scientific," non-supernatural, non-faith-producing Jesus does not exist, while, on the other hand, acknowledging that a careful historical analysis of the remembrances of Jesus is indispensable.[21] In this way, the differences between Johnson and Wright can be largely reconciled.

In short, we must come to terms with the miraculous. "To deny the miraculous is to deny historic Christianity."[22] In his book on the subject, C. S. Lewis avers, "A naturalistic Christianity leaves out all that is specifically Christian."[23] Indeed, Christianity is a supernatural faith, as I have written elsewhere:

> The central tenets of our faith all involve miracle: *Creation, Incarnation, Resurrection, Consummation*. One thinks of the clusters of miracles surrounding the Exodus, the ministries of Elijah and Elisha, the life of our Lord Jesus Christ, and the

---

20 Again, Paul Barnett would exemplify the latter view.
21 See Dunn's *A New Perspective on Jesus: What the Quest for the Historical Jesus Missed* (Grand Rapids: Baker Academic, 2005). And for a fuller treatment see Dunn's *Jesus Remembered*, Christianity in the Making, vol. 1 (Grand Rapids: Eerdmans, 2003).
22 Robert H. Stein, *Jesus the Messiah: A Survey of the Life of Christ* (Downers Grove, IL: InterVarsity Press, 1996), 18.
23 C. S. Lewis, *Miracles: A Preliminary Study* (New York: Macmillan, 1947), 69.

militant New Testament Church. Moreover, miracles have accompanied the historic Church throughout her history and have abounded in the Pentecostal/charismatic revival of recent decades. Christianity is rife with supernaturalism.[24]

Everything about Christianity involves the miraculous. The Bible is a supernatural book. It is the "God-breathed" book (2 Tim. 3:16). Its influence and longevity are nonpareil. And its story and power have been lauded by innumerable saints for millennia. Jesus himself is both a miracle and the miracle-worker par excellence.

Studying Christology entails examining mammoth, category-defying miracles. *The Incarnation*: God, the Word, "became flesh and made his dwelling among us" (John 1:14). *The Resurrection*: Has anyone ever risen from death alive forever more? *The Ascension*: Jesus ascending bodily into heaven. *Second Coming*: Jesus returning to earth in bodily form. And Jesus' earthly ministry was characterized by the working of miracles in a manner not known before or since. "In Mark alone 209 of the 661 verses deal with the miraculous."[25] And our experience of the presence of the risen Christ brings the miraculous full circle down to the present.

It is time for many of us Christian scholars to overcome our reticence about Jesus. If ever there was a time when a more doxological, discipleship approach to Christology was needed, it is now. With Western Christianity in precipitous decline, with blatant heresy being called "Christian scholarship," and with a widespread loss of nerve when it comes to affirming full biblical authority and the unique saving and ruling authority of our Lord and Savior Jesus Christ, the need for bold restatements of our Incarnational faith is greater than ever. The passion of every believer's life should be that of knowing Christ, and Christian scholarship's highest aim should be that of enhancing that passion and that process.

---

[24] Larry D. Hart, *Truth Aflame: Theology for the Church in Renewal*, rev. ed. (Grand Rapids: Zondervan, 2005), 195; utilizing in part: Gordon R. Lewis and Bruce A. Demarest, *Integrative Theology* (Grand Rapids: Zondervan, 1990), 2:104–5.

[25] Stein, *Jesus the Messiah*, 18.

KNOWING CHRIST

The apostle Paul, perhaps the greatest theologian of all time, was consumed with this passion:

> But whatever were gains to me I now consider loss for the sake of Christ. What is more, I consider everything a loss because of the surpassing worth of knowing Christ Jesus my Lord, for whose sake I have lost all things. I consider them garbage, that I may gain Christ and be found in him, not having a righteousness of my own that comes from the law, but that which is through faith in Christ—the righteousness that comes from God on the basis of faith. I want to know Christ—yes, to know the power of his resurrection and participation in his sufferings, becoming like him in his death, and so, somehow, attaining to the resurrection from the dead (Phil. 3:7–11).

Considering Paul's background and his original opposition to Christianity, this is an astounding declaration indeed!

Paul experienced a resurrection appearance of Christ, commissioning him to be an apostle. And this came part and parcel with his literal conversion to Christ on the road to Damascus. As Paul told King Agrippa, it was about noon as he was nearing Damascus when "I saw a light from heaven, brighter than the sun, blazing around me and my companions" (Acts 26:13). Paul also heard a voice, saying to him, "Saul, Saul, why do you persecute me?" to which Paul responded, "Who are you, Lord?" (Acts 9:4–5). The Lord replied, "I am Jesus, whom you are persecuting" (v. 5). *The NIV Study Bible* provides a helpful summary of the import of this event: "In rabbinic tradition such a voice from heaven would have been understood as the voice of God himself. The solemn repetition of Saul's name (v. 4) and the bright light (v. 3) suggested to him that he was in the presence of deity."[26] This was *the* formative event for the apostle and became the leitmotif of both his theological perspective in general and his Christology in particular.

---

26 *The NIV Study Bible* (Grand Rapids: Zondervan, 2011), 1841.

From a Roman prison Paul wrote to the believers at Philippi: "For to me, to live is Christ and to die is gain" (Phil. 1:21). Both in life and in death Christ was the meaning of Paul's life. For the apostle death was gain because he would depart to "be with Christ, which is better by far" (v. 23). And in life Paul's identity with Christ both in his crucifixion and resurrection was key: "I have been crucified with Christ and I no longer live, but Christ lives in me. The life I now live in the body, I live by faith in the Son of God, who loved me and gave himself for me" (Gal. 2:20). With the resurrection of Christ we can now experience him as "a life-giving Spirit" (1 Cor. 15:45 HCSB). And we experience Christ through the Holy Spirit:

> But you are not in the flesh; you are in the Spirit, since the Spirit of God dwells in you. Anyone who does not have the Spirit of Christ does not belong to him. But if Christ is in you, though the body is dead because of sin, the Spirit is life because of righteousness. If the Spirit of him who raised Jesus from the dead dwells in you, he who raised Christ from the dead will give life to your mortal bodies also through his Spirit that dwells in you (Rom. 8:9–11 NRSV).

Notice the progression of nomenclature in this passage: Spirit, Spirit of God, Spirit of Christ, and Christ. To have Christ is to have the Spirit. The "Spirit of him who raised Jesus from the dead" (the Father) will also raise our mortal bodies. And the Holy Spirit is the Spirit of God and the Spirit of Christ. Our experience of God is thoroughly Trinitarian and thoroughly Christ-centered. Through the indwelling of the Spirit we reach up with one hand toward the Father and cry "*Abba*, Father" (Rom. 8:15); and with the other hand extended toward the Son we say "Jesus is Lord" (1 Cor. 12:3).[27] The first man Adam became a living soul. But Jesus, "the last Adam," brings us resurrection life (see 1 Cor. 15:45)! Going back to Romans 8:9–11, we hear Paul telling the believer: (1) "you are in the Spirit"; (2) "the Spirit of God dwells in you"; (3) you "have the Spirit of

---

[27] See the following: James D. G. Dunn, *The Theology of Paul the Apostle* (Grand Rapids: Eerdmans, 1998), 264; Gordon D. Fee, *God's Empowering Presence: The Holy Spirit in the Letters of Paul* (Peabody, Mass.: Hendrickson, 1994), 841–45.

Christ"; (4) "Christ is in you"; (5) "the body is dead because of sin, the Spirit is life because of righteousness"; (6) the same God who raised Jesus from the dead "will give life to your mortal bodies also through his Spirit that dwells in you."

Through God's indwelling Spirit, Christ becomes real to us in the present. "The risen Jesus may not be experienced independently of the Spirit, and any religious experience which is not in character and effect an experience of Jesus Paul would not regard as a manifestation of the life-giving Spirit."[28] The Christian community becomes thereby a Christ-centered, Trinitarian community of faith, hope, and love. And Christ is the key for both Jew and Gentile: "through him both of us have access in one Spirit to the Father" (Eph. 2:18 NRSV). In fact, all authentic religious experience is (1) in the Spirit, (2) through the Son, and (3) to the Father. Together we can grow "in the knowledge of the Son of God and become mature" (Eph. 4:13). In other words, authentic Christianity is Christ-centered and Trinitarian.

The apostle John gives us a similar vision in his account of Jesus' Upper Room Discourse. Jesus was preparing his disciples for a new and more intimate relationship with him through the Paraclete, the Holy Spirit. He gives five distinct teachings on the Holy Spirit in this discourse, which depict what our life with God is all about: (1) John 14:15–24—through the Father's giving us the Spirit the Trinity takes up residence ("make our home," v. 23) within us; (2) John 14:25–26—Jesus3 continues his teaching ministry among us through the Father's sending us the Spirit; (3) John 15:26–27—Jesus sends the Spirit from the Father to empower our witness; (4) John 16:4–11—Jesus leaves the earth bodily (which is "for your good," v. 7) so that he can send the Holy Spirit, who will convict the world of sin; (5) John 16:12–15—The Holy Spirit guides us into all truth, the things of Jesus and the Father. And in the midst of these rich teachings Jesus gives us the beautiful allegory of the vine and the branches (John 15:1–8), in which Jesus is the vine, we are the branches, and the Father is the gardener. As we remain in Christ we bear fruit and glorify the Father.

---

28 James D. G. Dunn, *Jesus and the Spirit* (London: SCM Press, 1975), 323.

In concrete terms then, how do we know Christ today? We know him in *the Spirit*. We know him as he is beautifully portrayed to us in *the Scriptures*. We know him in *the* saints, the body of Christ. We encounter him in *the sacraments*. And we even encounter him in *society*, as we reach out to the stranger, the sick, the poor, and the powerless (Matt. 25:31–46). Luke Timothy Johnson gives beautiful expression to this vision:

> How, then, does Jesus now find continuing embodiment as life-giving Spirit? As all-powerful Lord, in any fashion he chooses! Jesus remains capable of surprise. But the ways in which Christians have come to recognize the face of the living Christ exist mainly within that assembly of those gathered in the name of Jesus who have drunk of the Spirit and have become "the body of Christ" (Rom. 12:5; 1 Cor. 6:14; 12:12–27; Eph. 1:23; 2:16; 4:4–16; 5:23, 30; Col. 1:18, 24; 2:17–19). Jesus is embodied in the texts that speak of him. Jesus is embodied in the sacraments. Jesus is embodied in the lives of the saints. Jesus is embodied in the little ones of the earth.[29]

CHRIST OUR CONTEMPORARY

Christ, then, is truly our contemporary. Ultimately, the appropriate question to ask is not "Who *was* Jesus?" but "Who *is* Jesus?" And we have already seen that many factors influence our approach to Christology, to knowing Christ. Here is a list of some of them:

1. Our view of Scripture and how it is to be interpreted
2. Our view of spirituality in general and spiritual experiences in particular
3. Our understanding of the supernatural, the transcendent
4. Our relation to other believers (the church)
5. Our orientation to people in need
6. What we bring with us from the past (conversion, etc.)
7. Our basic head/heart orientation

---

[29] Johnson, *Living Jesus*, 22.

In one sense, Christ is profoundly like us. He was a human being. In fact, I will be arguing later that he was and is more human than we are. Sin has actually diminished our humanity and marred the divine image in us. But in Christ we see perfect humanity, in right relation with God and with all other human beings. He *is* the image of God (Col. 1:15)! We were made by God and for God. Biblically, it is impossible to define humanity apart from God. And it was precisely because Jesus was one with the Father that he was complete in his humanity. Yet that also sets him apart. He is also unlike us. His sonship was unique: He was God's "one and only" Son (John 3:16). He was also sinless. "Can any of you prove me guilty of sin?" he challenged his opponents (John 8:46). Jesus preexisted as an eternal divine being, the Son of God. Then the Son became incarnate as Jesus of Nazareth. Jesus' postexistence after the resurrection and ascension also sets him apart. But the miracle of the incarnation continues into the ages: The preexistent Son of God took on human existence as Jesus of Nazareth, died for our sins, rose from the grave, and ascended back to the Father. He did not cease to be human when he returned to heaven. In fact, he blazed the trail for us, his followers!

But Jesus was more than human. He prompted faith and devotion even during his earthly ministry. He accepted praise and thanksgiving, and the earliest Christians worshiped him as God.[30] Believers for two millennia have done the same. Some, like Luke Timothy Johnson, may put the accent more on the "Christ of faith"—the resurrected Jesus and the Christ of Christian tradition—while others, like N. T. Wright, may stress more the "Jesus of history"—highlighting the incarnation *in history* and the importance of historical correctives to personal and traditional images. But all true believers confess and embrace Jesus as the divine-human Savior of the world. He is truly Christ our contemporary, and I cannot count the number of times I have personally seen him in action!

---

[30] Larry W. Hurtado has investigated this phenomenon thoroughly: *Lord Jesus Christ: Devotion to Jesus in Earliest Christianity* (Grand Rapids: Eerdmans, 2003); and *How on Earth Did Jesus Become God? Historical Questions about Earliest Devotion to Jesus* (Grand Rapids: Eerdmans, 2005).

My mind goes back to college days. As a basketball player for Oral Roberts University, I had heard rumors that we had recruited a very talented player from the state of Indiana, a basketball hotbed. When Bill Hull walked onto the court, I made two quick judgments. With all the evident beer fat, he might not even make the team. And with that sullen, "leave me alone," demeanor, he was going to be a tough one to reach for Christ. I was wrong on both counts. Three weeks after his arrival on campus he met the contemporary Christ. And while traveling with Oral Roberts on a ministry trip to Africa, Bill was called to preach. We became roommates. At that time Bill was not a serious student, but he was one of the best basketball players the university has ever had.

Bill graduated and became a player/coach for Campus Crusade for Christ's Athletes in Action basketball team. Then he went to seminary. He pastored, planted churches, and became one of the top five leaders of his denomination. Then Bill began to publish books and lead seminars on discipleship. He is now considered one of the top authorities on the subject—all because he met the contemporary Christ.

Ralph Bethea and I did our Ph.D. work at the same time at the Southern Baptist Theological Seminary. Ralph grew up in Kenya, his father being a medical missionary there for the Southern Baptist Convention. Later Ralph would return to Kenya with his wife and children. He had always had a burden for a breakthrough of the gospel in the Islamic world. He and twelve others began to pray regularly together for the Lord to give them a strategy. The Lord's instructions were simple: Go into the city and throughout the villages and ask people this simple question, "Is there anything Jesus can do for you?" They began to see incredible miracles.

A woman brought her baby onto the platform at a public meeting and asked Dr. Bethea, "Can your Jesus heal my baby?" Ralph looked at the horribly twisted legs of the baby and replied, "Yes, he can." But inside Ralph really didn't think anything was going to happen. They prayed, then looked at the baby—no change—the woman began to walk back to her seat, and the service continued. Suddenly she became hysterical and began to scream. The baby had almost jumped out of her arms, and when she pulled back the blanket, the baby's legs were absolutely straight! Later an imam whose son had been missing for months, asked "Can your Jesus help me find my son?" They prayed and at the end of the service his son was brought into the building. During the next two years miracles like these began to proliferate and more than 120,000 people came to Christ. In addition, more than two hundred new churches were planted—all because people began to discover what the resurrected Christ could do for them.

When I was a preschooler, my parents went into our small West Texas town one day and saw a tragic sight. A little girl was leading her drunken mother by the hand to the bar, where her drunken father was. Both adults were severe alcoholics. My parents asked their pastor to visit the couple. The pastor shared the good news of Jesus with the couple, led them in the sinner's prayer, and left. Then all hell broke loose in their home. They couldn't sleep all night. They felt like something was coming out of every pore of their bodies. The woman looked into a mirror and, seeing her sunken eyes, screamed in terror. But by the next morning they were completely delivered from alcoholism and never touched another drop. Immediately, they became bold witnesses, telling everyone they saw what Jesus had done for them. Later they would attend a Bible college to further train them in their newfound ministry!

These stories remind me of the gospel narratives and the Book of Acts. "Jesus Christ is the same yesterday and today and forever" (Heb. 13:8). Our next task then should be to step back into the past and study the Jesus of history—the Jesus who transformed history, who is the center of history, and who is still writing history today.

Lesson Two
The Historical Quests for Jesus

AN ANALYSIS OF HISTORICAL QUESTS PAST AND PRESENT

It is hard to put my Aunt Gay Hart in a category. She is a widow (her late husband flew in the lead plane on the D-Day invasion, I am told) in a small central Texas town who teaches Sunday School at the local Baptist church and a class on the Bible as literature at the local high school. She does some prison ministry work and just generally enjoys life. She defies categorization. A *New York Times* article on the separation of church and state contained these comments:

> Mrs. Hart is not, she said, just some small-town church lady.

> "I go to First Baptist," she said. "I wear a Pentecostal hairdo. I play the organ at the Episcopal church. When I could sing, I was the alto at Church of Christ. I have taught in a Catholic school. I am 77, and I am not a little old lady with a 15-year-old car that has 3,000 miles on it. I sky-dived last summer. I have a life, and I love this class."[1]

---

[1] Mark Oppenheimer, "Church and State, And Bible Class in Texas," *New York Times*, March 2, 2013, A17.

And the first thing we will learn as we survey the historical quests for Jesus is that he also defies categorization!

In fact, that has been precisely the problem in our historical quests. Michael J. McCylmond asserts that "Jesus is too large to be pigeonholed." He continues:

> The interpreter's most common and most characteristic error regarding Jesus is to narrow down the figure in the Gospels until he fits into some box chosen by the interpreter. My point about the first-century context applies to the twenty-first century as well. Jesus does not conform to any contemporary category, whether that of social activist, spiritual guru, alternative healer, ethical teacher, textual scholar, gadfly, hippie, corporate executive, political revolutionary, doomsday prophet, inspirational speaker, or commune founder. Jesus was and is uncategorizable, and this is one reason why he remains a perpetual challenge to believers and unbelievers alike, a figure instantly recognizable and yet ever elusive.[2]

> *People tend to create a historic person such as Jesus after their own image*

People tend to create a historic person such as Jesus after their own image. We portray him the way we would *like* him to be, but soon discover he refuses to be domesticated. I am on a sabbatical leave from the seminary in which I teach as I write these words. And I am anticipating traveling to some cultures that, while still Western, are quite different from my own. I will often not be familiar with the languages spoken, the pacing of life, some of the food, and the like. Think of being transported back to first-century Palestine—listening to Jesus and watching him in action. It would be like being on Mars.

First of all, he would not look like you have pictured him all your life. Then, he would be speaking in a strange tongue (either Aramaic or Hebrew) that you have probably never learned. At times

---

2 Michael J. McClymond, *Familiar Stranger: An Introduction to Jesus of Nazareth* (Grand Rapids: Eerdmans, 2004), 152.

he would shock you with his brusqueness in dealing with his religious opponents. At other times tears would no doubt come to your eyes as you watch him deal tenderly with a little child or someone desperately ill. You would quickly conclude that no work of history, no thorough biography, not even a video camera could fully capture what you are observing. And it would all seem so strange and foreign to you. And yet from our discussions of the previous chapter, I would also argue that Jesus would be familiar to you—the Jesus you have come to know and love in your Christian pilgrimage. To be sure, your time-travel experience will have provided countless additions and corrections to the picture of Jesus you have built up in your mind over the years, and you would never think of him in quite the same way again.

Our survey of the historical quests for Jesus of the past couple centuries will hopefully have a similar impact. In a thoroughly postmodern fashion, we will discover how profoundly our understanding is conditioned by our times and our culture. We will be both humbled and emboldened—humbled by the limitations of human knowledge and emboldened to pursue true knowledge of our Lord as never before. In terms of acquiring an authentic portrayal of Jesus, we will discover that the so-called Enlightenment of the eighteenth century in Germany and France was in reality the beginning of the "dark ages" of historical Jesus inquiry and that only in more recent decades have we made much progress in recovering our scholarly moorings in the West. Many times we are humbled by the often pre-critical and pre-modern voices of our Christian peers among the developing nations of Asia, Africa, and Latin America (along with those of Eastern Europe) who have a more immediate and accurate apprehension of who Jesus was and is. Nevertheless, the benefits of learning from our past far outweigh the perils of venturing into foreign places with strange-sounding voices.

THE FIRST QUEST OR THE "OLD QUEST"

Hermann Samuel Reimarus (1694–1768) was a child of his age, the Enlightenment, though not willingly so. As a devout and pious believer, he had hoped to maintain his traditional views of Jesus in the face of the challenges of his day. He set about privately to investigate the Bible's testimony to Jesus in hopes of salvaging his faith and even committed some of his findings to writing. These results he shared with only a few of his trusted friends. Later, after his death, some of his work would be made public by Gothold Ephraim Lessing (1729–1781). Unfortunately, Reimarus' efforts served only to reinforce his doubts and, with these newer approaches to Scripture, revise drastically who he thought Jesus really was and how Christianity really came about.

This professor of Semitic languages at Hamburg University had already imbibed deeply of the Enlightenment rationalism of his day, so that his quest for the real historical Jesus was already biased against accepting the Bible as divine revelation and as a trustworthy historical source. He concluded that Jesus' message and mission could be summarized with the words, "Repent, for the kingdom of heaven has come near" (Matt. 3:2). These words he interpreted as signifying that Jesus was seeking not to revise the Jewish religion but to renew it through repentance and preparation for God's imminent kingdom. Jesus was not a divine being revealing a Triune God, doing miraculous deeds, and rising bodily from the grave. He was simply a first-century Jewish revolutionary who sought to spread the unity of love with God that he himself enjoyed. He failed in that mission and there was no bodily resurrection. So his disciples, seeking to salvage their religious status, taught his soon return, which also did not happen.[3] "Thus, Christianity originated in a kind of double mistake," says Michael McClymond of Remarus' views, "in which Jesus first failed as revolutionary and then his followers mistakenly expected the immediate end of the world."[4] Christianity in the end was a fraud, then, a fabrication. Others would seek to mollify these results, but the die was cast. The stark contrast between a traditional Christianity, founded on divine revelation, and a revised edition, founded on reason alone would largely set the parameters for Jesus research for the next two centuries.

---

[3] See the excellent treatment of Reimarus in Hans Schwarz, *Christology* (Grand Rapids: Eerdmans, 1998), 8–14.
[4] McClymond, *Familiar Stranger*, 10.

In the nineteenth century, David Friedrich Stauss (1808–74) continued the Jesus quest with a series of books, beginning with the two-volume *Life of Jesus* in 1835. Unlike Reimarus, Strauss initially believed that there were truths to be found in the biblical texts. Yes, it was no longer acceptable to embrace the naïve supernaturalism of traditional Christianity. No, we cannot utilize the New Testament as such for reliable history— the birth, infancy, and child narratives, for example, being of little historical value. Miracles in general need to be seen as a mythology used by the early church to communicate spiritual truths. And the resurrection reports can be explained as hallucinations or "visions." So what is left? Jesus did truly think of himself as God's Messiah and he embodied what religion in general was all about— the unifying of God and humanity. Sadly, however, Strauss would ultimately capitulate to unbelief and embrace a thin humanism. And to understand our world, he would conclude, we should look to Darwin's theory of evolution.[5] Do not these views have a surprisingly modern ring?

And similar to our own times, the pendulum would swing from rationalism to romanticism. While extracting myth from Scripture seemed cold and sterile to some, the French Catholic, Ernest Renan (1823–92), provided a warm, affirming novel-like portrait of Jesus as the quintessence of humanity. His *Life of Jesus* (1863) was monumental in its impact, selling thousands of copies in its initial printing and going through numerous editions and translations. Rather than occupying himself with finding myth in the gospels, Renan set about to create a myth of Jesus of his own, right out of the gospels. This portrait was, as McClymond observes, "a mythicized Jesus that conformed to the cultural expectations of well-educated, late nineteenth-century western Europeans."[6] Jesus, then, represented the very best of what was truly human, having little to do with either Judaism or Christianity. He was the supremely God-conscious man who related to God as his father and taught humanity the path to earthly bliss. He was a teacher, not a messiah, savior, or apocalyptic prophet. He simply taught us the essence of true religion, which

---

5 Schwarz, *Christology*, 21–23.
6 McClymond, *Familiar Stranger*, 10–11.

was the fatherhood of God, the brotherhood of humanity, and infinite value of every person. Later, this classic liberal summary of the meaning of Jesus would be given eloquent expression in the extemporary and astonishingly informed lectures of Adolph von Harnack (*What Is Christianity?*). Jesus for Renan was a noble, yet tragic figure, who initially was popular but became increasingly unpopular toward his later years because of his high ethical demands.

As appealing as such romantic portraits of Jesus might be, nineteenth-century scholars refused to give up rigorous historical and literary analysis of the gospels themselves in the quest for the historical Jesus. H. J. Holtzmann (1832–1910) attempted a source-critical approach, concluding that Mark's gospel was written first and then later utilized by Matthew and Luke. His approach and his conclusions still hold sway today. He also rightly noted that the events of Caesarea Philippi (Mark 8) marked the turning point for Jesus' ministry. But as a child of his age, he concluded that Jesus was merely a teacher of ethics, a moral example—"Jesus as more the first Christian than the Christ," as Dunn has aptly summarized.[7] But keeping closer to the text inevitably moves one closer to the actual zeitgeist of Jesus' own day, which in part was thoroughly apocalyptic.

Johannes Weiss (1863–1914) continued in the nineteenth-century liberal tradition of creating a psychological portrait of Jesus as an ethical teacher and moral model. But his focus on the central theme of Jesus' teaching, the kingdom of God, nudged him in a new and more fruitful direction. Moving into the actual historical period of Jesus, we discover an apocalyptic worldview of a good world now dominated by demons and awaiting a deliverer, who will through a series of upheavals usher the world into end time judgment. This perspective, Weiss concluded, was what dominated Jesus' view of the kingdom of God. Weiss provided a full explication of this understanding of Jesus as an apocalyptic prophet in his *Jesus' Proclamation of the Kingdom of God* (1892). Jesus' preaching of an otherworldly kingdom and the imminent end of the world, according to Weiss, lay at the core of his

---

[7] James D. G. Dunn, *Jesus Remembered*, Christianity in the Making, vol. 1 (Grand Rapids: Eerdmans, 2003), 39.

message and ministry. This understanding stood in stark contrast to the traditional liberal, non-eschatological Jesus and set in part the future agenda of historical Jesus research.

William Wrede (1859–1906) came to the same conclusion as Weiss concerning the eschatological nature of Jesus' proclamation. But Wrede also moved in a more radical direction in relation to the historical usefulness of the New Testament gospels. His *Messianic Secret in the Gospels* (1901), for example, presents Mark's gospel as a theological construct, a fictitious account of a divine Jesus doing supernatural deeds. In his extreme skepticism, Wrede concluded that Jesus certainly did not think of himself as the Son of God and the Messiah and that the biblical gospels are unreliable as historical sources, thus bringing this original quest for the historical Jesus to a decisive turning point, if not a screeching halt—except for the explorations of one other key scholarly figure, Albert Schweitzer.

For a hundred years now, various lives of Jesus had emerged without any discernible consensus of opinion. Was Jesus an apocalypticist, a moralist, an ethicist? Do the gospels provide any trustworthy historical materials? What is the meaning of Jesus in the face of the acids of Enlightenment critical thought? Albert Schweitzer (1876–1965) stood forth to provide comprehensive summative insight into the efforts of the previous century and to set the agenda for the coming century. The title of Schweitzer's magisterial volume set his parameters: *The Quest of the Historical Jesus: A Critical Study of Its Progress from Reimarus to Wrede* (1906). Reimarus had acknowledged the gospels' depiction of Jesus as an apocalyptic figure but denied their historical veracity, while Wrede had demonstrated that denial of the eschatological portrait of Jesus in the New Testament was simply a duplicitous claim.[8] For his part, Schweitzer took as his starting point Weiss's thesis of Jesus as an apocalyptic prophet. According to Schweizer, Jesus secrecy revealed his messiahship to his disciples at his transfiguration, but Judas proceeded to communicate this event to the religious leaders. Jesus announced the imminent end of the earth, but ultimately attempted to force God's hand, as it were, by entering into suffering and death

---
8 Schwarz, *Christology*, 32.

on behalf of his people Israel. Schweitzer's descriptive language here is quite dramatic:

> There is silence all around. The Baptist appears, and cries: "Repent, for the Kingdom of Heaven is at hand." Soon after that comes Jesus, and in the knowledge that He is the coming Son of Man lays hold of the wheel of the world to set it moving on that last revolution which is to bring all ordinary history to a close. It refuses to turn, and He throws Himself upon it. Then it does turn; and crushes Him.[9]

In simplest terms, Schweitzer was announcing *failure*: (1) the failure of the entire quest for the historical Jesus up to Schweitzer's time and (2) the failure of Jesus in his end time mission. Jesus was simply misguided as a prophet and a tragic failure in his mission. Nevertheless, Schweitzer refused to give up Jesus' profound impact and influence down the centuries and retreated to a kind of mystical appeal to the ongoing power of the spirit of Jesus as we encounter his words. And the embers for a continued historical quest for Jesus were left burning in Schweitzer's groundbreaking work through his pointing us back to the gospels' portrayal of Jesus in such strong eschatological terms. But the quest entered hibernation at this point until Ernst Käsemann issued a new call in the mid-twentieth century.

THE "NO QUEST" PERIOD (FROM SCHWEITZER TO KÄSEMANN)

The first half of the twentieth century witnessed little interest in historical quests of Jesus. After all, the results of the original quest were paltry and largely contradictory. Enlightenment skepticism toward Scripture severely limited any constructive progress, and scholars saw much more promise in examining the life and background of the early church, for example, and exploring the dynamic of gospel preaching in the contemporary church. At the same time that Schweitzer was

---

[9] Schweitzer, *The Quest of the Historical Jesus* (1st ed.), 368–69; cited in Dunn, *Jesus Remembered*, 47. Later editions of Schweitzer's work omitted this well know passage.

pulling together the results of historical Jesus studies, Martin Kähler was arguing that the entire enterprise was an exercise in futility.

Kähler, a systematic theologian at the University of Halle, gave a now famous lecture to a group of pastors in 1892: *The So-Called Historical Jesus and the Historic Biblical Christ* (1892). "Historical" (*historische*) referred to the bare historical facts (*Historie*) without any ascribed significance. "Historic" (*geschichtliche*) pointed to a meaningful history (*Geshcichte*) of persons and events of significance. Since the gospels themselves were faith documents, the very best nineteenth-century questers could do with them was to derive the bare historical facts, rejecting the faith perspectives of the gospel writers themselves, and then foist upon these facts their own nineteenth-century "significance." Thus, the *Historie* would point, by assumption, to a more Ebionite or Arian Christ, a mere human Jesus without transcendent significance. In contrast, the real Jesus, argued Kähler, is the *historic* Jesus, the Christ who was preached and believed in by the earliest followers. True knowledge of Christ is independent of the work of the scholars and even the dogma of the church: It comes from believing in the Christ of the Bible. Hans Schwarz provides this lucid summary:

> Kähler concluded that we do not believe in Christ because of the Bible but we believe in the Bible because of Christ. Jesus Christ is the biblical Christ as he is mediated to us through the Bible. The biblical and historical Christ is the revealed Christ in his salvific action. Instead of grounding faith in the ever-changing results of historical Jesus research, the Christian faith is grounded in the whole biblical Christ.[10]

The New Testament gospels themselves evince an inseparable union between "the memory of the days of his flesh and the confession of his eternal significance."[11] And the proclamation of this good news produces a Spirit-engendered faith and true knowledge of Christ.

---
10 Schwarz, *Christology*, 40.
11 Kähler's words, cited in Veli-Matti Kärkkäinen, *Christology: A Global Introduction* (Grand Rapids: Baker Academic, 2003), 104; as quoted in Alister E. McGrath, *The Making of Modern German Christology 1750–1990*, 2nd ed. (Grand Rapids: Zondervan, 1994), 114.

Kähler was referring to the post-Easter faith of the early church. But James D. G. Dunn strengthens Kähler's argument by extending Jesus' impact to the *pre-Easter* faith—a faith-producing Jesus and the only Jesus there really is to discover in historical investigations![12]

I am reminded of the testimony of Billy Graham. Graham came to faith in Christ as a teenager. But later his colleague, Chuck Templeton, began to challenge Graham's confidence in the inspiration of Scripture with Templeton's questions and doubts. Finally, Graham knelt before God and acknowledged that he did not have all the answers. All he knew was that his life was changed when he placed his faith in the Christ of the Bible. And he resolved that from then on he would place his faith in the Bible in the same way. He accepted Christ by faith and the Bible that proclaimed Christ in the same manner, by faith: Kähler's precise point.

Ironically, one could turn Kähler's approach in a more radical direction, as did Rudolph Bultmann and Paul Tillich. Pushing aside the historical Jesus and calling for an existential faith, both Bultmann and Tillich, in effect, bifurcated faith from historical fact, which in the view of many leads in a more gnostic direction. The early Karl Barth (1886–1968), in his groundbreaking commentary on Romans, inadvertently contributed to this movement by his disdain of historical quests for the earthly Jesus. For Barth it is the preached Christ that saves, again a reverberation of Kähler. At least for Barth, it was a resurrected Christ who was preached. For Bultmann, Christ did not rise from the dead because, he says, dead men don't rise. Christ is a myth (Bultmann) or symbol (Tillich) and that is all that matters for an existential faith. But Barth, reacting to his liberal training, would beg to differ. The gospel of liberal and radical theology is no gospel at all: It is a thinly veiled humanism, blinded to the Christ-centered, Trinitarian faith of orthodox Christianity.

---

12 See Dunn's *A New Perspective on Jesus: What the Quest for the Historical Jesus Missed* (Grand Rapids: Baker Academic, 2005), 33–34 (and total presentation). This helpful précis of Dunn's approach serves as a prequel to his more comprehensive presentation in *Jesus Remembered* (Eerdmans, 2003).

THE NEW QUEST

Interestingly, it was Ernst Käsemann (1906–1998), a protégé of Bultmann, who would issue the call for a renewed quest for the historical Jesus. Käsemann's lecture, "The Problem of the Historical Jesus" (1954), became a milestone for the historical Jesus quest.[13] He agreed with Bultmann that a "life of Jesus" was beyond the pale of historical scholars. At the same time, he was convinced that much of the basic outline of Jesus' life and ministry was attainable and, even more important, that such historical work was essential to preventing Christian faith from devolving toward a more gnostic faith and docetic Christology.

Since the new questers would largely maintain Bultmann's more naturalistic approach, research tilted more toward the sayings of Jesus rather than a comprehensive presentation of his life and ministry, a characteristic that has continued to the present in the work, for example, of the Jesus Seminar. Good examples of the "New Quest" would be Günther Bornkamm and Joachim Jeremias. Bornkamm generally followed the path of Bultmann, with some deviations, in terms of a naturalistic portrayal of Jesus. One of his most important insights related to the faith perspectives of the gospels themselves. "We possess no single word of Jesus and no single story of Jesus, no matter how incontestably genuine they may be, which do not embody at the same time the confession of the believing congregation, or at least are embedded therein."[14] Dunn would argue that this reality does not, in fact, limit our findings: This is precisely who Jesus was—a faith-producing person! Jeremias' approach was unique in that he also focused on the sayings of Jesus, but additionally went on to couch Jesus carefully in his Jewish setting, one of Jeremias's greatest strengths.[15] In this regard Jeremias stood in sharp contrast to Bultmann. Further, Jeremias reached much more conservative

---

13 Ernst Käsemann, "The Problem of the Historical Jesus," in *Essays on New Testament Themes*, trans. W. J. Montague (Naperville, Ill.: Alec R. Allenson, 1964).
14 Günther Bornkamm, *Jesus of Nazareth* (1956; ET: London: Hodder & Stoughton, 1960), 14; cited in Dunn, *A New Perspective on Jesus*, 20.
15 See, for example, Joachim Jeremias, *New Testament Theology: The Proclamation of Jesus* (New York: Charles Scribner's Sons, 1971).

conclusions regarding the language and style of the sayings of Jesus in the Synoptics: "In the synoptic tradition it is the inauthenticity, and not the authenticity, of the sayings of Jesus that must be demonstrated."[16] My mentor, Dale Moody, liked to quote in class what Jeremias, during a visit to the seminary campus, said in response to the question, "What have you basically been trying to do in your scholarly work?" Jeremias quickly and somewhat humorously replied, "To refute Professor Bultmann!" Yet even Jeremias himself could not fully escape Bultmann's German rationalism, rejecting some (though certainly not all) of the miracle accounts in the gospels.

THE THIRD QUEST

Since the early 1980s a vastly variegated movement of historical Jesus studies has emerged, demonstrating that interest in the subject is as strong as ever.[17] At one extreme is the Jesus Seminar, whose widely publicized work (by design) is well known and often respected in general culture while most often disdained in mainstream New Testament scholarship. At the other extreme is a virtual phalanx of more conservative New Testament scholars who staunchly defend the reliability of the Scriptures and address head-on the challenges from the left. And in between these two are gradations of opinions across the continuum. Apart from the Jesus Seminar, this so-called Third Quest has found much more to trust historically in the gospels than previous quests. Perhaps the primary dividing line has been the willingness to place Jesus in his Jewish/eschatological setting. But more precisely, the field of scholars bifurcates into (1) the more skeptical and (2) the more (humbly) confident, when it comes to the New Testament in general and the synoptic gospels in particular. Returning to the opening themes of this volume, the ultimate dividing line is the supernatural. Those who reject miracles will take a more naturalistic approach in their use of historical and literary methods, while those

---

[16] Jeremias, *New Testament Theology*, 37.
[17] See Ben Witherington III, *The Jesus Quest: The Third Search for the Jew of Nazareth*, 2nd. ed. (Downers Grove, IL: InterVarsity Press, 1997). I obtained the date for the emergence of the Third Quest (early 1980s) from page 12 of this fine introduction to the movement.

more open to the possibility of the miraculous will attain strikingly different results with their use of these same methods.[18]

Reading from left to right, we begin with the famous (if not, infamous) Jesus Seminar. Founded in 1985 by Robert Funk and John Dominic Crossan, this consortium of New Testament scholars has utilized rather unorthodox means for coming to a rather unorthodox scholarly consensus on numerous historical/theological issues: They vote. Utilizing marbles to vote on Jesus' sayings, for example,—*red* signifying that Jesus said these words or something quite similar; *pink* indicating that Jesus probably said something similar to this saying; *gray* to express doubt that this is an actual saying, but the ideas are his (Jesus); and *black* to reject the saying as authentic at all. Beginning with extreme skepticism and an antisupernatural bias, the results are actually quite predictable. In terms of Jesus' sayings, then, a summary breakdown of results would be as follows: 50% black; 30% gray, 20% red or pink—only one in five authentic or probable. The deeds of Jesus fare even worse. Bottom line, we can eliminate, they conclude, the Lord's Prayer and Jesus' sayings from the cross, and reject out of hand Jesus' virgin birth, healings, miracles, and bodily resurrection—not much of the Good News left with these conclusions (actually none, as the apostle Paul would conclude). Publish these controversial results in newspaper interviews, television talk shows, popular newsmagazines, and the like, and you have a large built-in audience. But you have also lost your audience of the vast majority of New Testament scholars. Nonetheless, some of the major voices in this seminar deserve a hearing and provide helpful insights into who Jesus was, especially Marcus J. Borg and John Dominic Crossan. Unfortunately, one of the founders, Robert Funk, largely set the tone of the enterprise from the outset.

In effect, Robert Funk's vision is one of a completely revised Christianity, which is ironic since he himself was once a fiery preacher of fundamentalist Christianity in rural Texas. Now he would have us

---

18 See Paul Rhodes Eddy and Gregory A. Boyd, Ch. 1 "Miracles and Methods: The Historical-Critical Method and the Supernatural" in *The Jesus Legend: A Case for the Historical Reliability of the Synoptic Jesus Tradition* (Grand Rapids: Baker Academic, 2017), 39–90.

see Jesus as a mere man—a secular sage or social critic—and certainly not divine. Jesus could be viewed as a Jewish Socrates or a stand-up comic akin to Lenny Bruce. Jesus was certainly not resurrected, nor will we be resurrected. We need to be liberated from traditional Christian sexual morality (consensual, protected recreational sex is fine) and generate new symbols and stories for the faith. Paul Verhoeven, who was the director of *Basic Instinct* and *Showgirls*, is a voting member of the Jesus Seminar. Funk's forums throughout the country promote these sorts of views of Christianity in general and Jesus in particular.[19] In view of Funk's influence, it is difficult for me to see why scholars such as Borg or Crossan would have ever associated themselves with the seminar.

Marcus J. Borg puts things on a much more spiritual plain. The flyleaf of his first foray into the discussion describes his approach as follows: "This thought-provoking text presents a full and historical portrait of Jesus as charismatic, healer, sage, and prophet; as spiritual—and political—teacher."[20] Borg's vision of Jesus and Christianity is succinctly set forth in a conversation with N. T. Wright entitled *The Meaning of Jesus: Two Visions*.[21] Borg is a mystic and his Jesus is a mystic. The Jesus of history was not God and never thought of himself as God. God as Spirit is everywhere present, but especially present in Jesus. Easter means that Jesus' disciples continued to experience his presence after his death. Borg is indifferent concerning an empty tomb. Bodily resurrection sounds too much like resuscitation to Borg. Jesus was a mystic, healer, sage, prophet, and teacher with a merciful ministry of liberating the marginalized with a "politics of compassion."[22] And for us, Jesus' present-day followers, we too can enjoy an experiential relationship with God and be change agents in the world. We learn to see Jesus, God, and the world through

---

[19] I am indebted to journalist Jeffrey L. Sheller for much of the material on Funk and the Jesus Seminar scholars I present in this section. See his excellent volume, *Is the Bible True?* (HarperSanFrancisco/Zondervan, 1999), 184–91.
[20] Marcus J. Borg, *Jesus: A New Vision: Spirit, Culture, and the Life of Discipleship* (New York: Harper & Row, 1987).
[21] HarperSanFrancisco, 1999.
[22] Borg, *Jesus: A New Vision*, 196.

the "lens" of the Bible and the Christian tradition.[23] Through this approach and understanding, Borg, as a younger man, was able to move out of the agnosticism and even atheism into which he had fallen out of his traditional Lutheran heritage. He was able thereby to worship again and affirm the faith of the Nicene Creed, albeit with a few novel definitions of terms. Borg is an engaging personality, as is his colleague John Dominic Crossan.

Crossan's *The Historical Jesus: The Life of a Mediterranean Jewish Peasant* (1991) presents his vision of Jesus in eloquent, captivating language:

> He comes as yet unknown into a hamlet of Lower Galilee. He is watched by the cold, hard eyes of peasants living long enough at subsistence level to know exactly where the line is drawn between poverty and destitution. He looks like a beggar, yet his eyes lack the proper cringe, his voice the proper whine, his walk the proper shuffle. He speaks about the rule of God, and they listen as much from curiosity as anything else. They know all about rule and power, about kingdom and empire, but they know it in terms of tax and debt, malnutrition and sickness, agrarian oppression and demonic possession. What, they really want to know, can this kingdom of God do for a lame child, a blind parent, a demented soul screaming its tortured isolation among the graves that mark the edges of the village?[24]

Typical of liberal historical Jesus scholars in every generation, both Borg and Crossan give us a politically correct Jesus seeking to right the wrongs of society. For Crossan, Jesus is a revolutionary peasant resisting Roman economic and social oppression. He is a Jewish Cynic (adherent of the philosophy that virtue and self-control are the only good) who taught a wisdom aimed at undoing unjust social structures. Jesus was not interested in politics per se nor the afterlife: He wanted to make things better in this present life. In deriving this portrait of

---

23 Borg and Wright, *The Meaning of Jesus*, 239–40.
24 Crossan, *The Historical Jesus*, xi.

Jesus, Crossan rejects most of the gospel records as unreliable and leans heavily upon *Q* (a sayings source) and *The Gospel of Thomas* (a second-century gnostic sayings source). Most of traditional Christian teachings Crossan seems to view as problematic or simply unacceptable. Again, we find the vision of a revised Christianity typical of the Jesus Seminar. Crossan is perhaps the best known Jesus scholar in North America, due to his virtual omnipresence on television programs on the Jesus of history as well as his highly influential and well-drawn writing. His popular *Historical Jesus* rightly places Jesus in his Roman and Jewish contexts, something strictly intentional and strongly emphasized.[25] This is one of the strengths of his approach and an important contribution to the ongoing conversation, even though the Hellenistic world seems to overshadow the Jewish in his portrait of Jesus.

Transitioning from the Jesus Seminar to more traditional approaches to historical Jesus studies is like exploring the tropical paradise of Kauai. In the central part of the island you find possibly the wettest spot on earth (up to thirty-six *feet* of rain per year on Mount Wai'ale'ale), while the town of Waimea, some thirteen miles to the southwest on the leeward side of the island, is lucky to get nineteen inches of rain—a stark contrast, but you are still on the same beautiful tropical island! We are still studying the beautiful and mysterious Jesus of Nazareth when we move to the thoughts of E. P. Sanders on Jesus, but we have re-entered the more verdant Jewish atmosphere of the biblical gospels. The scholars we will now survey reflect a broad consensus on the Jewishness of Jesus, but will also evince strong differences of opinion. In contrast to the Jesus Seminar, Sanders prefers to study key events in the life of Jesus, which he is convinced we can ascertain, rather than to study the sayings of Jesus.

The key to understanding Jesus, according to Sanders, is his Jewish context.[26] Jesus was an eschatological, even apocalyptic, prophet who very much bought into a Jewish restoration theology. The end of the

---

[25] See his own discussion of his methodology and program in *The Historical Jesus: Five Views* (Downers Grove: IVP Academic, 2009), 105–07.

[26] See these two important and influential publications of Sanders: *Jesus and Judaism* (Minneapolis: Fortress, 1985); *The Historical Figure of Jesus* (London: Penquin, 1993).

age was imminent. God was going to break into history and rescue his people once and for all. Unfortunately for Jesus, he was seen as attacking the temple in his prediction of its destruction because of its corrupt practices, and Jesus was alienated for the Jewish leaders (not the Pharisees, Sanders says, in contradistinction to Mark's gospel) by his attitude and actions toward the temple. This ultimately led to his death. Sanders has little interest in the sayings of Jesus in his historical quest, nor for Jesus' miracles. In general, he rejects the authenticity of the miracle stories, taking a surprisingly skeptical, naturalistic approach. He also rejects the accounts of conflict between Jesus and the Pharisees as being read back into the story due to later church/synagogue controversies.[27] He rejects the general Christian interpretation of Judaism as a law religion and Christianity as a grace religion as basically anti-Semitic or at least anti-Judaism. Perhaps it would be more helpful to clarify this issue historically. Obviously, the biblical doctrine of grace encompasses both the Old and New Testaments. But just as Christians today often miss it, so the Jewish leaders of Jesus' day missed it as well. At this juncture, if would have been more helpful for Sanders to accept the narratives of conflict between the Pharisees and Jesus.

Continuing our reading of the Third Quest from left to right, we come to the voluminous project of the Catholic scholar, John P. Meier.[28] Originally, Meier had set out to produce a small work on the historical Jesus in preparation for a very large treatment of the gospel of Matthew. That small volume expanded to some 1600 pages and became the first volume of his total study of the historical Jesus. Meier does a good job anchoring Jesus in his proper Jewish setting and making full use of the biblical materials, in contrast to many of his predecessors in this field of study who have made spare use of the gospels and given more weight to non-canonical sources. Meier's theology is traditional and his conclusions are reserved and carefully documented. He has produced a goldmine of meticulously researched

---

[27] Witherington, *The Jesus Quest*, 118–32.
[28] See his massive four-volume work: *A Marginal Jew: Rethinking the Historical Jesus*, The Anchor Yale Bible Reference Library (New Haven, CT: Yale University Press, 1991, 1994, 2001, 2009).

material on Jesus and a standard reference in the field of historical Jesus studies. Anglican New Testament scholar N. T. Wright has done the same thing, providing a wide-ranging scholarly treatment of the historical Jesus as well as briefer works that make the results of his findings accessible to the popular market.

Wright's perspective and approach are unique because he comes to the task as a pastor, New Testament scholar, historian, and theologian. His central work has been in New Testament studies, but his broader work in historical, theological, and pastoral concerns has influenced the kind of literature he has produced and the focus of his work: Ultimately, Wright seems to want to promote true *discipleship* of Jesus, which from my own perspective is the greatest strength of all his writings. Additionally, one notes that N. T. Wright has come to a firm confidence in the basic reliability of the gospels, even though he does careful critical work and some of his conclusions have stirred controversies in conservative circles. Wright's *Jesus and the Victory of God*, the second volume in a projected six-volume series entitled "Christian Origins and the Question of God," has become known as one of the most important works of the Third Quest.[29]

Wright refuses to accept the Enlightenment rubric of historiography that faith and history are antithetical.[30] Indeed, the scholars we will be surveying for the remainder of this chapter have all adopted this approach. At the same time, Wright eschews the facile "writing off" of the original historical quest for Jesus and its progeny as unnecessary and wasteful. Rather, he agrees that often the right questions were being raised, even though the answers derived were often less than satisfactory.[31] Thus, Wright will utilize the eschatological insights of Weiss and Schweitzer, while at the same time attempting to alter or augment them where necessary in terms of where the evidence leads in his own opinion. In fact, his starting point is quite similar to those of Weiss and Schweitzer: Jesus in his Jewish/eschatological setting.

Wright's portrait of Jesus in his Jewish setting parallels precisely

---

29 N. T. Wright, *Jesus and the Victory of God* (Minneapolis: Fortress, 1996).
30 N. T. Wright, *The Challenge of Jesus* (Downers Grove, IL: InterVarsity Press, 1999), 15–16.
31 Wright, *The Challenge of Jesus*, 19–24.

that of Luke's gospel. Jesus saw Israel as God's chosen people. And he saw himself as God's long-awaited answer to their present plight (see, for example, Luke 4:14–30). At the same time, tensions and ultimate rejection arose because Jesus had a broader concept of God's kingdom than that of his own Jewish people: God's ultimate intention was to offer salvation to all persons, Jew and Gentile. Israel was simply not going to get the kind of king that they anticipated and longed for. Jesus' messiahship was different from what both a typical Jew and a typical Roman Gentile would expect. And yet, there were enough similarities to get him crucified! He easily became a disappointment to the Jew's more political and military expectations and a threat to the existing Roman rulers of Palestine. Wright summarizes Jesus' self-understanding as Messiah as follows:

> Jesus, then, believed himself to be the focal point of the people of YHWH, the returned-from-exile people, the people of the renewed covenant, the people whose sins were now to be forgiven. He embodied what he had announced. He was the true interpreter of the Torah; the true builder of the Temple; the true spokesperson for Wisdom.[32]

As Wright's scholarly project continues, his more developed Christology will emerge. His massive third volume in the Christian origins series, *The Resurrection of the Son of God*,[33] is a tour de force analysis of the meaning and historicity of the resurrection. Along with his many pastoral volumes, Wright's scholarly work urges Christians along a path of true discipleship in *this world*, the world Jesus came to redeem. At times one gains the impression that Wright seeks to correct distortions on both the left and the right when it comes to determining who Jesus truly is and what he came to do. Ultimately, Wright may find the need to speak in more ontological terms to balance out the more functional Christology that necessarily emerges from historical Jesus studies as such. Another giant on the Jesus studies scene who is equally influential is James D. G. Dunn.

---

32 Wright, *Jesus and the Victory of God*, 538.
33 Minneapolis: Fortress, 2003.

Dunn's approach to historical Jesus studies is rooted in his career-long interest in the beginnings of Christianity.[34] It is also influenced by his conviction that religious experience is formative of theology.[35] In terms of the Third Quest, his trilogy, *Christianity in the Making*, is his landmark contribution to the conversation, but numerous other writings of Dunn also clarify and amplify his thinking on the subject. *Jesus Remembered*, the first volume of his trilogy, has attracted wide attention and response.[36] He has also provided a methodological "prequel," as he calls it, to *Jesus Remembered* with his short, but substantive volume, *A New Perspective on Jesus: What the Quest for the Historical Jesus Missed*.[37]

For Dunn, it was Jesus' *experience* of God as his Father and of the eschatological Spirit that was formative of Jesus' self-understanding. And it was his followers' encounter with Jesus and the tumultuous events of his death and resurrection and their *experience* of the Spirit that were formative of their own understanding of who Jesus was and what he came to do. Early on, Dunn had reached these conclusions concerning Jesus:

> Jesus thought of himself as God's son and as anointed by the eschatological Spirit, because in prayer he experienced God as Father and in ministry he experienced a power to heal which he could only understand as the power of the end-time and an inspiration to proclaim a message which he could only understand as the gospel of the end-time.[38]

Dunn points out that the tendency of the Liberal portraits of Jesus to emphasize his sense of sonship without any mention of his consciousness of the Spirit—which *is* the eschatological dimension of

---

34 James D. G. Dunn, *Jesus, Paul, and the Gospels* (Grand Rapids: Eerdmans, 2011), xiii.
35 See, e.g., James D. G. Dunn, *Jesus and the Spirit: A Study of the Religious and Charismatic Experience of Jesus and the First Christians as Reflected in the New Testament* (London: SCM, 1975), 361.
36 James D. G. Dunn, *Christianity in the Making*, Vol. 1, *Jesus Remembered* (Grand Rapids: Eerdmans, 2003); Robert B. Stewart and Gary R. Habermas, *Memories of Jesus: A Critical Appraisal of James D. G. Dunn's* Jesus Remembered (Nashville: B & H Academic, 2010), which contains analysis from numerous leading scholars.
37 Grand Rapids: Baker, 2005.
38 Dunn, *Jesus and Spirit*, 67 (Dunn, as is often his practice, italicizes this important summary statement of his conclusions).

Jesus' ministry—distorted their understanding of who Jesus was. For Jesus the power of the Spirit at work through him was evidence of both the *presence* of the kingdom as well as its *imminence*. The already/not yet tension inherent in Jesus' proclamation was the result of this consciousness of the Spirit.[39]

Further, Dunn maintains that this dimension of religious experience, specifically experience of the Spirit, was formative of the theology of first-century believers—and should be so for twenty-first-century believers as well:

> In short, as religious experience was fundamental to and creative of the earliest Christian community, so religious experience was fundamental to and creative of the earliest Christian theology. Ever fresh religious experience in dynamic interaction with original witness to the Christ event was the living matrix of NT theology. Without the latter, faith all too easily becomes fanaticism and burns itself out. But without the former, without God as a living reality in religious experience, faith never comes to life and theology remains sterile and dead.[40]

Thus, our approach to New Testament theology in general, and to Christology in particular, should factor in both the objective historical revelation of Jesus and the experience of the Spirit. Calvary, the empty tomb, and Pentecost must be held together if we are to get at who Jesus truly was and is.[41] Perhaps the best term to use to characterize Dunn's approach to the historical quest for Jesus is the word "impact."

In both *Jesus Remembered* and *A New Perspective on Jesus*, Dunn argues that it was singularly this spiritual impact of Jesus that was formative of the New Testament writings. To quest for what Dunn would call a "non-faith-producing Jesus" is to miss him altogether—thus, the many distortions of past and present historical quests. And,

---

[39] Dunn, *Jesus and the Spirit*, 89–90.
[40] Dunn, *Jesus and the Spirit*, 361 (the concluding paragraph of the book).
[41] See Dunn's recent introductory volume in the Library of Biblical Theology series: *New Testament Theology: An Introduction* (Nashville: Abingdon, 2009), esp. Part II: The Determining Factors, Ch. 3 The Revelation of Jesus Christ and Ch. 4 The Experience of the Spirit.

going beyond Kähler (and Bultmann, Borg, et al.), Dunn would include both pre-Easter and post-Easter faith. Methodologically, Dunn argues strongly for greater exploration of the oral Jesus traditions that preceded the written gospels.[42] Oral tradition, the dynamic of memory, the impact of Jesus—it is these emphases in Dunn's writings that have drawn the greatest attention as well as criticism.

How much can we expect from memories, even in non-literary, aurally-oriented cultures? How much of the diversity among the reported sayings of Jesus can be ascribed to the oral transmission process? And does the emphasis on impact actually leave us one step short of the historical Jesus per se?[43] As for Dunn's efforts, his approach has produced one of the most complete and convincing portrayals of Jesus presently available.

Finally, brief mention must be made of the evangelical response to the ferment around the historical Jesus, both among scholars and in general culture. With almost every imaginable portrait of Jesus coming forth, one would expect those whose loyalties lie with a firm confidence in biblical authority, inspiration, and reliability to respond with appropriate critique and alternative scholarly perspectives. A growing library of usually careful research and statement has emerged. In terms of substantive scholarly responses to this ferment, Craig S. Keener and Darrell L. Bock should be mentioned.

Bock's numerous writings in this field of study are generally well known. His *Jesus according to Scripture: Restoring the Portrait from the Gospels* provides a full-orbed treatment of the portraits of Jesus to be found in all four gospels.[44] In addition, Bock has provided for the lay reader the results of a decade-long (1998–2008) study of Jesus by a group of leading biblical scholars, the IBR (Institute for Biblical Research) Jesus Group, meeting annually during the Society of Biblical

---

42 See James D. G. Dunn, *The Oral Gospel Tradition* (Grand Rapids: Eerdmans, 2013).
43 See, e.g., Markus Bockmuehl's questioning whether Dunn's emphasis on the impact of Jesus makes the historical quest for Jesus viable at all and Dunn's response that there is an "obvious linkage between the 'impact' made by Jesus and the Jesus who made that impact" in: Robert B. Stewart and Gary R. Habermas (eds.), *Memories of Jesus* (Nashville: B & H Academic, 2010), 42, 292.
44 Grand Rapids: Baker Academic, 2002.

Literature meetings.[45] Craig Keener has done similar work on his own with his massive study, *The Historical Jesus of the Gospels*.[46] Limiting himself to an examination of the Synoptic gospels, Keener leaves no stone unturned in his comprehensive treatment of the relevant historical materials.

What are the results of the renewed quest for the historical Jesus? Generally, confidence is being restored in the historical portraits of Jesus in the gospels and helpful corrections are being made. The Jewishness of Jesus is being re-emphasized. The eschatological setting of Jesus' message and ministry is finding fuller treatment. Only a few of the more prominent scholars, such as James D. G. Dunn, have taken the second step with a thorough study of New Testament Christology.[47] This may be the most urgent need at present. Veli-Matti Kärkkäinen summarizes the entire enterprise well: "The third quest is alive and well, and one hopes that those involved will begin to dialogue more widely with systematic theology."[48]

> What are the results of the renewed quest for the historical Jesus? Generally, confidence is being restored in the historical portraits of Jesus in the gospels and helpful corrections are being made.

The next step in our quest to know Christ better is to examine the life and ministry of Jesus as presented in the New Testament gospels. These narratives serve as the spine of all Christological reflection. They also serve as an amplification for, as well as a necessary corrective to, contemporary reflection on the significance of Christ. It is a rich journey indeed to enter again the pages of the New Testament and rediscover from these primary sources the person who has impacted this planet more than any other and whom millions confess to be their personal Lord and Savior.

---

45 Darrell L. Bock, *Who Is Jesus? Linking the Historical Jesus with the Christ of Faith* (New York: Howard Books, 2012).
46 Grand Rapids: Eerdmans, 2009.
47 James D. G. Dunn, *Christology in the Making: A New Testament Inquiry into the Origins of the Doctrine of the Incarnation*, 2nd ed., (Grand Rapids: Eerdmans: 1996).
48 *Christology: A Global Introduction* (Grand Rapids: Baker Academic, 2003), 108.

Lesson Three

The Life and Ministry of Jesus

A BRIEF SURVEY OF THE LIFE OF CHRIST

A video presentation would be best. We could move quickly from scene to scene: Bethelehem, Nazareth, the Jordan River, the Judean wilderness, Lake Galilee, Jerusalem, Gethesemane, the crucifixion, the empty tomb, mysterious appearances, the ascension. It is perhaps the best known story in human history. And too often the story gets lost in historians' discussions of minimalist versus maximalist approaches and in theologians' debates concerning substance, hypostasis, and the like. For two millennia the church has found the four gospels of the New Testament to be the best way to access this marvelous Christ event. In fact, for most Christians these narratives are God-given, actually "breathed out" by God, reliable, and totally gripping. They are the best means to knowing Christ savingly.

The purpose of this chapter is to provide exposure again to this story of stories. We will take a two-pronged approach. First, we will examine a thumbnail sketch of Jesus' life and ministry. Then we will survey selectively and in approximate chronological order the gospel accounts of Jesus. The gospels are *bioi*, ancient biographies which selected key events and sayings that best revealed what that person was like and placed these in approximate chronological order. In addition, Luke provides a two-part history of the life of Jesus and the early church, again utilizing the historiographical methods of his day. Taken together, these narratives reveal a unique personality of tremendous impact, both among his contemporaries and on down to the present.

OVERVIEW

It all began when the voice of prophecy—unheard for some four centuries—emerged from the Judean desert. The mysterious John the Baptist, who many thought might be the long-awaited Messiah, stood forth with a message of repentance. He portrayed himself as a forerunner to someone who would administer an end-time Spirit-and-fire baptism. But this someone would surprise everyone by his inauspicious beginnings.

> *It all began when the voice of prophecy—unheard for some four centuries—emerged from the Judean desert.*

Jesus of Nazareth, a Galilean peasant of Jewish descent, worked with his father as a builder and carpenter, loading and carrying rocks from the surrounding hills and cutting and shaping wood. He had four brothers (James, Joseph, Simon, and Judas), two of which would ultimately write books included in the New Testament (James and Judas), Jesus never authoring a book himself. And he had sisters, the number and names of whom we have no record. Evidently, his father, Joseph, died an early death, since he simply drops out of the narratives we have. And all kinds of rumors must have circulated about Jesus' mother, Mary. Was Jesus illegitimately conceived or did he really have a miraculous divine conception as was told by many? Nazareth was a small out-of-the-way, nondescript village, and Jesus himself was an unknown until about the last three years of his brief life, when both he and John (the baptizer) caught the attention, first of Jewish believers and then of the Roman governing officials. It is truly amazing that someone of such humble origins could have such historic impact.

The core events of Jesus' life and ministry can be easily encapsulated as follows:

- The preaching and baptizing ministry of John the Baptist
- The baptism of Jesus and launching of his ministry
- Jesus' Galilean ministry of teaching, preaching, and healing
- Jesus' Judean ministry, leading ultimately to conflicts with religious authorities in Jerusalem
- Jesus' arrest, trial, and crucifixion
- Jesus' resurrection, appearances, and ascension[1]

But as one moves through the stories of the gospels, it becomes abundantly clear that there is a transcendent dimension to this historical figure Jesus.

He is a man, a first-century Jewish man. But at the same time he is more than a man. He pre-existed as an eternal divine being, even before the creation of the cosmos. He rose from death and ascended back to Father. And he now reigns with the Father, while at the same time living—through the Holy Spirit—in those who believe in him. He was referring to his historical existence when he told his disciples, "The poor you will always have with you, but you will not always have me" (Matt. 26:11). But he would later say to these same disciples, "And surely I am with you always, to the very end of the age" (Matt. 28:20), referring to his glorified existence as the eternal Son of God—not two Jesuses, but one Jesus, at the same time both divine and human.[2] The Christ of faith and the Jesus of history are one and the same.

> He is a man, a first-century Jewish man. But at the same time he is more than a man. He pre-existed as an eternal divine being.

John's prophetic ministry, on the Old Testament model of Elijah, was short-lived, ending in imprisonment and death by beheading. Jesus' ministry would continue for a longer period of time, but would also end in a premature death by crucifixion. Jesus' j ministry was

---

1 See Mark L. Strauss, *Four Portraits, One Jesus: An Introduction to Jesus and the Gospels* (Grand Rapids: Zondervan, 2007), 404–405.
2 See Mark Allan Powell, *Introducing the New Testament: A Historical, Literary, and Theological Survey* (Grand Rapids: Baker Academic, 2009), 64–65.

focused primarily upon his own people, the Jews. He traveled from place to place, speaking in their synagogues. But he also spoke to the crowds he was attracting in an outdoor, rural setting. Jesus circulated among the smaller villages, such as Bethsaida or Capernaum, rather than targeting the larger cities, such as Sepphoris or Tiberias. He was a peasant, assuming the roles of a rabbi or a prophet, and ministering to other peasants.[3]

Though focused on Israel, he reached out to people largely disenfranchised by society: women, children, tax collectors, the infirm, the insane, prostitutes, and generally "sinners" of all sorts. He alienated the Jewish religious leaders with his attitudes toward Torah and Temple: Basically, he claimed to be the authoritative interpreter of the Law, its fulfillment, if you will. And he claimed an authority over the Temple as well, clearing it of those who had set up a market there, and putting his own bodily existence, or "temple," on par with the majestic structure that dominated the Jerusalem landscape. He announced that in his very person the kingdom of God had arrived and that one could only enter this rule or reign of God by aligning with Jesus himself. The common folk loved him, but their leaders were threatened by virtually all he said and did.

Jesus could be both compassionate and confronting, almost at the same moment. He was enigmatic, yet singularly uncomplicated. He was a commoner, utilizing folksy examples in his teaching and preaching. He could be humorous—for example, drawing the picture verbally of a person with a plank in their eye trying to help someone with a speck in their eye. He certainly was not "spooky," as some are today who aspire to be "spiritual"; otherwise, he would surely have repelled the children who flocked to him. Not weird but winsome, Jesus epitomized what a healthy human existence was all about—enjoying God, people, and God's creation. He came as a servant to all, setting the example for his followers.

He was known as a healer and an exorcist. He constantly dealt with hopeless situations—lepers, the blind, the mute, the paralyzed,

---

3 Powell, *Introducing the New Testament*, 66.

the demonized. His authority even extended to nature itself as seen in his turning water into wine and calming a storm on Lake Galilee. He even predicted his own death and resurrection. His kingdom ethic raised the bar above even the standards of the scribes and Pharisees. He claimed to be sinless, as we shall see. Both his words and his actions revealed a self-understanding that was considered blasphemous by his Jewish opponents. Literally, who did he think he was, claiming the authority to forgive sin and claiming a unique relationship with the Father that predated even his own earthly existence? In spite of his general benevolence toward all, the tide turned against him and his crucifixion became inevitable.

Jesus literally raised life and death issues. He raised the dead, predicted his own death, and rose from death himself. The kingdom he preached had both a present and a future dimension, referring to both God's rule here and now and to an end-time judgment, the results of which were all wrapped up in Jesus himself—again, life and death. As far as titles go, Jesus most often referred to himself in the third person as the Son of Man, with the mysterious, exalted figure of Daniel 7:13–14 as the backdrop. More privately, he portrayed himself as the Son of God and the Messiah. At his own death, justice was mocked by Jewish and Roman officials and his own disciples abandoned him. His demise was agonizing and ignominious. But his resurrection was glorious and mysterious—reflecting a light back upon an earthly life that could only be described as God's Shekinah Glory moving into the neighborhood (compare John 1:14 THE MESSAGE).

But there is much more to the story, which will become apparent as we move through the gospels' narratives and weave together the marvelous tapestry of Jesus' life and ministry. We will survey in turn Jesus' birth and youth, the beginning of his public ministry, his Galilean ministry, his travels outside Galilee, the Perean and Judean ministry, Jesus' last week and crucifixion, and Jesus' resurrection and ascension.[4] Even a brief perusal of these gospel accounts will reinforce

---

[4] I am utilizing here the very helpful outline provided by the following: Walter A. Elwell and Robert W. Yarbrough, *Encountering the New Testament: A Historical and Theological Survey* (Grand Rapids: Baker, 1998), 117–33.

the impression that Jesus was nonpareil and hopefully engender an even greater passion for being his followers. If we can become excited about our favorite sports figure or political candidate (though the latter is a little more difficult to come by these days), surely we should show some energy and enthusiasm about the greatest figure in human history, whose beginnings, though humble, point to the greatest miracle of all—the Word made flesh!

JESUS' BIRTH AND YOUTH (6 B.C.-A.D. 26)

Too often, when we read the New Testament, we come at these scriptures with the mentality that we are reading a fantasy by a Tolkien or Lewis—edifying as these writings may be!—rather than actual historical events. I will never forget standing before the pyramids of Giza and gaping in awe. They really are there, and we still wonder how they were built. It is helpful to remind ourselves that those structures had already been there some 2700 years when Mary and Joseph arrived in Egypt with their son, Jesus. That period of time from the building of the pyramids and Jesus' arrival in exile is longer than the span of time separating us from the events of the New Testament—amazing! The events surrounding Jesus' birth were also considered amazing (see the first two chapters each of Matthew and Luke), so amazing in fact that modern readers often view these stories more as literary and theological constructs than as actual historical events.

Take, for example, the magisterial study of these materials by the renowned New Testament scholar, Raymond E. Brown: *The Birth of the Messiah: A Commentary on the Infancy Narratives in Matthew and Luke*. No one does a better job of literary analysis and ferreting out the theological message of the infancy narratives.[5] And yet, following Brown's presentation to the end, one realizes that this very pious Catholic scholar actually places little historical credence in the events related by Matthew and Luke. The appearance of a mysterious star and the visit of magi, for example, carry no

---
5 New York: Doubleday, 1977.

historical weight, but much theological import.[6] But what if the history is as reliable as the theology? We are back to the issue of starting point already broached at the beginning of our explorations. Ultimately, historical and literary analysis should serve discovering the theological purpose of the writer. Matthew's infancy narrative is a good example.

Clearly the story of the magi, including the star and the dream (Matt. 2:1–12), was recorded by Matthew to emphasize God's sovereign orchestrating of events: God was bringing forth "the king of the Jews" (v. 2), "the Messiah" (v. 4), someone worthy of worship (v. 11)![7] Both the Jews and the Gentiles of all the nations awaited Jesus' appearance: His coming was of universal significance. And despite the machinations of Herod the Great, God was going to accomplish his sovereign purposes. Finally, the return of the holy family to Palestine was also divinely elicited, as they chose to settle in Nazareth, resulting in Jesus' being called a Nazarene, a term of derision foreshadowing the rejection that was to follow (v. 23).

Luke's infancy narrative achieves its historical and theological purposes in large measure by means of emphasizing the *contrasts* between Jesus and John the Baptist. John is "a prophet of the Most High" (Luke 1:76); Jesus is "the son of the Most High" (v. 32). John is "filled with the Holy Spirit even before he is born" (Luke 1:15); Jesus is *conceived* by the Holy Spirit (vv. 31–35). John will "go on before the Lord to prepare the way for him, to give his people the knowledge of salvation through the forgiveness of their sins" (vv, 76–77). John is merely the forerunner of the Messiah. Since the voice of prophecy had not been heard for some 400 years, it is understandable that many would mistake him for the Messiah. Paul encountered disciples of John at Ephesus some thirty-five years after Pentecost (Acts 19:1–7)! Thus, even the Johannine prologue would make special note of the contrast between John as a mere witness to the light and Jesus as the true light (John 1:1–14).

---

6 Brown does, however, provide a very helpful discussion of the astronomical possibilities (Brown, *The Birth of the Messiah*, 171–73)!
7 See Strauss, *Four Portraits, One Jesus*, 225.

Both the Matthean and Lukan infancy narratives make special note of the virginal conception of Jesus. Enlightenment rationalism often recoils from such a concept. Allowing for the supernatural, certainly God could have brought forth his incarnate, sinless Son in any manner he chose. But the Scriptures explicitly teach a *virginal* conception.[8] Both Jesus' entrance (virginal conception) and exit (resurrection and ascension) were supernatural. Remove the supernatural from the gospels and you no longer have the gospel. And yet, in the final analysis, the issue in this regard has more to do with our understanding of the authority and inspiration of Scripture than it does with Christology. Ultimately, we affirm the virgin birth doctrine because it is taught in the Bible.[9] We humbly acknowledge that God sovereignly chose to bring forth his Son in this manner, and we owe a singular debt to Mary for her willingness to suffer the stigma and to be "the Lord's servant" (Luke 1:38).

Finally, we must consider the boyhood of Jesus. The only biblical information we have is provided by Luke (ch. 2:41–52). Mary and Joseph found the twelve-year-old Jesus in the temple courts, conversing with the teachers. "Everyone who heard him was amazed at his understanding and his answers" (v. 47). Jesus said that he simply had to be in his "Father's house," something his parents could not understand at the time (vv. 49–50). Jesus' divine filial consciousness and sense of uniqueness was already evident. And yet his full and true humanity was also evident: "And Jesus grew in wisdom and stature, and in favor with God and man" (v. 52). This is, reliably, all we know about Jesus' boyhood. Later infancy gospels such as *The Protevangelium of James* and *The Infancy Gospel of Thomas* would relate fanciful tales of Jesus' manifesting divine powers, in poorly written accounts of no historical value. What we can speculate is that he lived an ordinary, unobtrusive life until he launched his public ministry. Perhaps Joseph, Jesus, and his four brothers plied their trade in nearby Sepphoris, a major city about

---

[8] See Raymond E. Brown, *The Virginal Conception & Bodily Resurrection of Jesus* (New York: Paulist Press, 1973) for a full treatment of this subject.

[9] Robert H. Stein, *Jesus the Messiah: A Survey of the Life of Christ* (Downers Grove, IL: InterVarsity Press, 1996), 80.

which we have abundant archeological information.[10] And it is also likely, given his Jewish and Hellenistic roots, that Jesus was trilingual, "speaking Aramaic in the home and with friends, using Hebrew in religious contexts, and conversing in Greek in business and governmental contexts."[11]

The gospel narratives shift quickly to the events which launched Jesus' public ministry. With John the Baptist we have the beginning of the end: He announces both the soon beginning of Jesus' ministry as well as the end of the age—coming judgment both within history with the fall of Jerusalem and at the end of history in the final judgment of the nations. In other words, according to John, the appearance of Jesus marks the beginning of end time events which continue to the present!

THE BEGINNING OF JESUS' PUBLIC MINISTRY (A.D. 26–27)

Following Luke's pattern of introducing John the Baptist first and then Jesus (see his infancy narrative), we are able to place Jesus both historically and eschatologically. The "word of God came to John" during "the reign of Tiberius Caesar" (Luke 3: 1–2), thrusting John forward as the Lord's forerunner announcing "God's salvation" (vv. 4–6). John preached a water baptism signifying repentance and forgiveness of sins. Jesus, John announced, would administer a Spirit-and-fire baptism bringing the judgment and salvation of the end time (vv. 16–17). "His winnowing fork is in his hand to clear his threshing floor and to gather the wheat into his barn, but he will burn up the chaff with unquenchable fire" (v. 17). Jesus the Baptizer, a seldom-discussed Christological title,[12] brings a holistic salvation, which in our various ecclesial traditions has been compromised by our regenerational (Reformed), sanctifying (Wesleyan), and empowering (Pentecostal/charismatic) emphases. Jesus' kingdom brings about a

---

10 See Richard A. Batey, *Jesus & the Forgotten City* (Grand Rapids: Baker, 1992).
11 Strauss, *Four Portraits, One Jesus*, 421.
12 See F. F. Bruce, *What the Bible Teaches About What Jesus Did* (Wheaton, Ill.: Tyndale, 1979), 44–45, on Jesus' continuing work.

cosmic redemption through an empowered church! Finally, Luke's genealogy of Jesus traces his line back to Adam, thus relating Jesus' saving significance to the whole of humanity (v. 37).

John preached and administered a baptism of repentance in preparation for the appearance of the Messiah. But when that day came, John was caught off guard by Jesus' request to be baptized by John. "I need to be baptized by you," John said. But Jesus persisted in order to "fulfill all righteousness" (Matt. 3:14–15). Jesus was identifying with John, with us, and with his Father. This public event in itself was a Messianic announcement, launching the Spirit-empowered Jesus on his end time mission. It was a corporate event in that Jesus was endorsing John's movement. But it was also a very personal and private event: "Just as Jesus was coming up out of the water, he saw heaven being torn open and the Spirit descending on him like a dove. And a voice came from heaven: 'You are my Son, whom I love; with you I am well pleased'" (Mark 1:10–11). Luke adds that Jesus was praying when this happened (Luke 3:21–22). A Trinitarian revelation, a spiritual anointing, the beginning of the Messianic Age—could there be a more significant revelation! But this spiritually high moment would lead directly into a stygian darkness of wilderness testing.

"Full of the Holy Spirit" (Luke 4:1), Jesus is taken by the Spirit into the wilderness where he is tempted by the devil, toward the end of a period of forty days of fasting (Matt. 4:1–11; Mark 1:12–13; Luke 4:1–13). The gospels are not explicit as to the rationale for this event. Moses was on the mountain for forty days of fasting when the Law was given (Deut. 9:9). Similarly, Jesus would inaugurate the new era of salvation with forty days of fasting. Satan's threefold temptation tested Jesus' faithfulness: Would he miraculously turn stones into bread to satisfy his physical hunger? Would he leap from the pinnacle of the temple in an effort to tempt the Father's protection? Would he bow down in worship to Satan to gain control of the nations? No, he answered the devil's lies with the truth of the Scriptures, resisted the devil's overtures, and won the victory.

Before surveying Jesus' ministry, something should be said concerning Jesus' family. Mary continued to loom large in the story of Jesus and the life of the early church. Joseph drops out of the narrative early on, presumably in death. Jesus, therefore, probably inherited a fatherly role in the family. He had four brothers: James, Joseph, Simon, and Judas, as well as sisters, though the number is uncertain (Matt. 13:55). At one point early in his ministry, his family sought to seize him, thinking he had lost his mind (Mark 3:21). Later, his own brothers would bait him to go publically to Jerusalem, knowing the imminent danger that awaited him there (John 7:1–9). But these same siblings would become followers of Jesus, James becoming the leader of the Jerusalem church and authoring a book of the New Testament and Judas (Jude) also penning a book included in the New Testament canon.

There was an indefinite period of time (perhaps a year) between Jesus' baptism and his return to Galilee, after the arrest of John, to begin his public ministry. These were probably months of spiritual consolidation similar to the longer sojourns of Moses and Paul before assuming their respective leadership roles. What would transpire in the two to three years of ministry to follow would literally shake the world—an astounding fact given the modest parameters of his travels and his ignominious death. But then—as Christians of all ages aver—no one else ever spoke as he spoke, performed such astounding miracles, taught as he taught, loved as he loved, died as he died, or came out of the grave alive forevermore, as he did!

THE GALILEAN MINISTRY (A.D. 27–29)

Jesus' first major task was that of calling the twelve founding apostles to be his disciples. He wanted their companionship and he wanted to send them out on mission (Mark 3:13–19). Luke tells us that Jesus spent the entire night in prayer before making these momentous selections from among his followers (Luke 6:12–16). The parallel with the twelve patriarchs of Israel was obvious. But one apparent implication of his actions is often overlooked: Jesus' vision of a future church spreading the gospel of the kingdom across the globe.[13] Jesus had returned to Galilee, after the arrest of John the Baptist by Herod Antipas, to launch an extensive ministry in Galilee, headquartered in Capernaum (Matt. 4:12–13; Mark 1:14). A survey of selected events during this period will prove quite illuminating as to who Jesus is and what he set out to accomplish.

Jesus' inaugural sermon in his hometown synagogue proved to be singularly inauspicious: He was run out of town (Luke 4:16–30)! Most preachers I know would have abandoned their calling had they been similarly treated by their home church after their first sermon. But such rejection was to epitomize Jesus' ministry. It was the *content* of Jesus' message that day that got him into trouble. He claimed to be fulfilling in his own person Isaiah's prediction of the coming Messiah (Isa. 61:1–2). As with most prophets in Scripture, Jesus confronted the parochial concerns of his hearers and engendered their wrath. "What happens in Nazareth prepares for what will happen in Jerusalem," observes David E. Garland. "[Prophets] speak the truth that people often do not want to hear."[14] In this instance, Jesus predicted his own rejection, similar to that of Elijah and Elisha in their day, for announcing that God's saving plan included the Gentiles (vv. 23–20).

Jesus' authoritative words and actions astounded everyone. Walking by Lake Galilee, he sees Simon and Andrew casting their net and simply says, "Come, follow me, and I will send you out to fish for people" (Mark 1:16–17). He issues a similar call to James and John, the sons of Zebedee (vv. 19–20). In both instances these fishermen immediately leave their work to follow Jesus. Then Mark proceeds to give us a glimpse into a typical day in the life and ministry of Jesus (vv. 21–34). Again, his *authority* is on display.

First, they go to Capernaum, where on the Sabbath "Jesus went into the synagogue and began to teach. The people were amazed at his teaching, because he taught them as one who had authority, not as the teachers of the law" (Mark 1:21–22). Jesus claimed personal authority

---

[13] Stein, *Jesus the Messiah*, 120–22.
[14] David E. Garland, *Luke: Zondervan Exegetical Commentary on the New Testament*, Clinton E. Arnold, gen. ed. (Grand Rapids: Zondervan, 2011), 208.

for his teaching instead of appealing to previous rabbis, as their scribes did. Immediately (*euthus*, a Greek term Mark uses repeatedly throughout his narrative to enforce the sense of immediate *action*), a crisis ensues as a demonized man confronts Jesus and Jesus delivers him (vv. 23–24).

> The people were all so amazed that they asked each other, "What is this? A new teaching—and with authority! He even gives orders to impure spirits and they obey him." News about him spread quickly over the whole region of Galilee (vv. 27–28).

The Christological import is obvious. Jesus is unique. The authority implicit in his words and actions is nonpareil. It was difficult to be indifferent to him. Responses, both positive and negative, were strong. Immediately (again, *euthus*), Jesus goes to Peter's house and proceeds to heal Peter's mother-in-law of a fever (vv. 29–31). The whole town gathers and Jesus heals and delivers them all (vv. 32–34). This pattern of Jesus' dominical authority pervades Mark's gospel.

Jesus departed Capernaum and immediately launched into his first preaching tour (Mark 1:35–39; Luke 4:42–43). Matthew provides the following summary of these travels: "Jesus was going all over Galilee, teaching in their synagogues, preaching the good news of the kingdom, and healing every disease and sickness among the people" (Matt. 4:23 HCSB; cf. 9:35). I have commented elsewhere on these words and their implications for Jesus' followers, the church:

> Matthew's gospel accents Jesus' teaching role, coupling five great teachings of Jesus with a related narrative section. Before the first two of them, the Sermon on the Mount (Matt. 5:1–7:29) and the Mission Discourse (Matt. 9:35–10:42), Matthew provides a programmatic summary of Jesus' ministry. In both instances Jesus is described as (1) teaching in their synagogues, (2) preaching the good news of the kingdom, and (3) healing every disease and sickness (Matt. 4:23; 9:35). As the Body of Christ, shouldn't we expect to

continue that ministry? "Jesus Christ is the same yesterday and today and forever" (Heb. 13:8).[15]

Jesus taught and preached, but he also healed and delivered. His fame spread: "So they brought to Him all those who were afflicted, those suffering from various diseases and intense pains, the demon-possessed, the epileptics, and the paralytics. And He healed them all" (Matt. 4:24 HCSB). The churches of the developing nations in Asia, Africa, and Latin America have perpetuated Jesus' ministry in this regard and with amazing results!

So Jesus was a preacher, healer, exorcist, and wonder-worker—and he was the quintessential teacher. Matthew's gospel displays this ministry well in the distinctive teaching sections of his narrative. Perhaps the best known of Jesus' messages is the Sermon on the Mount (Matt. 5–7). A broad overview of the sermon reveals a poignant characteristic of Jesus' person and preaching: He was *provocative*; he demanded decision. The sermon depicted a choice of *two*: two kinds of righteousness (5:20–48); two kinds of piety (6:1–18); two treasures: earth/heaven (6:19–21); two kinds of persons: blind/sighted (6:22–23); two masters: God/money (6:24); two gates, roads, and destinies (7:13–14); two kinds of prophets or teachers (7:15–20); and two houses/foundations (7:24–27).[16] Thus, Jesus' teaching, preaching, and healing ministry also brought with it *controversy*.

Luke's "Sermon on the Plain" (Luke 6:17–49) shares similarities with the Sermon on the Mount, but is shorter. Some of Matthew's sermon account is scattered elsewhere in Luke's gospel. Both set the disciples' kingdom agenda and ethic. Both are daunting! Jesus, as a traveling preacher, probably repeated himself often and adapted his teaching to the setting and audience. Any honest traveling preacher today will admit to the same practice. And, besides, the core message bears repeating. Ultimately, it is singular: the gospel of the kingdom. Jesus' preaching was authoritative and necessarily divisive. He was preemptive of everything the Pharisees, Sadducees, teachers of the law

---

15 Larry Hart, *Christianity in 3D* (Tulsa: Truth Aflame Press, 2014), 122.
16 See John R. W. Stott, *Christian Counter-Culture: The Message of the Sermon on the Mount* (Downers Grove, IL: InterVarsity Press, 1978).

represented. He claimed to be the *fulfillment* of it all! The religious establishment may have been largely put off by Jesus's teaching, but common folk heard him gladly.

> Jesus, as a communicator, was never boring. He refused to drone on, citing one rabbi after another, in paralyzing prose that put his hearers to sleep. His language and images were fresh, drawn from nature and everyday life. He was colorful, unpredictable, sometimes humorous. He utilized proverbs, metaphors, similes, puns, riddles, paradox, hyperbole, and irony. He always kept you a little off balance and forced you to think. He is simply the most delightful and disturbing teacher you will ever hear. No one has matched him in the history of civilization, nor will they ever. The uniqueness of Jesus' teaching alone is positive proof that we are dealing here with someone who is more than a man. He is God's one and only Son.[17]

Both Matthew and Luke provide interesting perspectives on our next selected event in Jesus' Galilean ministry: the healing of the centurion's servant (Matt. 8:5–13; Luke 7:1–10). Luke highlights three centurions of exemplary faith in his salvation-history narrative: the one in this story (Luke 7:9); the one at the cross (23:47); and Cornelius (Acts 10).[18] Matthew provides a *Readers' Digest* version of the slave's healing with some variations from Luke. Scholars debate explanations for these variances, such as the process of oral tradition and the redacting work of the gospel writers. But the central message is clear: faith recognizes Jesus' authority and his saving gospel is available to *all*, regardless of social status (cf. the healing of the man with leprosy in Matt. 8:1–4, which precedes this account), gender, nationality, religion, and the like. Jew and Gentile, slave and free, male and female, rich and poor, powerful and helpless—all are candidates for Jesus' kingdom. Both accounts inform us that Jesus was amazed at the centurion's faith (Matt. 8:10; Luke 7:9). The centurion evinced humility, feeling unworthy to have Jesus in his home, and faith,

---

17 Hart, *Christianity in 3D*, 122–23.
18 Garland, *Luke*, 292.

recognizing Jesus' authority. Jesus needed only to speak the word for his slave to be healed. Jesus took the occasion to confront publically Israel's unbelief, her failure to acknowledge Jesus' authority. Again, neutrality toward Jesus was an impossibility.

Jesus' authority set him apart. He claimed the right to forgive sins. He dispelled spiritual darkness, rebuking and silencing demons. He healed people in every sort of distress. He raised the dead to life. And he even exercised authority over nature, as our next event illustrates: the calming of the storm on Lake Galilee.

I have a vivid memory of a reenactment of this story (Matt. 8:23–27; Mark 4:35–41; Luke 8:22–25). That morning, I read Mark's account, from the Good News translation, to my little daughter. And that afternoon, in a little inflatable pool in the backyard, we decided to act out the story. First, I said, we need a storm; so we proceeded to make big splashes in the little pool. Playing the role of the disciples, I cried very dramatically, "Jesus, we're going to die. Don't you care?" My little daughter, playing the role of Jesus, was so caught up in my histrionics she simply yelled, "Yeah!" Then we returned to the script: Still splashing the water vigorously, we quoted Jesus saying, "Wind, be quiet! Waves, be still!" The story continues with Jesus' rebuking his disciples' fearful unbelief and the disciples' asking, "Who is this?" They were amazed at his authority over nature. A short time later, Jesus would determine that it was time to expand his mission, so he sends out the twelve.

Jesus commissioned his apostles, empowering them to duplicate the very ministry he himself was doing—healing the sick, driving out demons, even raising the dead (Matt. 10:1–16; cf. Mark 6:7; 3:13–19; Luke 6:12–16; 9:2–5; 10:3). Matthew provides the full discourse (Matt. 10:1–42). "Jesus called his twelve disciples to him and gave them authority to drive out impure spirits and to heal every disease and sickness" (v. 1). He commissioned them to go "to the lost sheep of Israel" (vv. 5–6). Later he would commission them to go to all the nations (Matt. 28:18–20). It would be a faith journey with opposition, persecution, rejection, and division (vv. 9–42). They would be "like sheep among wolves"; so they should be "as shrewd as snakes and as innocent as doves" (v. 16). It was a disciple-making call of taking up one's cross and following Jesus, of losing one's life for his sake (vv. 38–39).

Meanwhile, John the Baptist is languishing in prison. He hears reports of Jesus' miraculous ministry, but his questions linger. Jesus has not turned out to be the kind of messiah everyone was expecting—and John is still in jail! So he sends messengers to Jesus to ask, "Are you the one who is to come, or should we expect someone else?" (Matt. 11:3; Luke 7:20). Jesus' reply introduces a whole new paradigm (Matt. 11:2–6; Luke 7:18–23). The salvation he is bringing is cosmic in scope. His kingdom entails not merely military conquest and political power. It is veritably the restoration of the entire creation, the transformation of a fallen planet. In describing his ministry, he alludes to key passages in Isaiah (35:5–6; 61:1; 26:19; 29:18–21) which depict the transformation of the universe into an eternal Edenic state. Thus, when Jesus was healing the sick, casting out demons, raising the dead, commanding nature, and proclaiming the good news to the poor, this was the literal inbreaking of the kingdom of God.[19]

Luke, historian and theologian,[20] describes Jesus' continuing work in Galilee with these words:

> After this, Jesus traveled about from one town and village to another, proclaiming the good news of the kingdom of God. The Twelve were with him, and also some women who had been cured of evil spirits and diseases: Mary (called Magdalene) from whom seven demons had come out; Joanna the wife of Chuza, the manager of Herod's household; Susanna; and many others. These women were helping support them out of their own means (Luke 8:1–3).

Luke alone provides us with this important information. In fact, throughout his two-volume work he highlights the role of women.

---

[19] Mark L. Strauss, *Jesus Behaving Badly: Puzzling Paradoxes of the Man from Galilee* (Downers Grove, IL: InterVarsity Press, 2015), 28–33.

[20] See the pioneering work by I. Howard Marshall: *Luke: Historian and Theologian* (Grand Rapids: Zondervan, 1971).

Branching out again into the surrounding towns and villages, Jesus initiates a new phase of his Galilean ministry. What Luke takes pains to note is the fact that Jesus' band of followers included numerous women, many of whom also provided financial support for the ministry.

It is difficult to overstate the significance of such an arrangement—women disciples traveling the countryside with Jesus and his male disciples and providing financial support. Some of them may have come from desperate circumstances, but others evidently came from the upper strata of society. All were committed followers of Jesus. They would be with him to the very end (Luke 24:1–12). By his actions more than his words, Jesus continually challenged the status quo. "While a large crowd was gathering and people were coming to Jesus from town after town," Luke continues, "[Jesus] told this parable" (Luke 8:4). The parable Luke relates is one of Jesus' most important teachings and one of the few parables, evidently, for which Jesus provides an *interpretation* (vv. 5–15).

Jesus provides an allegory of the diversity of responses to his kingdom message.[21] Again, his teaching is universal in scope: God spreads the message of his kingdom among all kind of folk, and only about a fourth of them (to use modern statistical analysis, with probable distortion!) respond appropriately. Followers of Christ today would do well to remind themselves that fallen human nature has not changed and that the church can anticipate a similar response to our evangelistic and discipleship efforts.

The Galilean ministry continues as Jesus sends out the Twelve to do precisely the kind of ministry he has been doing—casting out demons, healing the sick, and announcing the kingdom of God (Luke 9:1–9): "So they set out and went from village to village, proclaiming the good news and healing people everywhere" (v. 6). When they returned, they "gathered around Jesus and reported to him all they had done and taught" (Mark 6:30; cf. Luke 9:10). There is so much hustle and bustle

---

[21] Craig L. Blomberg, *Interpreting the Parables* (Downers Grove, IL: InterVarsity, 1990), 226–29.

LEARNING CHRIST 69

(to the point of missing meals) that Jesus says to them, "Come with me by yourselves to a quiet place and get some rest" (Mark 6:31). Jesus valued the principle of rest. What happens next, however, becomes one of the most significant miracles of Jesus' ministry.

Unable to avoid the pursuing crowds, Jesus proceeds to teach and heal them until late in the day. Then the need for food becomes obvious. Five thousand men, plus women and children, swelling the number of mouths to feed to around two thousand, need sustenance. And Jesus knows just how to provide it (Matt. 14:13–21; Mark 6:32–44; Luke 9:10–17; John 6:1–15). He takes five loaves and two fish and multiplies them as they are served; there are twelve basketfuls left over. It is a well-known story. And apparently it was also well-known to the early church in that it is the only miracle of Jesus recorded in all four gospels. The Synoptics each include it, and John adds additional interesting details. (It is helpful to correlate the accounts to get the full picture.) This nature miracle is rife with symbolism. It is an adumbration of the Messianic Banquet to come! One is reminded of the manna in the desert provided by God through Moses (Exod. 16; Num. 11), of Elisha's feeding of the hundred (2 Kings 4:42–44), and the miraculous catch of fish Jesus made possible when he called his first disciples (Luke 5:1–11)—the beginning of Israel, the restoration of Israel, the beginning of Jesus' end time ministry.[22] We should also note the role of the Twelve (Luke 9:12), the twelve basketfuls left over, and the sheer bounty of the event. And God still uses us fallible human beings today to accomplish his miraculous saving purposes in the earth!

Walter A. Elwell and Robert W. Yarbrough provide a helpful concluding summary of this period of Jesus' ministry:

> This phase of the Galilean ministry ended after the Passover of A.D. 29 when Jesus became embroiled in two major conflicts—one with the fickle crowd that wanted to make him a king because he had fed them in the wilderness, and the other with the religious leaders over some questions

---

[22] Darrell L. Bock, *Jesus according to Scripture: Restoring the Portrait from the Gospels* (Grand Rapids: Baker Academic, 2002), 217.

of ritual law. This latter conflict heated up to such a degree that the Jewish authorities in Judea began devising ways to take Jesus' life (John 7:1).[23]

JESUS' TRAVELS OUTSIDE GALILEE (A.D. 29)

As we continue our selective journey through Jesus' life and ministry, we want to examine two key events that occurred during the brief time he journeyed outside of Galilee. One is clearly a turning point in Jesus' whole ministry (Peter's confession of Jesus' messiahship at Caesarea Philippi) and the other a precursor of the revelation of Jesus' future eschatological glory (the Transfiguration).

Careful students of Mark's gospel have generally observed a key turning-point and transition in Mark's presentation, with the Caesarea Philippi account (Mark 8:27–30). Luke's narrative of both events (Caesarea Philippi and the Transfiguration) provides an insight that neither Mark nor Matthew take note of: *Jesus was praying when they occurred* (Luke 9:18, 29). (Later we will explore in depth this salient characteristic of Luke's two-volume narrative.) But Matthew's rendering of the Caesarea Philippi story is the most complete and will form the backdrop for our theological observations.

Jesus was about to embark on his fateful journey to Jerusalem. He wanted to consolidate his relationship with his disciples and their understanding of his person and mission. He chose to travel northeast to a scenic but pagan community at the headwaters of the Jordan, Caesarea Philippi, for a private retreat with his disciples. Such an unlikely location for such a momentous revelation! He begins with a diagnostic question: "Who do people say the Son of Man is?" (Matt. 16:13). Referencing himself as "Son of Man" is strategically ambiguous enough to guard against the crowds conscripting him to be a military king. Then he asks, "Who do you say I am?" (v. 15). In typical fashion, Peter speaks up first: "You are the Messiah, the Son of the living God" (v. 16). And Jesus congratulates Peter for receiving this revelation from

---

23 Elwell and Yarbrough, *Encountering the New Testament*, 124.

the Father (v. 17). If only the conversation had stopped there, but unfortunately it does not.

Jesus goes on to predict his coming suffering, death, and resurrection and Peter steps forth again in response: "Peter took him aside and began to rebuke him. 'Never, Lord!' he said. 'This shall never happen to you!'" (v. 22). Jesus' rejoinder is chilling: "Get behind me, Satan!" (v. 23). From congratulations to being called Satan for opposing the purposes of God—Peter is much like us all in our spotty spiritual performances! Frank Matera, addressing the Markan version of this event, summarizes well what is happening in this story: "In effect, the Gospel of Mark redefines messiahship in terms of suffering, death, and resurrection."[24] Again, we see Jesus preparing his church, under Peter's leadership initially (see the first half of the Book of Acts), with a clearer understanding of who he is and what he came to do. And Jesus couches his call to self-denial and cross-bearing in eschatological terms. The Son of Man is going to come in his Father's glory and some standing there would see a glorious manifestation of kingdom glory *before they died!* He was referring to his Transfiguration (Matt. 16:27–28; Mark 8:38–9:1; Luke 9:26–27).

That the Synoptic writers intended to join the events of Caesarea Philippi and the Transfiguration is clearly indicated by their linking them in a precise timeline, something not attempted elsewhere until the passion narratives. "After six days" (Matt. 17:1; Mark 9:2) and "About eight days after Jesus said this" (Luke 9:28) are the descriptive phrases used. Each event further informs the other. In the broadest strokes both stories deal with Jesus' suffering and glory. The Transfiguration is epochal, comparable to Moses on Sinai. Indeed, in both there is a terrifying manifestation of divine glory and speech. And both Moses and Elijah are subordinated to Jesus: "This is my Son…listen to him!" (Matt. 17:5; Mark 9:7; Luke 9:35). This high point in Jesus' ministry, shared only with his inner circle of Peter, James, and John, is theological to the core—an archetype of Incarnational Christology.

---

[24] Frank J. Matera, *New Testament Christology* (Louisville: Westminster John Knox Press, 1999), 18.

THE PEREAN AND JUDEAN MINISTRY (A.D. 29–30)

> In the fall of A.D. 29, Jesus knew that the time had arrived for him to go to Jerusalem to fulfill the purpose of his life, which was to die and rise again for the sins of the world.[25]

Thus, Elwell and Yarbrough aptly summarize the beginning and import of Jesus' fateful journey to Jerusalem. We will be drawing almost solely from the gospels of Luke and John for the narrative of this phase of Jesus' ministry. The best place to begin is with Luke's famous "Travel Narrative," beginning with Luke 9:51: "As the time approached for him to be taken up to heaven, Jesus resolutely set out for Jerusalem." What ensued immediately was rejection by the Samaritans (vv. 52–56). "As the baptism (3:21–22) introduced the first period of Jesus' ministry, which begins with the rejection at Nazareth, the transfiguration (9:28–36) introduces the second period of his ministry, which begins with his rejection in Samaria."[26] It is impossible to trace the historical and geographical sequence of the numerous events that follow. But correlating Lukan and Johannine materials we will be able to highlight significant events that further enhance our Christological purposes as well as give perspective as to the etiology of the historic episodes of the Passion Week.

Jesus knew that when he made his way from Galilee to Judea the die was cast, "because the Jewish leaders there [Judea] were looking for a way to kill him" (John 7:1). Cruelly, his own brothers baited him to go to Jerusalem because they "did not believe in him" (v. 5). It was September or October, and the culminating festival of the year, Tabernacles, was about to begin. Jesus did not go up with his brothers, but went secretly later. About halfway through the week he began to teach in the temple precincts. The results were controversy and division. Then came "the last and greatest day of the festival" (v. 37), a day of great pomp and circumstance. A solemn procession from the Gihon spring with a golden pitcher filled with water led through the Water Gate to the altar, where the water was then poured

---

[25] Elwell and Yarbrough, *Encountering the New Testament*, 126.
[26] Garland, *Luke*, 408.

out, symbolizing such end time prophecies as Ezekiel 47:1–12 and Zechariah 14:8. Earlier, a choir had sung of joyfully drawing water from the wells of salvation (Isa. 12:3) at the spring of Gihon. At that exact moment of the culminating outpouring at the Temple a loud voice was heard. Here is how John reports it (John 7:37–38 NJB):

> On the last day, the great day of the festival, Jesus stood and cried out:
>
> Let anyone who is thirsty come to me!
>
> Let anyone who believes in me come and drink!
>
> As scripture says, "From his heart shall flow streams of living water."

John clarifies that Jesus was speaking about the Holy Spirit (v. 39). In other words, if you are thirsty for the living water of salvation, Jesus was saying, come to *me* and drink. Like the rock in the wilderness (Exod. 17:17; Num. 20:1–13) from which came life-giving water, Jesus is our rock. As Paul wrote: "they drank from the spiritual rock that accompanied them, and that rock was Christ" (1 Cor. 10:4). Earlier Jesus had informed the woman at Jacob's well in Sychar that he could give her "living water" that would become "a spring of water welling up to eternal life" (John 4:10, 14).[27]

Next, Jesus encounters a man born blind (John 9). This classic healing story, the sixth of John's seven "signs," typifies John's feel for the dramatic. In a single chapter we encounter a healing saga with numerous lessons. The disciples' defective theology shows up immediately with the query, "Rabbi, who sinned, this man or his parents, that he was born blind?" (v. 2). Following popular religious notions (as well as the theology of Job's friends!), they assumed that personal sin was the cause of this tragedy. Jesus corrects these notions and proceeds to utilize a strange method to heal the man. It is fascinating to observe the response of those around him as well as

---

27 For a detailed discussion of this event see: Dale Moody, *Spirit of the Living God* (Philadelphia: Westminster, 1968), 161–64; C. Marvin Pate, *The Writings of John* (Grand Rapids: Zondervan, 2011), 102–03.

the man's growing awareness of Jesus' identity to the point of worship and personal trust (v. 38). The most important lesson is the danger of spiritual blindness: The Pharisees, the "back to the Bible" crowd of Jesus' day, were informed and warned by Jesus of their spiritual blindness and continuing guilt (vv. 40–41). The man's words, "One thing I do know. I was blind but now I see!" (v. 25), have become timeless and descriptive of the saving light of Jesus received by countless saints through history—including John Newton ("Was blind, But now I see").

Shifting back to Luke's gospel, we next encounter Jesus' sending out of the seventy-two disciples, two by two, in preparation for the harvest (Luke 10:1–24). They return with joy, amazed that even the demons are subject to them in Jesus' name (v. 17). Luke's high Christology is reflected in Jesus' unique heavenly perspective: "I saw Satan fall like lightning from heaven."[28] Then Jesus gently corrects them with the words: "Do not rejoice that the spirits submit to you, but rejoice that your names are written in heaven" (v. 20). Jesus further responds with what scholars have described as "a Johannine bolt out of the blue"—a revelation of the intimate relation between the Son and the Father, typical of John's narratives, but very atypical of the Synoptics. Jesus rejoices in the Holy Spirit and says:

> I praise you, Father, Lord of heaven and earth, because you have hidden these things from the wise and learned, and revealed them to little children. Yes, Father, for this is what you were pleased to do.
>
> All things have been committed to me by my Father. No one knows who the Son is except the Father, and no one knows who the Father is except the Son and those to whom the Son chooses to reveal him (vv. 21–22).

Again, we are encountering Luke's high Christology, typical in this regard to Johannine Christology. David Garland summarizes well the main idea of this entire account: "The successful mission of the seventy-two in proclaiming the presence of God's reign and the

---

[28] Garland, *Luke*, 432.

revelation about Jesus as God's Son reveal that the advance of God's reign is unstoppable and Jesus will ultimately triumph."29

Finally, we come to the turning point of Jesus' ministry, the "last straw," as it were, in terms of the animosity of the Jewish leaders: the raising of Lazarus from the dead (John 11). This, of course, was one of Jesus' most spectacular and memorable miracles. It is important to note that only three raisings of the dead by Jesus are recorded in all four gospels: Luke alone tells us of the raising of the widow's son at Nain (Luke 7:11–17); all three Synoptics relate the story of the raising of Jairus's daughter (Matt. 9:18–26; Mark 5:21–43; Luke 8:40–56); and John alone relates, in typical dramatic fashion, the raising of Lazarus (John 11). The story would make a great movie. It could be entitled "The Seventh Sign." It could provide the lead-up in terms of Jesus' friendship with Mary, Martha, and Lazarus and also dramatically portray how precipitous the resuscitation was: now the Jewish leaders have concluded that both Jesus (11:53) and Lazarus (12:10–11) must be killed. From this point on the cross is inevitable.

John powerfully depicts the momentous events surrounding this miracle, the seventh of his "sign" stories, and includes the fifth of his famous "I am" sayings, "I am the resurrection and the life" (11:25). The narrative is rife with Christological content. Martha confesses: "I believe that you are the Messiah, the Son of God, who is to come into the world" (v. 27). The account brings the central Christian tenet of *resurrection* to the fore, and foreshadows Jesus' resurrection. Of course, Lazarus was only resuscitated; he would die again. But Jesus himself uses the occasion to teach on the ultimate hope of resurrection (11:23–25).

JESUS' LAST WEEK AND CRUCIFIXION (APRIL A.D. 30)

The last week of Jesus' life is the intentional focus of all four gospels. So much space is devoted to this period of time that Martin Kähler

---
29 Garland, *Luke*, 422.

was surely correct to describe the gospels as "passion narratives with extended introductions."[30] The gospels relate the gospel—the good news that Jesus' death and resurrection brought the forgiveness of our sins and eternal life. They also show that Jesus' life and ministry is integral to that good news as well. They are our indispensable aid to true daily discipleship. And they all emphasize, by shear space alone, the centrality of the cross.

Expectations were high as Jesus neared Jerusalem. People thought that the kingdom of God could appear at any moment (Luke 19:11: "the people thought that the kingdom of God was going to appear at once"). "Six days before Passover, Jesus came to Bethany," relates John (John 12:1). Here a dinner was given and Mary anointed Jesus' feet with perfume. Judas objected, but Jesus said it was "for the day of my burial" (vv. 1–8). "Meanwhile a large crowd of Jews found out that Jesus was there and came, not only because of him but also to see Lazarus, whom he had raised from the dead," so the chief priests decide Lazarus must be killed as well (vv. 9–11). So Jesus spends Friday with his dear friends in Bethany, a village about two miles from Jerusalem on the eastern slope of the Mount of Olives, and Saturday, enjoying a Sabbath rest. Passion Week begins with Jesus' triumphal entry into Jerusalem.

> Expectations were high as Jesus neared Jerusalem.

Now for the first time Jesus is making his messiahship quite public. Instead of walking with the rest of the festival pilgrims into Jerusalem, Jesus *rides* into the city on a donkey—an event which has come to be known as the Triumphal Entry (Matt. 21:1–11; Mark 11:1–11; Luke 19:29–44; John 12:12–19). He was deliberately fulfilling the prophecy of Zechariah 9:9 (cf. Matt. 21:4–5): "Rejoice greatly, Daughter Zion! Shout, Daughter Jerusalem! See, your king comes to you, righteous and victorious, lowly and riding on a donkey, a colt, the foal of a donkey." The crowds greet him, waving palm branches and shouting,

---

30 Martin Kähler, *The So-Called Historical Jesus and the Historic Biblical Christ* (Philadelphia: Fortress, 1964 [1896]) 80, fn. 11; cited in James D. G. Dunn, *Jesus, Paul, and the Gospels* (Grand Rapids: Eerdmans, 2011), 54. Note Dunn's helpful discussion: 54–56, 62, 73.

"Hosanna! Blessed is he who comes in the name of the Lord! Blessed is the king of Israel!" (John 12:13). Thus, this momentous day is known as Palm Sunday. Jesus came not as a conquering warrior king, but a lowly spiritual king. His disciples did not understand all this at first (John 12:16), but the Pharisees "said to one another, 'See, this is getting us nowhere. Look how the whole world has gone after him!'" (v. 19). "Jesus entered Jerusalem and went into the temple courts. He looked around at everything, but since it was already late, he went out to Bethany with the Twelve" (Mark 11:11).

The next morning (Monday) Jesus left Bethany to return to Jerusalem. He would perform two very disturbing acts this day—one private and one public—that would communicate dramatically God's judgment upon Israel and the Temple. The first of these acts was the cursing of the fig tree, related only by Matthew and Mark (Matt. 21:18–22; Mark 11:12–14, 20–24). This private event surely had an immense impact on the disciples who observed it and marveled at it. The public event was the clearing of the temple courts, which obviously drew enormous public attention and response. Mark utilizes an intercalation or "sandwiching" of these events to drive home their intent and import. It was a deliberate provocation on the part of Jesus which escalated the tensions between Jesus and the Jewish leaders. It would prove Jesus' undoing in terms of their desire to do away with him. Tensions would continue to grow this Tuesday of Passion Week as Jesus entered into a series of disputes with the chief priests, scribes, elders, Pharisees, Herodians, and Sadducees (Matt. 21:23–23:36; Mark 11:27–12:40; Luke 20:1–47).

As Jesus was leaving the temple that day, the disciples drew attention to its splendid structures. "Look, Teacher! What massive stones! What magnificent buildings!" one of them said (Mark 13:1). "Do you see all these great buildings?" replied Jesus. "Not one stone here will be left on another; everyone will be thrown done" (v. 2). What could be more shocking for the disciples to hear? Later that evening, on the Mount of Olives, the disciples came to him and asked when this would take place "and what will be the sign of your coming and of the end of the age?" (Matt. 24:3). Jesus' response is often called the Olivet Discourse (cf. Matt. 24:1–25:46; Mark 13:1–37; Luke 21:5–36). The key to discerning its message is that Jesus addressed *both* questions that evening: (1) when the destruction of Jerusalem would take place and (2) what would be the sign of his coming and of the end of the age. They were two different events, the former being illustrative of the latter. With the fall of Jerusalem, we have the end of traditional Judaism in terms of the centrality of the temple and the continuing of the sacrificial system. It was truly a cataclysmic event. Jesus had mourned over Jerusalem, foreknowing what was to come (Matt. 23:37–39; Luke 13:34–35). But Jesus also spoke of the end of the age and of his second coming. The way these teachings are woven together makes for difficult interpretation at times!

Of course, historically some in the church have waxed eloquent on end-time teachings with elaborate charts and virtual, if not deliberate, date-setting. Jesus' caution in this regard is well taken: "But about that day or hour no one knows, not even the angels in heaven, nor the Son, but only the Father" (Matt. 24:36; Mark 13:32). The obverse side of the coin, however, is that Jesus' teaching here is important: We should be watching (Matt. 24:45–51), waiting (Matt. 25:1–13), and working (Matt. 25:14–30).[31]

Luke alone provides a summary of Jesus' teaching activity during Passion Week: "Each day Jesus was teaching at the temple, and each evening he went out to spend the night on the hill called the Mount of Olives, and all the people came early in the morning to hear him at the temple" (Luke 21:37–38). Jesus' continued popularity, let alone the topics of his teaching, would obviously be problematic for the Jewish leaders. So the final plot begins for the lynching of Jesus by crucifixion. Jesus warns his disciples: "As you know, the Passover is two days away—and the Son of Man will be handed over to be crucified" (Matt. 26:2). Jewish officials begin scheming feverishly as to how to "arrest Jesus secretly and kill him," but "not during the festival," they decide for fear of the people's rioting (Matt. 26:4–5; Mark 14:1–2).

---

[31] I owe these points to Millard J. Erickson, found in his excellent treatment of the "Second Coming of Christ" in Walter A. Elwell, ed., *Evangelical Dictionary of Theology* (Grand Rapids: Baker, 1984), 992–95.

Then Judas Iscariot, one of the Twelve, approaches the chief priests and officers of the temple guard, volunteering to hand Jesus over to them secretly for the price of thirty pieces of silver (Matt. 26:14–16; Mark 14:10–11; Luke 22:3–6). Luke alone informs us of the spiritual dynamics of this treachery: "Then Satan entered Judas, called Iscariot, one of the Twelve" (Luke 22:3). Judas then approached the Jewish officials and "discussed with them how he might betray Jesus" (v. 4).

It is now Thursday, the first day of the Festival of Unleavened Bread, and Jesus sends Peter and John to make preparations for the Passover meal (Luke 22:8; see Matt. 26:17–19; Mark 14:12–16; and Luke 22:7–13 for all the details). Jesus and the Twelve meet in a large upstairs room of a prearranged home in the city (Mark 14:15; Luke 22:12). As they enter into the meal, Jesus says, "I have eagerly desired to eat this Passover with you before I suffer" (Luke 22:15). The atmosphere is swirling with conflicting emotions. Before the evening is out Jesus will have instituted the Lord's Supper, rebuked the disciples for their jealousy, washed the disciples' feet, revealed Judas as the betrayer, predicted the disciples' desertion and Peter's denial, delivered his extensive Upper Room Discourse, and prayed his High Priestly Prayer (Matt. 26:20–35; Mark 14:17–31; Luke 22:14–38; John 13:1–17:26). With his last supper with the disciples becoming the Lord's Supper, we have one of the most significant events of the Passion Week. Jesus was also providing the full perspective on the meaning of his sacrificial death. What is sometimes neglected is the importance of his Upper Room Discourse. The Paraclete teachings embedded in this address do much to explain the role of the Holy Spirit in bringing the saving impact of the Passion through the church to the world. The teaching culminates with powerful prayer. Then, John indicates the next important step in Jesus' passion pilgrimage: Gethsemene: "When he had finished praying, Jesus left with his disciples and crossed the Kidron Valley. On the other side there was a garden, and he and his disciples went into it" (John 18:1).

What a dismal journey it must have been as Jesus moved through the dark streets of the city, through the Kidron Valley, and up the slopes of the Mount of Olives to Gethsemane (Matt. 26:36; Mark

14:32). Now he is driven to agonizing prayer in preparation for the unspeakable suffering to follow (Matt. 26:36–46; Mark 14:32–42; Luke 22:39–46). The completeness of his humanity is fully evident. He takes with him his inner circle of Peter, James, and John, sharing with them: "My soul is overwhelmed with sorrow. Stay here and keep watch with me" (Matt. 26:38; Mark 14:34). Angelic help is sent to him from heaven to give him strength, as his sweat becomes like drops of blood (Luke 22:43–44). Christ's divinity is also on display in the intimate relationship with the Father in prayer. He embodies and exemplifies in his own person how one truly walks with God and one's companions through the challenges of life. Then the dastardly plot of evil continues with the arrival of Judas and the mob who have come to arrest Jesus.

It is late Thursday evening, very dark. Judas would betray Jesus with a kiss and Jesus' disciples would desert him, but not before Peter flails a sword, cutting off the right ear of the servant of the high priest—an act that Jesus rebukes and condemns, thus proving the true nonviolent nature of his kingdom and his mission (Matt. 26:47–56; Mark 14:43–52; Luke 22:47–53; John 18:2–12). Typically, John's account is quite dramatic and adds rich detail found nowhere else. A portion of it bears repeating (John 18:4–8):

> Jesus, knowing all that was going to happen to him, went out and asked them, "Who is it you want?"
>
> "Jesus of Nazareth," they replied.
>
> "I Am," Jesus said. (And Judas the traitor was standing there with them.) When Jesus said, "I Am," they drew back and fell to the ground.
>
> Again he asked them, "Who is it you want?"
>
> "Jesus of Nazareth," they replied.
>
> Jesus answered, "I told you, 'I Am.'" If you are looking for me, then let these men go."[32]

---

[32] I have combined the NIV and CEB renderings of this passage.

Careful readers of John's gospel will note the leitmotif of "I Am," which is found throughout his gospel. These men, both Jews and Gentiles, are knocked to the ground by their encounter with divine majesty. It is also important to note Jesus' pastoral concern for his disciples. With this arrest, the process is in place for Jesus' lynching.

From late Thursday night to early Friday morning, Jesus would go through the mockery of both Jewish and Roman "trials"—a parody of justice. At the same time, these events proved quite revelatory. First, the depravity of humanity is documented in this the worst crime ever committed. Sinful humanity condemned the sinless Son of God to a tortuous death. Royalty was treated like riffraff. The best that human civilization had to offer in terms of religion (Israel) and government (Rome) produced this worst of all tragedies. Second, the purity and nobility of Jesus stand in stark contrast to human sinfulness. The details of the story have proven memorable (Matt. 26:57–27:26; Mark 14:53–15:15; Luke 22:54–23:25; John 18:13–19:16). One thinks of Peter's denials, Judas' suicide, Pilate's dilemma, Jesus' scourging, and the soldier's mockery. The accounts of the crucifixion itself are surprisingly subdued. Original readers of the gospels would be poignantly aware of the unspeakable brutality. Today, it often takes a movie's graphic display of the event to remind us of the sufferings of our Lord. Combining the accounts of the four gospels, the Seven Sayings of Jesus from the Cross have been traditionally highlighted.[33]

1. **"Father, forgive, for they do not know what they are doing"** (Luke 23:34): Jesus' prayer for the soldiers as they drive the cruel spikes into his body.
2. **"Truly I tell you, today you will be with me in paradise"** (Luke 23:43): Jesus' gracious promise to one of the criminals.
3. **"Woman, here is your son...Here is your mother"** (John 19:26–27): Jesus' committing his mother to John's care.
4. **"My God, my God, why have you forsaken me?"** (Matt. 27:46; Mark 15:34): Jesus' cry of dereliction.
5. **"I am thirsty"** (John 19:28): Jesus' cry of physical agony.

---

[33] See, e.g., Bruce M. Metzger's *The New Testament: Its Background, Growth, and Content* (Nashville: Abingdon Press, 1965), 125–26.

6. **"It is finished"** (John 19:30): Jesus' cry of completion and victory.
7. **"Father, into your hands I commit my spirit"** (Luke 23:46): Jesus' calm and confident surrender to his Father.

THE RESURRECTION AND ASCENSION OF JESUS (APRIL–JUNE A.D. 30)

As the beginning of the Sabbath approached that Fridday evening, Joseph of Arimathea, a rich man who was also both a member of the Jewish Council and a secret disciple of Jesus, approached Pilate about taking Jesus' body. Nicodemus accompanied Joseph and helped prepare Jesus' body for burial in Joseph's own newly prepared tomb in a garden near where Jesus had been crucified. The men placed Jesus' body in the tomb and the stone was rolled in place. Mary Magdalene and the other women who had been with Jesus since his Galillean ministry followed Joseph and saw where Jesus had been laid (Matt. 27:57–61; Mark 15:42–47; Luke 23:50–56; John 19:38–42). Matthew adds that the next day the chief priests and the Pharisees approached Pilate about securing the tomb so that Jesus' followers could not steal the body and claim that Jesus' predictions of his resurrection had been fulfilled. Pilate gave them a guard, whom they posted, after having sealed the stone in front of the tomb (Matt. 27:62–22). And that was the end of it. Jesus had been silenced. His followers' hopes had been dashed. The hostile Jewish leaders had dealt definitively wth "that deceiver" (Matt. 27:63)—or so they thought. Jesus' body rested quietly in the tomb that Sabbath, but on the first day of the new week remarkable and disturbing things began to take place.

The first people the risen Lord revealed himself to were *women*. This is remarkable in view of the social and legal conventions of the day. Women were the first to witness the empty tomb. Hearing their report, Peter and John raced to the garden to see the very same thing—an empty tomb (Matt. 28:1–8; Mark 16:1–8; Luke 24:1–11; John 20:1–10). Mark, strangely, does not follow-up with resurrection appearances, but the other gospels and Paul provide numerous reports. Together, their witness had great impact. It was this combination of eyewitnesses to the empty tomb and resurrection appearances that proved decisive. As Bruce Metzger concludes: "The evidence for the resurrection of Jesus Christ is overwhelming."[34]

The gospels contain two kinds of stories related to Jesus' resurrection: (1) empty tomb reports and (2) resurrection appearances. It is the genius of the New Testament that both kinds of evidence are provided to indicate why the early believers had such strong convictions concerning such a strange phenomenon completely foreign to human experience. These saints were even willing to lay down their lives for these beliefs. The stories themselves are often difficult to correlate, which actually lends even greater credence to their not being merely contrived. In his massive study of the resurrection, N. T. Wright comes to the same conclusion:

> Neither the empty tomb by itself…nor the appearances by themselves, could have generated the early Christian belief. The empty tomb alone would be a puzzle and a tragedy. Sightings of an apparently alive Jesus, by themselves, would have been classified as visions or hallucinations, which were well enough known in the ancient world.… However, an empty tomb and appearances of a living Jesus, taken together, would have presented a powerful reason for the emergence of the belief.[35]

And, again, it is fascinating to note Jesus' priority of women. John relates the tender encounter between Jesus and Mary Magdalene in the garden (John 20:11–18). Space does not allow recounting all these amazing encounters found in the closing chapters of the gospels and Paul's "resurrection chapter" (1 Cor. 15), but their witness is uniformly powerful and convincing.[36]

But in one sense the story is just beginning. There are mysterious accounts of the forty days between Jesus' resurrection and ascension in which Jesus prepares his disciples for their end-time mission. The four

---

34 Metzger, *The New Testament*, 126.
35 N. T. Wright, *The Resurrection of the Son of God* (Minneapolis: Fortress, 2003), 686.
36 See the helpful summary and charting of these events in: *Four Portraits, One Jesus*, 513.

gospels tell us only about what Jesus *began* to do and teach (Acts 1:1). He would continue his earthly ministry through his church. Thus, the gospels conclude their saga of the greatest life ever lived with the themes of commission and empowerment.

Mark dramatically concludes his gospel with an open ending: "Trembling and bewildered, the women went out and fled from the tomb. They said nothing to anyone, because they were afraid" (Mark 16:8). The reader is left with questions concerning exactly what is next! Actually, Mark has already hinted at the answer. The heavenly messenger instructs the women, "But go, tell his disciples and Peter, 'He is going ahead of you into Galilee. There you will see him, just as he told you'" (v. 7). In Galilee, the disciples will see the risen Lord and receive their disciple-making commission. Thus, Mark seems to want the reader to follow that same road of encounter and commission. Later copyists, seemingly having missed his point, would supply longer endings that *did* include resurrection appearances and the ascension (vv. 9–20), but the earliest and best manuscripts and witnesses to the gospel do not include these additions, even though they probably contain reliable tradition.

Matthew concludes his gospel with the women at the empty tomb and the guard's report (Matt. 28:1–15) and then proceeds immediately to the disciples on the mountain in Galilee receiving the Great Commission (vv. 16–20). Among John's empty tomb and resurrection appearance accounts we find the Easter Sunday story in which Jesus suddenly appears to ten of his disciples, hiding behind locked doors "for fear of the Jewish leaders" (John 20:19). He greets them and then says, "As the Father has sent me, I am sending you" (v. 21). "And with that he breathed on them and said, 'Receive the Holy Spirit'" (v. 22). Again, the Great Commission motif should be noted. Luke expands on this theme—and understandably so, since he is writing a two-volume historical narrative of both the life of Jesus and the launching of the early church. His dramatic Easter Sunday evening narrative has Jesus concluding his talk by referring to the disciples' preaching repentance and the forgiveness of sins to all the nations, of their being his witnesses, and of their empowerment to do so (Luke 24:47–48).

Luke continues with these themes in Acts as Jesus teaches on a global Spirit-empowered witness (Acts 1:1–8). And an ascension tradition is associated with two of the four gospel writers.

Since Mark has written more of a gospel tract with a mysterious ending calling for the reader's response, he deliberately leaves out resurrection appearances and the ascension. Later copyists would, of course, supply them. The ascension account reads as follows: "After the Lord Jesus had spoken to them, he was taken up into heaven and he sat at the right hand of God. Then the disciples went out and preached everywhere, and the Lord worked with them and confirmed his word by the signs that accompanied it" (Mark 16:19–20). Luke provides *two* accounts of the ascension. In his gospel he has Jesus leading his disciples to the vicinity of Bethany, blessing them, and then ascending. Their response is telling. Instead of grieving his departure and floundering with what to do next, they show evidence that Jesus has prepared them well: "Then they worshiped him and returned to Jerusalem with great joy. And they stayed continually at the temple, praising God" (Luke 24:50–53). Luke expands the narrative in Acts. Jesus was "taken up before their very eyes, and a cloud hid him from their sight" (Acts 1:9). Then, these words:

> They were looking intently up into the sky as he was going, when suddenly two men dressed in white stood beside them. "Men of Galilee," they said, "why do you stand here looking into the sky? This same Jesus, who has been taken from you into heaven, will come back in the same way you have seen him go into heaven (vv. 10–11).

The disciples would continue to follow Jesus' instructions, remaining in Jerusalem until they are empowered and launched into their global mission (Acts 1:12–2:41).

Thus, the ascension would end one era and begin another. Jesus would pour out the Holy Spirit on his fledgling congregation and they would proceed to turn the Roman Empire upside down. No longer with them physically, now seated on his throne of authority, he would nevertheless be with them spiritually: "And remember, I am with you always, to the end of the age" (Matt. 28:20 NRSV). Jesus' life was nonpareil: "Jesus did many other things as well. If every one of them were written down, I suppose that even the whole world would not have room for the books that would be written" (John 21:25). But his disciples—extending down to the present day!—would "do even greater things than these, because I am going to the Father" (John 14:12). That is how strongly invested in us Jesus is! If anyone wants to know this Jesus—to learn this Jesus—they can read the gospel stories and they can pray. They can also consult his church, which continues to embody his ministry in the twenty-first century and will continue to do so until he returns. But full knowledge comes only with becoming a fully-devoted follower of Jesus yourself!

Lesson Four

The Witness of the New Testament

NEW TESTAMENT PORTRAITS OF JESUS CHRIST

Having surveyed the life and ministry of Jesus, we have already had opportunity to glimpse the diversity of perspectives on Jesus Christ within the New Testament itself. Each of the gospel writers, we discovered, has distinctive emphases, which dictate how materials are redacted to serve those purposes. The next logical step, therefore, would be to allow each writer to speak for himself and to flesh out more fully the portrait of Christ they produced. Then, quite naturally, we should expand our parameters to the entire New Testament. It is a rich and rewarding journey into the very heart of the Scriptures, for Christians read *both* the Hebrew Scriptures and the New Testament with Christological lenses!

We will begin with Mark's portrait of Christ, since there is wide consensus that he wrote the first gospel. But prior to our mining the riches of Mark's Christology, it might be helpful to consider briefly what the four gospels of the New Testament *taken together* have to tell us about Jesus. I am drawing here on the insights of two New Testament specialists who have loomed large in the theater of international scholarly opinion: Mark L. Strauss and N. T. Wright.

First, this comprehensive yet concise overview offered by Mark Strauss:

> Each of the four gospels…paints a unique portrait of Jesus Christ. Each provides special insight into who he is and what he accomplished. The Gospels exhibit both unity and diversity, bearing witness to the same Jesus (unity) but viewing him from unique perspectives (diversity). What are these four unique portraits? At the risk of oversimplifying, we may say that Matthew presents Jesus as the *Jewish Messiah*, the fulfillment of Old Testament hopes; Mark portrays him as the *suffering Son of* God, who offers himself as a sacrifice for sins; Luke's Jesus is the *Savior for all people,* who brings salvation to all nations and people groups; and in John, Jesus is the *eternal Son of God*, the self-revelation of God the Father. These are not contradictory portraits but complementary ones. Having four Gospels gives us a deeper, more profound understanding of Christology—the nature of Jesus' person and work.[1]

Then these colorful comments from N. T. Wright:

> John's gospel is designed to bring you to your knees in wonder, love and praise. Luke's is meant to make you sit up and think hard about Jesus as Lord of the whole world. Matthew's is like a beautifully bound book which the Christian must study and ponder at leisure, steadily reordering one's life in the process. Mark's is like a hastily printed revolutionary tract, stuffed into a back pocket, and frequently pulled out, read by torchlight, and whispered to one's co-conspirators. You need all four. You never know when you are going to have to call on them.[2]

As we transition to a consideration of Mark's gospel, N. T. Wright's spirited summary seems singularly appropriate:

---

[1] Mark L. Strauss, *Four Portraits, One Jesus: An Introduction to Jesus and the Gospels* (Grand Rapids: Zondervan, 2007), 24.
[2] Tom Wright, *The Original Jesus: The Life and Vision of a Revolutionary* (Grand Rapids: Eerdmans, 1996), 144.

Mark is the shortest, the darkest, the strangest of the Gospels. It's the Gospel for the cynic-in-a-hurry. It tells you the story (Who is Jesus? Why did he die?), sharpened to a point. And it leaves you with the challenge: follow him.... Mark takes you by the scruff of the neck and tells you, breathlessly, that this is urgent and important and you'd better listen carefully.[3]

Thus, Mark's presentation thrusts us immediately into the heart of Christology—the good news that is at the core of Scripture and that created the church.

THE CHRISTOLOGY OF MARK

Perhaps one of the benefits of modern biblical scholarship is the promotion of Mark's gospel to the head of the class after centuries of neglect. "The most concise, vivid, and in some ways exciting of the Gospels, it has been rather neglected throughout the history of the church."[4] Being the shortest of the gospels, the instinct was too often to consult the fuller presentations of the other three gospels. But sometimes less is more. Lawyers, journalists, and sometimes (miraculously) even preachers and theologians have learned and applied this wise principle!

Mark's narrative sets a unique tone. It "tells a mysterious story enveloped in apocalyptic urgency, a story that focuses relentlessly on the cross and ends on a note of hushed, enigmatic hope."[5] It is a sophistic presentation that demands much of the hearer or reader. What he does *not* say is just as important as what he *does* say. It is an action-oriented gospel, repeating the term "immediately" (*euthus*) as it moves quickly from episode to episode. He depends on the narrative of events itself to communicate his theology and often reverts to the "historical present"

---

[3] Wright, *The Original Jesus*, 142.
[4] Walter A. Elwell and Robert W. Yarbrough, *Encountering the New Testament: A Historical and Theological Survey* (Grand Rapids: Baker Books, 1998), 88.
[5] Richard B. Hays, *Reading Backwards: Figural Christology and the Fourfold Gospel Witness* (Waco: Baylor University Press, 2014), 17.

(Jesus "says/does" instead of "said/did") to draw the reader into the story. These characteristics of his work dictate how one ferrets out his Christology: "The Christology of Mark's Gospel is in the story it tells."[6] Richard B. Hays recommends the liturgy of the Greek Orthodox Church for its drawing participants into Mark's process as he leads readers "through a mysteriously allusive reading of Israel's Scripture, into recognizing Jesus as the embodiment of the God of Israel."[7]

Thus, Mark's Christology, more often than not, is an implicit Christology, an enacted Christology. We have already encountered this dynamic in our survey of the life and ministry of Jesus. Jesus often evinced a unique authority in his words and deeds. Mark was a pioneer in this endeavor of presenting Christ in this manner. Mark's is truly a "gospel" Christology. James D. G. Dunn even argues that Mark unilaterally defined what is meant by "gospel" from the very first verse:

> Almost consciously and deliberately, Mark in effect was introducing a new genre to the literature of the ancient world. This is no longer simply a biography (*bios*) of a great man, but a *Gospel*, the account of a particular man's mission which made salvation possible, a book which itself is a means to salvation. It is Mark who, whether knowingly or intentionally or not, made the transition from "gospel" to "Gospel."[8]

There is further evidence that Mark's presentation reflects a strong "eyewitness" dynamic. Papias (*c.* 30–160 A.D.) is quoted by Eusebius (*c.* 260–340 A.D.) as stating that Mark relied on the apostle Peter's teaching and preaching, thus suggesting an even stronger element of primitive Jesus tradition.[9] "The Marcan tradition is thus said to be based on Mark's memory of the teaching of Peter."[10]

---

6   Frank J. Matera, *New Testament Christology* (Louisville: Westminster John Knox Press, 1999), 24.
7   Hays, *Reading Backward*, 32–33.
8   James D. G. Dunn, *Jesus, Paul, and the Gospels* (Grand Rapids: Eerdmans, 2011), 53.
9   See Richard Bauckham, *Jesus and the Eyewitnesses: The Gospels as Eyewitness Testimony* (Grand Rapids: Eerdmans, 2006), ch. 2 "Papias on the Eyewitness" for a complete analysis of the evidence.
10 Michael F. Bird, *The Gospel of the Lord: How the Early Church Wrote the Story of Jesus* (Grand Rapids: Eerdmans, 2014), 103.

Key themes of Mark's "enacted" Christology would include Jesus' *authority*, his *supernatural ministry* of healings and exorcisms (the spiritual warfare motif looming quite large), and the widely acknowledged *messianic secret* feature, which serves Mark's penchant to veil his Christology and allow the reader to gradually discover Jesus' identity. He begins his narrative with these programmatic words: "The beginning of the good news about Jesus the Messiah, the Son of God" (Mark 1:1). As the story moves along and culminates in the Passion Week, one gradually gains a more complete understanding of precisely what these Christological titles mean. Surprisingly, Mark brackets his gospel with the same theme with which he begins it: "And when the centurion, who stood there in front of Jesus, saw how he died, he said, 'Surely this man was the Son of God!'" (Mark 15:39). Thus, *Messiah* and *Son of God* form the Christological spine of Mark *with* the later addition of *Son of Man*. We will take these titles in order.

Jesus had to deal incessantly with the preconceived notions of messiahship of his day. Mark's gospel depicts this conflict and subtly corrects misconceptions. He declares that Jesus is the Messiah in the very first verse, but fails to mention it again until the turning-point of the gospel (Mark 8:27–30), where Peter at Caesarea Philippi answers, "You are the Messiah" (v. 29). Thus, Mark entitles his gospel by utilizing the title Messiah, but the first time it actually appears in the *narrative* is here. Next, we find Jesus instructing John with these words: "Truly I tell you, anyone who gives you a cup of water in my name because you belong to the Messiah will certainly not lose their reward" (Mark 9:41). The key phrases in this story (vv. 38–41) are "in your name" and "in my name." In the process of teaching an inclusive spirit among his followers, Jesus drives home that his distinctive name among his disciples is *Messiah*.

Then we find Jesus confronting the teachers of the law with a probing question (Mark 12:35–37). Utilizing a verse that became key to the church's communication of the gospel, Psalm 110:1, Jesus sets up almost a riddle to be solved: Who is David's "lord" in this passage? Jesus wanted them to understand that the Messiah was not just a human descendent of David. In effect Jesus is telling them,

I am David's Lord! Later before the Sanhedrin, Jesus will again allude to Psalm 110:1. When the high priest asks him, "Are you the Messiah, the Son of the Blessed One?" Jesus replies, "I am. And you will see the Son of Man sitting at the right hand of the Mighty One and coming on the clouds of heaven" (Mark 14:61–62). "Jesus hints that the Messiah son of David is a divine, transcendent figure...."[11] Later, as Jesus hung on the cross, the chief priests and teachers of the law would mock him, saying, "Let this Messiah, this king of Israel, come down from the cross, that we may see and believe" (Mark 15:32). They had derided him, saying, "He saved others, but he can't save himself!" (v. 31). The irony was that Jesus chose not to save himself precisely because he wanted to save others. That is the kind of Messiah he was—a suffering Messiah.

The second Christological title that Mark highlights is *Son of God* (Mark 1:1). God himself identifies Jesus as "my Son" at (1) Jesus' baptism (1:11) and (2) the Transfiguration (9:7). Combining all these with the centurion's declaration (15:39), and we have, as David Garland has pointed out, a beautiful bracketing:

"Son of God" (1:1)

"My Son" (1:11)

"My Son" (9:7)

"Son of God" (15:39)

"The title 'Son of God' provides the primary category for understanding Jesus' identity in Mark's gospel since this is how God identifies him in the narrative."[12]

It is important to note as well Jesus' use of the Aramaic term *abba*. Mark alone transliterates this term of intimacy and endearment in relating Jesus' prayer in Gethsemane. Jesus addresses God there as "*Abba*, Father" (Mark 14:36). Joachim Jeremias, a specialist in this

---

[11] David E. Garland, *A Theology of Mark's Gospel: Good News about Jesus the Messiah, the Son of God* (Grand Rapids: Zondervan, 2015), 245.

[12] Garland, *A Theology of Mark's Gospel*, 227–28.

field of Aramaic studies in relation to the New Testament, relates this helpful summary:

> The complete novelty and uniqueness of *Abba* as an address to God in the prayers of Jesus shows that it expresses the heart of Jesus' relationship to God. He speaks to God as a child to its father: confidently and securely, and yet at the same time reverently and obediently.[13]

Evidently, this example of Jesus' intimacy must have strongly impacted his disciples: Later Paul would describe our own intimacy with God in the Spirit and through Christ in precisely the same terms (Rom. 8:15; Gal. 4:6)![14]

The third Christological title highlighted by Mark is *Son of Man*. It is the genius of Mark that he blends this title into his gospel to further refine what is meant by the previous two titles, Messiah and Son of God. The emphasis in Mark is on the *suffering* of the Son of Man. Thus, the titles Messiah and Son of God must be viewed in this same light. To be sure, the note of *authority* is also present (Mark 2:10, 28), but the overarching emphasis is on messianic suffering (Mark 8:31; 9:12, 31; 10:33–34, 45; 14:21, 41). The backdrop of this title must surely be Daniel 7:13–14, which clearly refers to an exalted being, yet is ambiguous enough for Jesus to supply his own definition to the concept with reference to himself. And the key to it all is the cross: Mark's Christology is cruciform. Frank J. Matera expresses it well:

> Son of Man is the necessary complement to Messiah and Son of God, ensuring that neither title will be interpreted apart from Jesus' death and resurrection. For Mark, Jesus is the Messiah, the Son of God, because he fulfills the destiny of the Son of Man. Were Jesus not to fulfill this destiny, he would not be God's messianic Son. Markan Christology, then, can be summarized in the terms "Messiah," "Son of

---

[13] Joachim Jeremias, *New Testament Theology: The Proclamation of Jesus* (New York: Charles Scribner's Sons, 1971), 67.
[14] Garland, *A Theology of Mark's Gospel*, 234–35.

God," and "Son of Man." And yet, none of these can be understood adequately apart from Mark's narrative; for the Christology is in the story, and through the story we learn to interpret the titles.[15]

Thus, Mark's portrait of Jesus introduces us to the Messiah and Son of God, who authoritatively forgives sins, heals the sick, raises the dead, casts out demons, and commands nature. This is a *supernatural* Jesus. But he is also the enigmatic Son of Man, who veils his full identity during his earthly ministry, gives his life as a ransom for many in suffering, death, and resurrection, and who will return one day in heavenly clouds of glory. Could there be a more intriguing, attractive Lord: "Ruler of all nature…Beautiful Savior! Lord of the nations! Son of God and Son of Man! Glory and honor, Praise, adoration, Now and forever more be Thine!"[16]

THE CHRISTOLOGY OF MATTHEW

If Mark takes us on a whirlwind tour of the life and ministry of Jesus, Matthew asks us to slow our pace, give Jesus a careful hearing, and contemplate more deliberately Christ's person and work—even to the point of consideration of the newly formed Jew/Gentile church that is forming even as he writes. He evinces substantial literary and linguistic abilities. He knows how to mesh complex structures into a coherent message of Christ's bringing (and *being*) the end-time salvation for humankind. Perhaps the best way to get at Matthew's Christology is to begin with how he utilizes Mark's presentation and radically augments it. Fully 90 percent of Mark is found in Matthew. But Matthew's tendency is to pare down Mark's stories and add his own. Large teaching sections are included along with extensive expansion of Mark's beginning and ending. The result is a gospel some 60% larger than its predecessor.[17]

---

[15] Matera, *New Testament Christology*, 26.
[16] *Fairest Lord Jesus* in *The Hymnal for Worship & Celebration* (Waco: Word Music, 1986), #88.
[17] Larry W. Hurtado, *Lord Jesus Christ: Devotion to Jesus in Earliest Christianity* (Grand Rapids: Eerdmans, 2003), 316–17.

Matthew is a careful, meticulous, and deliberate editor. He moves collections of teachings and stories about to drive home his points, differing somewhat chronologically at times from Mark, though basic chronology remains intact.[18] He quotes the Old Testament from the Greek Septuagint when incorporating other Synoptic materials, but translates the Hebrew Scriptures into Greek on his own at other points in his presentation. "This suggests that the author was proficient in Hebrew as well as Greek and that his primary Bible was the Hebrew Scriptures."[19] The design of a literary work often indicates its effectiveness of communication. "Among the four Gospels, Matthew shows the most evidence of careful structure and design. The author is clearly a skilled literary artist."[20] The Jewishness of Matthew's gospel has often been noted with his numerous fulfillment quotations and allusions.[21] Matthew's fivefold structure, alternating teaching and narrative, parallels Moses' fivefold Pentateuch, though Matthew's actual intent in this regard is conjectural.

> Matthew is a careful, meticulous, and deliberate editor.

The opening verse of the gospel sets the agenda: "This is the genealogy of Jesus the Messiah, the son of David, the son of Abraham" (Matt. 1:1). At the outset, we encounter a very *Jewish* story: a genealogy of a Jewish boy, born into a family with a rich Jewish heritage which includes the founder of Israel, Abraham, and Israel's greatest king, David. Furthermore, this child is "born king of the Jews," as the Magi state (Matt. 2:2). Notice Jesus is announced in the opening chapters of Matthew's gospel as someone who is *born* a king, not who will become a king someday. The startling news is that Jesus *is* the Messiah, the long-awaited savior-king of Israel. And he has the right pedigree: he is the son of David and the son of Abraham. But David is the key to the genealogy.

---

18 See Mark Allan Powell's helpful presentation on these characteristics and comparisons in: *Introducing the New Testament: A Historical, Literary, and Theological Survey* (Grand Rapids: Baker Academic, 2009), 110–11.
19 Strauss, *Four Portraits, One Jesus*, 218.
20 Strauss, *Four Portraits, One Jesus*, 215.
21 Strauss, *Four Portraits, One Jesus*, 218 (helpful chart). Mark L. Strauss has provided a treasure-trove of helpful materials for the study of all four gospels.

Demonstrating his penchant for structure, Matthew selectively presents a tripartite genealogy of fourteen names each. "Thus, there were fourteen generations in all from Abraham to David, fourteen from David to the exile to Babylon, and fourteen from the exile to the Messiah" (Matt. 1:17). According to the Jewish practice of *gematria* (which takes the numerical value of each letter and adds them together), the numerical value of David's name is fourteen—another way of identifying Jesus as the Davidic Messiah of God's exilic people Israel!

Matthew's gospel makes much of Jesus' being the Son of David: (1) Jesus heals two blind men, who are calling out to him, "Have mercy on us, Son of David!" (Matt. 9:27); (2) Jesus heals a demon-possessed man who is both blind and mute, and the astonished observers exclaim, "Could this be the Son of David?" (Matt. 12:22–23); Jesus heals a demon-possessed daughter of a Canaanite woman who has addressed him, "Lord, Son of David" (Matt. 15:22); Jesus heals two blind men, who had twice shouted out to him, "Lord, Son of David, have mercy on us!" (Matt. 20:30–31); (4) Jesus asks the Pharisees whose son is the Messiah, and they reply the "son of David"; then using Psalm 110:1, Jesus challenges them to perceive that he is the divine Messiah who is David's "Lord" (Matt. 22:41–46). Notice how many times Jesus is addressed as *lord* in these passages, and there are others. Repeatedly in Matthew's gospel, people are kneeling in worship and petition before Jesus and addressing him reverentially as Lord: Matt. 2:2; 8:2; 9:18; 14:33; 15:25; 20:20; 28:9, 17.[22]

Thus in Matthew, Jesus is presented as the Son of David, the exalted Messiah. He is the Lord and King who deserves worship. Perhaps the church will recapture one day Matthew's genius in demonstrating the absolute need for Jesus: The Jews need Jesus; the church needs Jesus; the world needs Jesus. "Remember that *the fundamental solution in the gospel is that Jesus is Messiah and Lord*; this means that there was a fundamental need for a ruler, a king, and a lord."[23] And there still is!

---

22 I. Howard Marshall, *New Testament Theology: Many Witnesses, One Gospel* (Downers Grove, IL: InterVarsity Press, 2004), 112–13.

23 Scot McKnight, *The King Jesus Gospel: The Original Good News Revisited* (Grand Rapids: Zondervan, 2011), 137

Jesus is also introduced prominently in Matthew as the *Son of* God. Comparing Mark and Matthew, it is interesting to note that Mark immediately introduces Jesus with this title (Mark 1:1), whereas Matthew begins with "Jesus the Messiah the son of David, the son of Abraham" (Matt. 1:1). "Interestingly, Matthew omits from this pedigree his preeminent title for Jesus, that of the 'Son of God.' The reason is that this latter title is of such importance that Matthew will allow no one other than God himself to be the first to utter it, at Jesus' baptism (3:17)."[24] Without question, Matthew's use of this title is distinctive. In one of his most important Christological passages, Matthew provides a glimpse into the inner sanctum of the Father/Son relationship: Matthew 11:25–29. Jesus juxtaposes divine sovereignty and human freedom as well as those who are worldly wise and those who are his humble disciples. He reveals his unique relationship with the Father and teaches the revelatory basis of true knowledge of God—a knowledge that only Jesus himself can make possible. His statements disturb those scandalized by his authoritative claims and they comfort those who accept his gracious call to find rest in him. "Jesus assumes an unheard-of relationship to God," observes Frank J. Matera.[25]

Just as in the church of the patristic period, the title Son of God in Matthew epitomizes who Jesus is. Mark Allan Powell provides this helpful summary:

> Matthew's Gospel places special emphasis on the identity of Jesus as the Son of God. As in Mark, in Matthew's Gospel God speaks twice from heaven (at Jesus' baptism and at his transfiguration), and both times God calls Jesus "my son" (3:17; 17:5; cf. 2:15). But Matthew has expanded on this theme by adding a story of virgin birth that presents Jesus as God's son in an almost literal sense (1:18) and by including accounts of the disciples confessing Jesus to be the Son of God (cf. Matt. 14:32–33 with Mark 6:51–52; Matt. 16:16

---

[24] Jack Dean Kingsbury, *Jesus Christ in Matthew, Mark, and Luke* (Philadelphia: Fortress, 1981), 64–65.

[25] Matera, *New Testament Christology*, 36.

with Mark 8:29). Ultimately, Jesus' identity as God's Son in Matthew is closely linked to the story of his crucifixion: Jesus claims that the reason his enemies want to kill him is that he is the Son of God (21:33–46), and sure enough, he is later sentenced to death for claiming to be God's Son (26:63–66). On the cross, he is mocked by opponents who claim that such a fate proves that he is not the Son of God (27:40, 43), but ironically, the manner of his death leads others to confess that he is indeed the Son of God (27:54).[26]

From Matthew's infancy narrative we learn early on that Jesus' very name is revelatory: Joseph is instructed by the angel of the Lord to "give him the name Jesus, because he will save his people from their sins" (Matt. 1:21), Jesus being the Greek form of Joshua, meaning "the LORD saves." Thus, Matthew introduces Jesus as the Savior. Then, he adds these words: "All this took place to fulfill what the Lord had said through the prophet: 'The virgin will conceive and give birth to a son, and they will call him Immanuel' (which means 'God with us')" (vv. 22–23). Here Matthew makes the momentous claim that Jesus uniquely mediates the very presence of God. We have already seen how often people are found reverencing Jesus in Matthew. To this we could add how Jesus himself taught that he would be with his disciples: "For where two or three gather in my name, there am I with them" (Matt. 18:20). Jesus also made this promise as he sent them forth into the world with the task of making disciples of all nations: "And remember, I am with you always, to the end of the age" (Matt. 28:20 NRSV).

Matthew's use of *Son of Man* is roughly equivalent to that of Mark, although more references to it are found in Matthew since he drew on more material and produced a longer narrative.[27] Interestingly, the Caesarea Philippi event is pivotal in both gospels (Mark 8:11–21; Matt. 16:1–12). Matthew alone includes the title Son of Man: "Who do people say the Son of Man is?" (Matt. 16:13). In Matthew "Son of Man" is found nine times before this event and

....

26 Powell, *Introducing the New Testament*, 114–15.
27 Marshall, *New Testament Theology*, 113.

twenty times afterward.[28] The stress here is on Jesus' path to suffering and glory. As the Son of Man, Jesus would go to the cross, rise from the dead, return to the Father, and—very importantly—come again in glory.[29]

One salient feature of Matthew's portrait of Jesus is that of Jesus as *teacher*. Matthew alone provides five extensive discourse sections, followed by a narrative section:

1. The Sermon on the Mount (5:1–7:29): Narrative: (8:1–9:34)
2. The Mission Discourse (9:35–10:42): Narrative (11:1–12:50)
3. The Kingdom Parables (13:1–52): Narrative (13:53–17:27)
4. Various Sayings (18:1–35): Narrative (19:1–22:46)
5. Eschatological Discourse (23:1–25:46): Narrative (26:1–28:20)[30]

Matthew's gospel also contains two virtually identical summary depictions of Jesus' ministry (Matthew 4:23; 9:35) as *teacher, preacher, and healer*. Though not prominent, a *wisdom* motif can be found in this regard (cf. the previously cited Matt. 11:25–30) as well. Jesus was the quintessential teacher. But he also proclaimed the kingdom and demonstrated its presence with signs and wonders. Jesus was the quintessential preacher and healer as well. "For Matthew, Jesus is *the* Teacher, called so by himself (10:24–25; 23:10) and by others (8:19; 19:16; 22:16, 24, 36; 26:18). His whole public ministry was directed toward instructing the people."[31]

Larry W. Hurtado summarizes well Matthew's portrait of Jesus and the impact it has had:

> It is not difficult to see why Matthew became the favorite Gospel rendition of Jesus in many early Christian circles. Matthew gave his readers an august Jesus who

---

28 Leon Morris, *New Testament Theology* (Grand Rapids: Zondervan Academie Books, 1986), 124.
29 Any serviceable concordance will provide the copious references to "Son of Man" in Matthew.
30 Adapted from: Leon Morris, *New Testament Introduction* (Downers Grove, IL: InterVarsity Press, 1970), 48–50.
31 Elwell and Yarbrough, *Encountering the New Testament*, 83.

delivered authoritative teachings, fulfilled biblical prophecy, demonstrated his power in miracles, received divine vindication in his resurrection, then commissioned his followers to pursue a worldwide mission and also assured them of his continuing, powerful presence as they did so. That the author made a rather full appropriation of Mark does not reduce the significance of his own literary contribution to the devotion that Christians have offered to Jesus from the late first century to the present day.[32]

THE CHRISTOLOGY OF LUKE

When you think of Luke, think of history, theology, art, music, and literature. Think of beauty, refined culture, and the best expressions of the humanities. At the same time, think of a medical doctor doing missionary work with the great apostle Paul. Imagine a Pentecostal style of spirituality with signs and wonders, prophetic utterances, speaking in tongues, and the like—as reported by Luke in both his gospel and the Book of Acts.

When you think of Luke, think of history, theology, art, music, and literature.

Ernest Renan (1823–92), the French Catholic, called Luke's gospel "the most beautiful book in the world." Renan was the Dan Brown of his day, writing up his own very popular, novel-like—"de-supernaturalized"—version of Jesus as the best expression of humanity. But he was not wrong to capture the beauty of Luke's portrait of Jesus. Leon Morris has noted the "wonderfully attractive account of the ministry of Jesus…[Jesus] as a warm and winsome figure" that Luke provides us.[33]

But Luke was much more than a biographer. He was a careful historian who penned a seamless two-volume account of the life and ministry of *both* Jesus and the early church. In more recent decades,

---
32 Hurtado, *Lord Jesus Christ*, 340.
33 Morris, *New Testament Theology*, 157.

we have begun to appreciate the fact that Luke was also a theologian, providing a distinctive, comprehensive perspective on our gospel-faith-and-life. He was also a "man of letters," writing in a very polished Greek literary style. (I noticed that we started with John, not Luke, in beginning Greek class in seminary!) But where do art and music come in? Well, for one, tradition holds that Luke was "a painter who produced numerous portraits of the Virgin Mary that are treasured as sacred relics in churches throughout Europe and the East."[34] The study of such works is fascinating, though many Western Protestants may remain somewhat skeptical of authenticity. And Luke also has inspired the music traditions of Christendom with his own inclusion of hymns in his infancy narrative (the Magnificat, etc.). Luke could even be thought of as a "food critic," with meals and table fellowship figuring much more prevalently in his narrative![35]

Luke penned *one* massive work—Luke-Acts—comprising some 27 percent of the New Testament, the most of any author. He is the only Gentile writer in the Bible. And he has provided a portrait of Christ and the church of universal appeal. Powell, in his inimitable style, has summed up well Luke's contribution:

> One way to appreciate the impact that this book has had on religion and culture is to try to envision what Christianity would be like without it. Can we imagine Christmas without the shepherds or a baby in a manger? Liturgy without the Magnificat? A church year without Ascension or Pentecost? How many favorite Bible stories would we lose? Zacchaeus, Mary and Martha, the good Samaritan, the prodigal son—all would be gone forever.[36]

In contrast to Matthew, who utilizes some 90 percent of Mark, Luke utilizes only about half of Mark. About half of Luke conveys content that cannot be found anywhere else, including five miracle stories and seventeen parables.[37] Also, Luke expands the parameters of

---

34 Powell, *Introducing the New Testament*, 147.
35 Powell, *Introducing the New Testament*, 158–59.
36 Powell, *Introducing the New Testament*, 147.
37 Powell, *Introducing the New Testament*, 154.

his gospel beyond the others to include the birth of John the Baptist and the ascension. Then, of course, he goes on to provide the story of the early church in the Book of Acts. Both Luke and Matthew expand Mark with materials at the beginning and end, and Luke tends to "polish" Mark's form and content. Instead of large teaching sections, as in Matthew, Luke disperses Jesus' teachings throughout his narrative.

Nevertheless, "Luke presents the same basic Christology as in the other Synoptic Gospels."[38] With all the sharing of sources, one would expect a lot of commonality in Christology among the Synoptics—and there is. Even so, with Luke we enjoy expanded vistas: Jesus' concern for the poor and the outcast and for women. We see Jesus warning against the dangers of riches. We see him often in humble, dependent prayer. We see him as a Spirit-empowered person and as the paradigm as such for the church. People are always thanking and praising God in Luke-Acts. Luke alone provides the expanded story of Jesus' pouring out his Spirit, who guides and empowers the church on her end-time mission. We will do three things to attempt to access Luke's Christological insights. First, we will move quickly through his narrative, noting Christological highlights. Then, we will examine key Christological titles. Finally, we will attempt a broad summary of the Christology of Luke.

Luke's introduction (Luke 1:1–4) indicates that he is relating the traditions, presumably both oral and written, of people who were both "eyewitnesses and servants of the word" (v. 2). "Eyewitnesses" (*autoptai*) here has no juridical import, but rather simply indicates "firsthand observers of the events."[39] "With this in mind," Luke adds, "since I myself have carefully investigated everything from the beginning, I too decided to write an orderly account" (v. 3). "It seems that the principle of eyewitness testimony 'from the beginning' was remarkably important for the way that the traditions about Jesus were transmitted and understood in early Christianity."[40] Thus, unlike

---

[38] Marshall, *New Testament Theology*, 146.
[39] Bauckham, *Jesus and the Eyewitnesses*, 117.
[40] Bauckham, *Jesus and the Eyewitnesses*, 124.

Renan's fanciful portrait of Jesus many centuries later, Luke's purpose was to demonstrate the truth and historical reliability of the gospel. In other words, he stayed close to his sources instead of dreaming up a pleasing tale.

As Luke moves into the infancy section of his narrative (Luke 1:5–2:52), he shifts from a very polished literary style of Greek to a more Semitic style, similar to that of the Septuagint: In other words, he very skillfully transports us into the Old Testament world of pious Judaism. Persons such as Zechariah and Elizabeth, Mary and Joseph, Simeon and Anna represent the faithful remnant of Israel awaiting the fulfillment of God's promises. John, filled with the Holy Spirit from his mother's womb, is "a prophet of the Most High" (Luke 1:76), will go before the Lord "in the spirit and power of Elijah" (v. 17). Jesus, conceived by the Holy Spirit (vv. 31–35), is "the Son of the Most High" (v. 32), who will be given "the throne of his father David" (v. 32). He is "the Son of God" (v. 35). He is the "Savior," "the Messiah, the Lord" (Luke 2:11). He calls the Temple "my Father's house" (v. 49). Salvation has come for both Jew and Gentile (Luke 1:69, 71, 77; 2:30; cf. 3:6). Thus, Luke's infancy narrative serves as "an overture for the symphony which follows, setting the theological stage for the rest of the Gospel and for Acts."[41]

And there is much singing, joy, and rejoicing that accompanies this good news! Four times, under the inspiration of the prophetic Spirit, singers (Mary, Zechariah, the angels, and Simeon) announce the good news of salvation—a salvation which lifts the lowly, a salvation for both Israel and the Gentiles, a salvation wrought through God's Messsiah: The *Magnificat* (1:46–55); The *Benedictus* (1:68–79); *Gloria in Excelsis* (2:14); and The *Nunc Dimittis* (2:29–32).[42] "The infancy material has a note of joy and tells the story from the perspective of Mary."[43] Gabriel informs Zechariah that John "will be a joy and delight to you, and many will rejoice because of his birth" (Luke 1:14). John "leaped for joy" in Elizabeth's womb (v. 44), when Mary

---

41 Strauss, *Four Portraits, One Jesus*, 264.
42 These titles are derived from the first words of the Latin translation of each hymn.
43 Darrell L. Bock, *A Theology of Luke and Acts* (Grand Rapids: Zondervan, 2012), 67.

greeted her. Mary responds in song to Elizabeth: "My soul glorifies the Lord and my spirit rejoices in God my Savior" (vv. 46–47). When Elizabeth gives birth to John, her relatives and neighbors "shared her joy," rejoicing that God had shown her mercy (vv. 57–58). The angel says to the terrified shepherds: "Do not be afraid. I bring you good news that will cause great joy for all the people" (Luke 2:10). And Luke brackets his gospel with joy, reporting that at Jesus' ascension his disciples "worshiped him and returned to Jerusalem with great joy" (Luke 24:52).

Luke concludes the infancy narrative with a summary statement: "And Jesus grew in wisdom and stature, and in favor with God and man" (Luke 2:52). David E. Garland observes that Luke balances the divine with the human with these words. Jesus' miraculous conception and exalted status is placed alongside his developing as a complete human being. Problems, even heresies, emerge when this balance is lost. The *Infancy Gospel of Thomas*, with its fanciful tales of Jesus' boyhood, is an example of the compromise of Jesus' complete humanity. The tendency among some modern scholars to deny Jesus' divinity is an example of the equal and opposite error to be avoided. "What is important from Luke's summary statement is that the life of Jesus reveals what a human life full of God's Spirit and wisdom looks like."[44]

In his next section (Luke 3:1–4:13) Luke displays Jesus' pedigree and preparation for ministry through his accounts of (1) Jesus' baptism, (2) his genealogy, and (3) the temptation narrative. After four centuries of a silent prophetic voice, John the Baptist steps onto the scene with a message and baptism of repentance (Luke 3:1–20). He takes pains to differentiate himself from Jesus: "I baptize you with water. But one who is more powerful than I will come, the straps of whose sandals I am not worthy to untie. He will baptize you with the Holy Spirit and fire" (v. 16). His words that follow make it clear that he is speaking in eschatological terms: The Spirit-and-fire baptism that Jesus brings is the beginning of the end times, and they continue to

---

[44] David E. Garland, *Luke: Zondervan Exegetical Commentary on the New Testament*, Clinton E. Arnold, gen. ed. (Grand Rapids: Zondervan, 2011), 147.

this day. Jesus' entire saving ministry is in purview here, and John is contrasting it with his own. It is the difference between water baptism and Spirit baptism. Before his ascension, Jesus himself picks up this contrast: "For John baptized with water, but in a few days you will be baptized with the Holy Spirit" (Acts 1:5).

When Jesus himself is baptized, a great revelatory event transpires. Luke alone tells us that it was while Jesus was praying that this great event happened: "And as he was praying, heaven was opened and the Holy Spirit descended on him in bodily form like a dove. And a voice came from heaven: 'You are my Son, whom I love; with you I am well pleased'" (Luke 3:22). This places Luke's Christology in a Trinitarian context. It also highlights the unique sonship of Jesus. Luke's genealogy (vv. 23–38) further amplifies this, placing Jesus and his ministry in a broad, universal context going back to "Adam, the son of God" (v. 38). Then immediately comes Jesus' wilderness temptations. "Part of Jesus' qualifications to be a representative for humanity and son of Adam/Son of God is that he successfully overcomes the temptations of Satan."[45] Jesus further qualifies himself to be the one to bring salvation to all of humanity. Perhaps we should give a little more attention to the prayer that accompanied Jesus' monumental baptism event.

Luke makes much of Jesus' prayer life. This emphasis would lend credence to the view that Luke's is a "Spirit Christology," in terms of interpreting Jesus' earthly ministry. Prayer and the Spirit are inextricably linked throughout Luke-Acts. Jesus himself links the two in his teaching on prayer. It is a unique phenomenon in Lukan theology. *While Jesus is praying* in the waters of the Jordan at his baptism, the Holy Spirit descends upon him (Luke 3:22). Jesus, "full of the Spirit" is "led by the Spirit into the wilderness" (Luke 4:1). In his hometown synagogue Jesus interprets his identity and ministry in terms of Isaiah's messianic prophecy: "The Spirit of the Lord is on me, because he has anointed me" (Luke 4:18–19; Isa. 61:1–2). After the wilderness testing, Jesus returns to Galilee "in the power of the Spirit" (v. 14). As Jesus' ministry begins to attract the masses, he does

---
[45] Bock, *A Theology of Luke and Acts*, 69.

something completely counterintuitive to modern-day American evangelical pragmatism: "But Jesus often withdrew to lonely places and prayed" (Luke 5:16).

Only Luke informs us that Jesus *spent the entire night* in prayer before he selected the Twelve apostles (Luke 6:12–16). Only Luke tells us that it was *while Jesus was praying* that Peter had his great revelation at Caesarea Philippi that Jesus is "God's Messiah" (Luke 9:18–20). Only Luke tell us that "while he [Jesus] was *praying*" he was transfigured (vv. 28–29). Luke provides two glimpses into Jesus' extensive teachings on prayer: In the first (Luke 11:1–13), Jesus culminates with his ask/seek/knock teaching, but surprises us by saying, "how much more will your Father in heaven give the Holy Spirit to those who ask him!" (v. 13)—prayer and the Spirit! The second teaching (Luke 18:1–14) begins with these words: "Then Jesus told his disciples a parable to show them that they should always pray and not give up" (v. 1). Luke's account of Jesus' prayer on the Mount of Olives as he prepares for Calvary is quite poignant (Luke 22:39–46). Finally, two of Jesus' last sayings from the cross are prayers: (1) "Father, forgive them for they do not know what they are doing" (Luke 23:34) and (2) "Father, into your hands I commit my spirit" (v. 46). This pattern of prayer continues throughout Acts (Acts 1:14; 2:42; 4:24–31; 6:4; 8:15; 9:11; 10: 2, 4, 30–31; 12:5, 12; etc.). In this emphasis Luke gives no evidence of an adoptionistic Christology. He simply provides a profound insight into how Jesus functioned in his humanity. In this regard, Jesus' Spirit-empowered, Spirit-led, and prayerful life becomes paradigmatic for his followers!

An extended section follows in which Luke portrays Jesus' Galilean ministry (Luke 4:14–9:50). Jesus' rejection in Nazareth (Luke 4:14–30) came as a result of his messianic claims (Isa. 61:1–2; 58:6) as his prophetic rebuke of Israel nearly cost him his life. What follows are myriad events demonstrating Jesus' unique *authority* to do such things as drive out demons (vv. 31–37), heal the sick (vv. 38–44), command nature and call his disciples (Luke 5:1–11), forgive sins and heal paralysis (vv. 17–26), announce himself as "Lord of the Sabbath" (Luke 6:5), pronounce blessings and woes (vv. 17–26), raise the dead (Luke 7:11–17), calm a raging storm on Lake Galilee (Luke 8:22–25), restore a demon-possessed man (vv. 26–39), and feed the five thousand (Luke 9:10–17). And these are only selective examples from this extended section! Joel Green summarizes well the import of these narratives: "[They relate] how Jesus, empowered by the Spirit, understood the nature of his vocation and engaged in its performance by means of an itinerate ministry balancing proclamation and miraculous activity and occasioning a division between supporters/disciples and opponents."[46]

This unit in Luke's presentation is followed by an even larger one: his travel narrative couched as a journey to Jerusalem (Luke 9:51–19:44). "As the time approached for him to be taken up to heaven, Jesus resolutely set out for Jerusalem" (Luke 9:51). Jesus literally "set his face" in fierce determination to go to Jerusalem and to the cross. Jerusalem—the holy city of which Luke makes much in his narrative—is the center of the Jewish religion and the place from which the gospel will be launched to the ends of the earth. "From this point onward Jesus is portrayed much more as a teacher alternating between instruction of his followers and controversy with his opponents."[47]

Luke 9:51 to 19:27 has often been called the "Gospel for the Outcast" and contains numerous parables as well that illustrate this theme: The Good Samaritan (Luke 10:29–37); The Rich Fool (Luke 12:13–21); The Great Banquet (Luke 14:16–24); Lost Coin, Lost Sheep, Lost Son (Luke 15:1–32); The Rich Man and Lazarus (Luke 16:19–31); The Persistent Widow (Luke 18:1–8); and The Pharisee and the Tax Collector (vv. 9–14). The story of Zaccheaus (Luke 19:1–10), a despised chief tax collector, is a fitting culmination of this section, which ends with these words: "For the Son of Man came to seek and to save the lost" (v. 10).[48] In effect, this verse is the "central theme of the writings of Luke…Jesus came to save."[49]

---

46 Joel Green, *The Gospel of Luke*, NICNT (Grand Rapids: Eerdmans, 1997), 197; cited in: Bock, *A Theology of Luke and Acts*, 69.
47 Marshall, *New Testament Theology*, 134.
48 Strauss, *Four Portraits, One Jesus*, 274–75.
49 I. Howard Marshall, *Luke: Historian and Theologian* (Grand Rapids: Zondervan, 1970), 116.

As Jesus approaches Jerusalem, he weeps over a city facing divine judgment because she did not "recognize the time of God's coming to you," (Luke 19:44). "The statement reflects a high Christology, since it is Jesus who visits Jerusalem."[50] Thus, Jerusalem becomes the scene of the last great redemptive drama: Jesus' Passion, Resurrection, and Ascension (Luke 19:45–24:53). Jesus immediately enters into controversy with the religious establishment (Luke 19:45–21:38). "Every day he was teaching at the temple. But the chief priests, the teachers of the law and the leaders among the people were trying to kill him. But they could not find any way to do it, because all the people hung on his words" (Luke 19:47–48). Jesus' authority is challenged, and the Jewish leaders seek ways to entrap him. But Jesus continues to teach at the very temple whose impending doom he predicts, couching his prophetic teaching in eschatological terms. The cross is inevitable now.

Luke's account of Jesus' betrayal and death is filled with pathos and a sense of ultimate tragedy and injustice. Satan takes control of Judas who collaborates with the chief priests and officers of the temple guard (Luke 22:1–6). Then the scene shifts to the Passover meal, which Jesus invests with new meaning centered on his very person and atoning work (vv. 7–38). Jesus goes to the Mount of Olives and enters into agonizing prayer. He is arrested there, and Peter denies Jesus three times at the house of the high priest (vv. 39–62). Soldiers mock Jesus, and Jesus' trials are a mockery of justice (Luke 22:63–23:24). Luke's portrayal of the events of the crucifixion, death, and burial of Jesus is vivid (Luke 23:26–56). Reactions to these events are widely variegated: Some watch in idle curiosity, others mock, one of the thieves believes, a soldier sees Jesus' innocence. The earth turns dark, and the temple curtain is rent asunder. Jesus is given a dignified burial by Joseph of Arimathea. The whole narrative raises a question: What should the reader's response be to all of this?[51] We will need to devote an entire chapter in this volume to explore the meaning of these events. Then comes Easter!

---

50 Garland, *Luke*, 774.
51 Bock, *A Theology of Luke and Acts*, 78–79.

Jesus rises from the dead (Luke 24:1–49), an event without parallel in human history—alive forevermore! The women discover the empty tomb. Others receive resurrection appearances, including the ten disciples on Easter Sunday night. Luke's account of this appearance is significant in terms of the evidence that Jesus himself offers (showing them his hands and feet and eating broiled fish in front of them) and also because of the Scripture study he conducts! He wanted them to understand the necessity that the Messiah must suffer and rise from the dead (vv. 36–49). Finally, Jesus ascends and the disciples return to Jerusalem "with great joy," and they stay "continually at the temple, praising God" (vv. 50–52). Jesus is vindicated and the disciples are vivified. The church will soon be launched on her worldwide, end-time mission (Acts).

THE CHRISTOLOGY OF JOHN

Paul Trebilco, in his authoritative study of *The Early Christians in Ephesus from Paul to Ignatius*, states rather modestly that "a number of leading personalities of early Christianity have a connection with Ephesus and the range of New Testament and early Christian texts which are linked with Ephesus is probably greater than that of any other city in which there was an early Christian community."[52] Ephesus indeed can be categorized as one of the key cities of early Christianity. Think of the important biblical characters associated with this city: Paul, Timothy, perhaps even Paul's traveling companion Luke, Apollos, Priscilla, Aquila, John, and Mary the mother of Jesus. Paul began the Christian saga there with his extensive missionary work. Then John would later settle there with Mary the Lord's mother, according to tradition.

Ephesus itself was a major center of the ancient world. Third in size only to Rome and Alexandria, Ephesus was a large cosmopolitan center of travel, trade, and commerce, where pagan deities and Roman emperors were worshiped at elaborate temples and where a large

---

[52] Paul Trebilco, *The Early Christians in Ephesus from Paul to Ignatius* (Grand Rapids: Eerdmans, 2004), 1.

Jewish community had been established. Then came the Christians. As their gatherings began to develop, predictably tensions mounted with the Jewish community losing converts to this fledgling sect. Later, false (gnostic) teachers would be attracted to this key center of early Christianity, spreading their distortions of the Christian message. It was in this fermenting context that the apostle John would pen his memories of Jesus and his understanding of the Christian faith. His simple, yet profound gospel would powerfully address this religious and cultural scene as well as the rapidly expanding Christian movement. "John became the heroic pastor-theologian of Asia Minor."[53]

As Ephesus was the most important city of Asia Minor, "so the church in Ephesus was the most important in Asia Minor, and possibly the most influential church in the world at the end of the first century AD."[54] Considering the spiritual giants who ministered there, this should be no surprise. Centuries later, a major church council would be held there. Even today the archeological site draws millions of pilgrims from across the globe, and numerous scholars are still mining its archeological riches. John's writings in the New Testament apprise us of the central *fact* of the Christian faith and movement: Jesus Christ. They demonstrate the relevance of the church's Christology to the cultural and religious challenges of the day. And Ephesus served as an ideal microcosm of the larger historical context in which Christianity was birthed and in which Christianity spread.

It is easy to imagine how profound John's influence would have been in such a context. He penned a gospel—unique among the four—that evinced both simplicity and profundity. Augustine said John's gospel is deep enough for an elephant to swim in it, but shallow enough for a child not to drown in it. How true! Children today can read it and assimilate much, while scholars continue to be amazed at its structure and substance. Clement of Alexandria called

---

[53] So comments Gary Burge, a noted Johannine scholar, in his helpful introduction to John in the *NLT Illustrated Study Bible* (Carol Stream, IL: Tyndale House Publishers, Inc., 2015), 1892. Burge uses almost the exact same words in his helpful commentary on John: Gary M. Burge, *The NIV Application Commentary: John* (Grand Rapids: Zondervan, 2000), 22.

[54] G. R. Beasley-Murray, *The Book of Revelation*, NCB (Greenwood, SC: Attic Press, 1974), 73.

it a "spiritual gospel," acknowledging the depth of its spiritual and theological teaching. At the same time, more recent scholarship has often affirmed the solid historical moorings of John's gospel and appreciated the chronological clues it provides. It is serene, yet serious in tone. In many ways, it "touches all the bases"—theologically, spiritually, and practically—for the church both then and now. Its goal is *faith*.

"Jesus performed many other signs in the presence of his disciples, which are not recorded in this book. But these are written that you may believe that Jesus is the Messiah, the Son of God, and that by believing you may have life in his name" (John 20:30–31). John's good news comes to us by means of *signs* Jesus performed, miracles that signify who he is and what he has come to do. And John relates them so that the reader may *believe*. But this saving faith has *content*: "that Jesus is the Messiah, the Son of God." The result is "life in his name." And at the core of John's message is Christology: Jesus the Messiah, the Son of God. In addition to signs, John relates extensive sections in which Jesus himself elaborates on these themes. The result is a poignantly powerful presentation of the gospel. But unique to John's portrait of Jesus is the prologue that places Jesus in cosmic perspective as the preexistent Word (Logos).

"In the beginning was the Word, and the Word was with God, and the Word was God" (John 1:1). John takes us back to the beginning (cf. Gen. 1:1) and frames it in explicitly Christological terms. Literally *everything* was made through Christ (v. 3): This cannot be said about any other human being! Now it becomes necessary to factor *Jesus* into our very definition of God. He is presented here as a preexistent divine being. But we are getting a little ahead of ourselves. First, we must get the lay of our Johannine literary and theological landscape. Only then can we effectively explore the details of his Christology.

John's design is deceptively simple. The book divides neatly into two halves: chapters 1–12 and chapters 13–21. These units have often been titled "The Book of Signs" and "The Book of Glory" respectively. Add to this the further delineation of a prologue (John 1:1–18) and an epilogue (John 21:1–25) and we have the complete picture. The result is as follows:

1. Prologue (1:1–18)
2. The Book of Signs (1:19–12:50)
3. The Book of Glory (13:1–20:31)
4. Epilogue (21:1–25)

Not only is John's design simple, so is his manner of writing. Utilizing a very simple grammar, syntax, and vocabulary he manages to communicate the most profound truths. He paints a portrait of stark contrasts—a dualism of darkness and light, truth and lies, life and death, time and eternity. Simple words like *believe, life, know, witness, the world, light, glory,* and *abide* take on deceptive depth of meaning.[55]

I also see John providing "bookends" for his Christ-centered, cross-centered narrative. Early on, John the Baptist announces Jesus with these programmatic words: "Behold, the Lamb of God who takes away the sin of the world!…this is he who baptizes with the Holy Spirit…this is the Son of God" (John 1:29–34 ESV). Then toward the end of his narrative John provides the only report of "a sudden flow of blood and water" issuing forth from Jesus' pierced side (John 19:34). And John makes much of the fact that he was an eyewitness to this fact (v. 35). Utilizing a soteriological water-metaphor which looms large in his gospel, John provides an easily discernable pattern:

1. Blood: "Behold, the Lamb of God who takes away the sin of the world!"
2. Water: "This is he who baptizes with the Holy Spirit."

Then he ties it all together with: "This is the Son of God." This same pattern is repeated in his first epistle: "Water and blood came out from the side of Jesus Christ. It wasn't just water, but water and blood. The Spirit tells about this, because the Spirit is truthful" (1 John 5:6 CEV). One is reminded of the living water Jesus offers the woman at Jacob's well in Sychar (John 4:1–26) and Jesus' cry of invitation at

---

[55] Strauss, *Four Portraits, One Jesus*, 299–300.

the Festival of Tabernacles, which John also clarifies as an offer of the Holy Spirit (John 7:37–39). In other words, Jesus alone can baptize in the Holy Spirit. He alone can give living water—eternal, abundant life! He alone is the Baptizer. And he can do this because he alone is also the Lamb of God who shed his blood for our redemption. He alone is the one and only Son of God.

The overture of the Johannine Christological symphony is found in the first eighteen verses (John 1:1–18). It culminates with the announcement of the most stupendous miracle of all: "The Word became flesh and made his dwelling among us" (John 1:14). "This is *a clear assertion of the historicity and reality of the incarnation.*"[56] With this sole use of *Logos*, John provides a cosmic cast to his portrait of Jesus: He is the creator of everything that is! "The first word about creation is Genesis 1, but the final word is John 1."[57] John's use of *Logos*, a practice that would continue in the post-apostolic period in the work of Justin Martyr, a second-century Greek apologist, and others, was genius.

> The overture of the Johannine Christological symphony is found in the first eighteen verses (John 1:1–18).

To both Jew and Greek the Logos was both the originator of the universe and the one who gave order to it. John utilizes this concept to communicate in the most exalted terms imaginable just who Jesus Christ really is. He is the preexistent divine being (both "God" and "with God" [v. 1]) through whom the universe was created. He is the supreme revelation of God, and—most amazing of all!—he became flesh and "tabernacled," or "pitched his tent," among us. He is literally God incarnate![58]

Millard Erickson provides a helpful Christological summary of John's prologue with terms such as preexistence, deity, creative work,

---

56 James D. G. Dunn, *Unity and Diversity in the New Testament: An Inquiry into the Character of Earliest Christianity* (Philadelphia: Westminster, 1977), 300 (Dunn's italics).
57 Paul K. Jewett, *God, Creation, and Revelation* (Grand Rapids: Eerdmans, 1991), 494.
58 Larry D. Hart, *Truth Aflame: Theology for the Church in Renewal*, rev. ed.(Grand Rapids: Zondervan, 2005), 305–06.

incarnation and revelatory work.[59] And Andreas J. Köstenberger provides an extensive treatment of this creation/new creation theme.[60] He summarizes well John's tack in using *Logos* terminology: "As a comprehensive Christological designation, the expression "the Word" encompasses Jesus' entire ministry, placing all of Jesus' works and words within the framework of both his eternal being and existence and God's self-revelation in salvation history."[61]

Another way that John captures this eternal perspective on Jesus is with his inclusion of the "I AM" sayings.

1. **"I am the bread of life"** (John 6:35, 48; with variants on the metaphor throughout the pericope (vv. 25–59): Bread was the staple of life in first-century Palestine and a perfect metaphor for who Jesus is—he *is* the bread that alone brings full satisfaction in life (v. 35), and he gave his life "for the life of the world" (v. 51). He came that we might have life in full abundance (John 10:10). What could be more appealing to a world hungering and thirsting for real life! It is found in Jesus and in Jesus alone.
2. **"I am the light of the world"** (John 8:12; cf. 9:5, which lacks the emphatic pronoun "I"): Jesus continues with: "Whoever follows me will never walk in darkness, but will have the light of life" (John 8:12). *Light* and *life* loom large in John's portrait of Jesus, beginning with the prologue (John 1:4–9). This is an audacious claim from Jesus, but true because of who he is. It is also true that those who follow have the light of life.
3. **"I am the gate for the sheep"** (John 10:7): "I am the gate; whoever enters through me will be saved"; Jesus makes another audacious and exclusive claim, that he alone is the way into the saving presence of God.
4. **"I am the good shepherd"** (John 10:11, 14): Jesus knows his sheep and lays down his life for them (vv. 11, 15); his sheep also know him (v. 14). Christianity is ultimately about knowing Jesus.

---

[59] Millard J. Erickson, *The Word Became Flesh: A Contemporary Incarnational Christology* (Grand Rapids: Baker, 1991), 26–27.
[60] Andreas J. Köstenberger, *A Theology of John's Gospel and Letters* (Grand Rapids: Zondervan, 2009), 336–54.
[61] Köstenberger, *A Theology of John's Gospel and Letters*, 338.

5. **"I am the resurrection and the life"** (John 11:25): Jesus does not merely bring the resurrection and life, he *is* the resurrection and the life. Jesus goes on to say: "Anyone who believes in me will live, even after dying. Everyone who lives in me and believes in me will never ever die" (v. 26 NLT).
6. **"I am the way and the truth and the life"** (John 14:6): Jesus makes the exclusive claim of being *the* way, truth, and (eternal/abundant) life, adding: "No one comes to the Father except through me."
7. **"I am the true vine"** (John 15:1): Jesus adds: "and my Father is the gardener." Verse 5 reads: "I am the vine; you are the branches." Only by our remaining in him do we have life and bear fruit.

In all seven of these sayings Jesus speaks in relational terms. How we are related to him is the difference between death and life, darkness and light, barrenness and fruitfulness. We also find the words "I AM" on the lips of Jesus in other contexts (John 8:24, 28, 58; 13:9). When Jesus averred, "Before Abraham was born, I am!" the Jews "picked up stones to stone him" (John 8:58–59). Such a claim to deity was blasphemous—unless he *was* deity!

Jesus also did "signs" and "works" that pointed to his identity. Some see seven signs (*sēmeia*) in the first half of the gospel, the Book of Signs, but the precise identity is disputed. There are numerous other references to signs and to Jesus' working of miracles, but they all serve the same purpose:

> Ultimately, all signs point to *Jesus* as the true messenger of God, the giver of life, a reality that finds its fullest expression in Jesus' resurrection from the dead, but a reality that is already given preliminary expression in the signs performed during Jesus' public ministry. According to John, the "signs," including the temple clearing, are revelatory pictures of Jesus' true identity: he is the Christ, the Son of God (cf. 20:30–31).[62]

---

62 Köstenberger, *A Theology of John's Gospel and Letters*, 333.

The Jewish setting of John's Christological saga is never lost sight of, but rather dominates his portrait. Jesus is the ultimate *fulfillment* of the institutions of Judaism (ritual purification, the temple, a rabbi, a holy well: John 2:1–4:54) and the festivals of Judaism (Sabbath [ch. 5], Passover [ch. 6], Tabernacles [chs. 7–9], Dedication [ch. 10]).[63] John's stated purpose, in part, is for the reader to believe that Jesus is "the Messiah, the Son of God" (John 20:31). Similar to the Synoptics, John prominently portrays Jesus as the Messiah. Twice John uses the Greek transliteration (*messias*) of the Hebrew term *mashiach* (John 1:41; 4:25), a device found nowhere else in the New Testament. Nineteen other times John uses *christos*/Christ, the traditional translation of Messiah, signifying the Anointed One.[64] Frank J. Matera skillfully summarizes John's distinctive understanding of this concept:

> In the Fourth Gospel, the Messiah is the one who comes from above, the one whom God sent into the world. Thus, although the crowd raises the correct question when it debates about Jesus' origin, it does not understand the full significance of its own question. The Messiah's origin is not a matter of Davidic lineage but of descent from above. Jesus is the Messiah because he is the one whom God sent into the world, the Son of Man who comes from above, God's Word made flesh.[65]

Thus, the Messiah in John's gospel is presented as being of *divine origin*. He is the Son sent from the Father. The divine name of "Son" (*huios*) "occupies a central role in the Christology of John's gospel."[66] Nathanael declares: "Rabbi, you are the Son of God; you are the king of Israel" (John 1:49). Three times Jesus refers to himself as the "Son of God" (John 5:25; 10:36; 11:4). Martha expressed belief in Jesus as "the Messiah, the Son of God, who is to come into the world" (John 11:27). The Jewish leaders asked that Jesus be crucified for blasphemously claiming to be the "Son of God" (John 19:7). And as we have already seen, John's very purpose was for readers to believe in Jesus as Messiah and Son of God (John 20:31).

---

63 See Gary Burge's masterful commentary (*NIV Application Commentary: John*), including his helpful diagram of John in this volume (p. 45).
64 Strauss, *Four Portraits, One Jesus*, 328.
65 Matera, *New Testament Christology*, 230–31.
66 Köstenberger, *A Theology of John's Gospel and Letters*, 380.

But John goes a step further. He reserves the term *huios* (Son) for Jesus alone. Paul has no problem referring to God's sons and daughters as *huioi*, but John prefers *tekna* (children; cf., e.g., John 1:12). He even goes one step further to guard Jesus' unique sonship by conjoining the adjective *monogenēs* (only; unique; one and only) with the Son (John 1:14, 18; 3:16, 18). "For God so loved the world," writes John, "that he gave his one and only Son, that whoever believes in him shall not perish but have eternal life" (John 3:16). Jesus expressed his sonship in terms of his unity with the Father and his being sent by the Father. In one of the most poignant controversy stories in John's gospel these dynamics come powerfully to the fore.

Jesus had healed the invalid at the pool of Bethesda, and his Jewish opponents immediately challenge his authority to do such things on the Sabbath (John 5:16–30). "The Son" is mentioned some nine times in this story, most often with respect to his unique relationship with the Father. It is a story worth careful study because it illustrates the dynamics of all that has been said thus far about Jesus as the unique Son of God. Toward the end of the story, Jesus refers to himself as the "Son of Man" (v. 27).

"Son of Man" seemed to be Jesus' preferred way of referring to himself, and John's gospel follows the same path as the other gospels in this regard. However, John adds a nuance of usage of this title that is unique to his portrait of Jesus. There is a movement back and forth from heaven to earth in John's portrayal of the Son of Man. Jesus as the Son of Man is sent from heaven to earth, where he is "lifted up" on the cross in a saving sacrifice. He then is raised from death and returns to heaven, from which he will return in glory (John 1:51; 3:13–14; 5:27; 6:27, 53, 62; 8:28; 9:35; 12:23, 34; 13:31).[67] Jesus, as the exalted Son of Man of Daniel 7:13, has *authority* from above to carry out his ministry and manifests God's *glory*, both by his going to the cross and rising from the dead and by his conquering return at the end of the age. John wants us to see the *glory* of Jesus' humble earthly life and ignominious death. Some have conjectured that perhaps one reason he omits the

---

[67] See Köstenberger, *A Theology of John's Gospel and Letters*, 386–88 for a detailed, helpful analysis of these texts.

Transfiguration is so that readers would not be distracted from seeing the glory of God's Suffering Servant in his earthly life and saving death.

With such an exalted view of Jesus, some might anticipate that John would neglect the full *humanity* of Christ. But this is far from the case. A good example is John's dramatic account of disputes with the Jewish leaders in which Jesus makes stupendous claims about himself (John 8:12–58). He owns his unique, unparalleled relationship with the Father (vv. 12, 16, 19, 23, 26, 29, 42, 51) and alludes to his preexistence (v. 38). He claims to be "sent" by the Father (vv. 16, 26, 29, 42) as well as to be sinless (v. 46)! His culminating "blasphemous" announcement was the last straw: "I tell you the truth, before Abraham was even born, I AM!" at which they tried to stone him (vv. 58–59 NLT). Yet in the midst of these scandalous claims Jesus refers quite casually and naturally to his complete humanity: "As it is you are looking for a way to kill me, a man who has told you the truth that I heard from God" (v. 40).[68] I have summarized elsewhere John's perspective on Jesus' complete humanity:

> Even though John's writings give the most explicit portrayal of Christ's divinity, they also provide strong testimony to his humanity. Christ is the preexistent Word, to be sure (John 1:1–5), but he is also the Word who "became flesh and lived among us" (v. 14). The "Word of life," asserts John, is something "which we have heard, which we have seen with our own eyes, which we have watched and touched with our own hands" (1 John 1:1 NJB). This crassly *physical* description would have scandalized the heretics of John's day, who could not countenance the concept of the enfleshment of the Word of God. But John's Jesus gets tired (John 4:6) and thirsty (v. 7; 19:28). He shows great emotion—at Lazarus' tomb, for example (11:33–38). And he dies a real death (19:34). John's Jesus is as far from the gods of Greek mythology as the east is from the west. Jesus' humanity is real and complete; it is no disguise.[69]

---

[68] Hart, *Truth Aflame*, 313–14.
[69] Hart, *Truth Aflame*, 314.

Finally, we must consider John's portrait of Jesus as the Paraclete (*paraklētos*; advocate). Careful students of John will already know that in John's gospel Jesus refers to the *Holy Spirit* with this term. It is only in 1 John that *Jesus* is explicitly referred to as the Paraclete (1 John 2:1). The Upper Room Discourse contains five Paraclete Sayings, which can be displayed and summarized as follows:

1. **HELPER**: John 14:15–24—Through the Father's giving us the Spirit the Trinity takes up residence within us.
2. **TEACHER**: John 14:25–26—The Father will send us the Spirit to continue Jesus' teaching ministry among us.
3. **WITNESS**: John 15:26–27—Jesus sends the Spirit from the Father to empower our witness.
4. **JUDGE**: John 16:4–11—Jesus leaves the earth bodily in order to send the Spirit, who will convict the world of sin.
5. **GUIDE**: John 16:12–15—The Holy Spirit guides us into all truth, the things of Jesus and the Father.

Contemporary theologians have largely neglected the interlacing of Pneumatology and Christology that is found in John and which helped nudge the church in a Trinitarian direction.

For example, in the first Paraclete Saying Jesus says: "On that day you will realize that I am in my Father, and you are in me, and I am in you" (John 14:20). Is Jesus speaking of his resurrection or of the subsequent giving of the Spirit? In either case, he is speaking of a profound unity between himself and his followers. Jesus goes on to say: "Anyone who loves me will obey my teaching. My Father will love them, and we will come to them and make our home with them" (v. 23). In other words, through the indwelling of the Paraclete, the Holy Spirit, Jesus and the Father will also make their home in the believer (cf. the Vine and Branches teaching to follow: John 15:1–8). Jesus' *sending* of the Spirit and the Spirit's mediating role, communicating Christ and the Father to us, also loom large in these teachings. This is a profoundly pneumatological, trinitarian presentation of the glorified Christ and his profound union with his followers. *It should not be left out of any full-orbed presentation of Johannine Christology.*

It is also important to note in this opening Paraclete Saying that Jesus refers to the Holy Spirit as "another advocate" (John 14:16: *allos*=another of the same kind, versus *heteros*=another of a different kind; and *paraklētos*=Paraclete, Advocate). In other words, through the Holy Spirit, Jesus, also a Paraclete, will continually be with his disciples. In John's first epistle he describes Jesus as our Paraclete with the Father, saying, "we have an advocate [*paraklētos*] with the Father, Jesus Christ, the Righteous One. He is the atoning sacrifice for our sins, and not only for ours but also for the sins of the whole world" (1 John 2:1–2). A paraclete or advocate is someone who is called alongside to help or defend, as a defense lawyer does in court. What a wonderful ministry of our Lord!

We have devoted more space by far to John's Christology because in large measure it is the capstone of New Testament Christology. Much more could (and probably should) be said, but the general parameters and impact of John's witness must suffice for our purposes here. Now we must turn to another theological giant in the New Testament, the apostle Paul, and explore his rich Christology.

THE CHRISTOLOGY OF PAUL

The apostle Paul was a Christ-intoxicated man. His personal encounter with Christ—which was both a conversion and a resurrection appearance commissioning him as an apostle—has impacted millions of people in every generation. It was what prompted him to pen some twenty-five percent of the New Testament. It launched his empire-wide missionary enterprise, which would ultimately cost him his life. He suffered much for his witness to Christ. And his Christological contribution is essential to our full understanding of the gospel and the Christian life. Consider Paul's passion, proclamation, and perspective:

> *The apostle Paul was a Christ-intoxicated man.*

PAUL'S PASSION:

I want to know Christ—yes, to know the power of his resurrection and participation in his sufferings, becoming like him in his death, and so, somehow, attaining to the resurrection from the dead (Phil. 3:10–11).

I have been crucified with Christ and I no longer live, but Christ lives in me. The life I now live in the body, I live by faith in the Son of God, who loved me and gave himself for me (Gal. 2:20).

PAUL'S PROCLAMATION:

Jews demand signs and Greeks look for wisdom, but we preach Christ crucified: a stumbling block to Jews and foolishness to Gentiles, but to those whom God has called, both Jews and Greeks, Christ the power of God and the wisdom of God.... Christ Jesus, who has become for us wisdom from God—that is, our righteousness, holiness and redemption (1 Cor. 1:22–24, 30).

Paul, a servant of Christ Jesus, called to be an apostle and set apart for the gospel of God—the gospel he promised beforehand through his prophets in the Holy Scriptures regarding his Son, who as to his earthly life was a descendant of David, and who through the Spirit of holiness was appointed the Son of God in power by his resurrection from the dead: Jesus Christ our Lord (Romans 1:1–4).

PAUL'S PERSPECTIVE

The Scriptures tell us, "The first man, Adam, became a living person. But the last Adam—that is, Christ—is a life-giving Spirit (1 Corinthians 15:45 NLT).

One new humanity (Eph. 2:15).

All things have been created through him and for him (Colossians 1:16).

Clearly, Paul thought in cosmic terms when it came to Christ Jesus—everything from creation to new creation, even a new humanity! Getting a handle on his far-reaching Christology is a daunting task. Let us begin with a definition of Paul's gospel, Paul's theology, Paul's Christology: *Christ crucified*. That is it. Enough said? Not at all. Paul wrote a quarter of the New Testament explicating this theology, and scholars past and present have produced prodigious tomes exploring it. To a large degree Paul became the spokesperson for Christianity, explaining in-depth how God brings salvation to humankind. And he always brings us to the cross. In this regard, his writings parallel the four gospels, which also put the accent on Passion Week. To be sure, Paul has very little to say about the life and ministry of Jesus, but he does delineate the gospel for us in unmistakable terms. Christ crucified: What are we to make of this pregnant phrase?

First, *Christ*: In Paul's writings this term is no longer simply a Greek translation of a Hebrew word. It is now a proper name. Our tendency to refer to Jesus as simply "Christ" we owe solely to Paul. And he uses this name often: "Out of 529 occurrences in the New Testament, 379 are found in the Pauline epistles; thus, he has the extraordinary proportion of just under 72 percent."[70] Paul's frequent use of "Jesus" (214; second only to John: 237 times) links to Jesus' humanity and earthly ministry. *Combining* the two names, typical of Paul, brings the complete picture: "Christ Jesus" (83 times); "Jesus Christ" (26 times); "Lord Jesus Christ" (54 times); "Christ Jesus our Lord" (8 times). The last two combinations (total 62 times), forming the full Christological name can be found only 19 times in the rest of the New Testament.[71]

The second word, *crucified*: Paul preached "the gospel of Christ," and for Paul it was Christ's *death* that "gave the proclamation of Christ its character as 'gospel.'"[72] "The Gospel according to Paul," which is perhaps the best title for Paul's Roman epistle, highlights this centrality. Paul places a paragraph-long sentence (in the original) at the outset of his carefully planned letter (Rom. 3:21–26) which focuses

---

[70] Morris, *New Testament Theology*, 39.
[71] Morris, *New Testament Theology*, 40.
[72] James D. G. Dunn, *The Theology of Paul the Apostle* (Grand Rapids: Eerdmans, 1998), 183.

strongly on Christ's death. Then, chapters 5–8 explicate this salvation with the death of Christ as the central motif. But Paul also strongly emphasizes the resurrection, mentioning it some 17 times throughout the Roman epistle. His opening words set the agenda:

> Paul, a servant of Christ Jesus, called to be an apostle and set apart for the gospel of God—the gospel he promised beforehand through his prophets in the Holy Scriptures regarding his Son, who as to his earthly life was a descendant of David, and who through the Spirit of holiness was appointed the Son of God in power by his resurrection from the dead: Jesus Christ our Lord (Rom. 1:1–4)

As here in Romans, so throughout Paul's letters, the death and resurrection of Jesus form the heart of Paul's Christology. James D. G. Dunn expresses well the inseparability of the two:

> If the cross of Jesus stands at the centre of Paul's theology, so also does the resurrection of Jesus. Christ crucified is also he whom God raised from the dead. More to the point, the significance of the one cannot be grasped in isolation from that of the other. Without the resurrection, the cross would be a cause for despair. Without the cross, the resurrection would be an escape from reality. Unless the one died the death of all, the all would have little to celebrate in the resurrection of the one, other than to rejoice in his personal vindication.[73]

Paul's Christology was cruciform in its objective message and pneumatological in its subjective application. Paul's strong Jewish roots are evident, but one also sees a comfort on the part of Paul with his surrounding Hellenistic culture. Still his message would be scandalous to his Jewish audience and moronic to his Hellenistic hearers (1 Cor. 1:22–24).

At the core, Paul's theology is soteriological. In this regard, Paul and Luke hold much in common in terms of Christology—which

---
[73] Dunn, *The Theology of Paul the Apostle*, 235.

should not surprise us since they were co-laborers in missionary enterprise! I have argued elsewhere that the leitmotif of *Christ as Savior* provides a unifying dynamic for the Christological symphony. Christ's saviorhood guards both (1) the unity of his person in his humanity and divinity and (2) the unity of his person and work. Jesus as Savior is the divine-human deliverer of humanity.[74] What Jesus *does* for us defines to a large degree who he *is*. At this juncture it is important to caution American readers of this text: Our culture thinks so much in individualistic terms, it is often very difficult for us to grasp the corporate dimension of Christ's saving work. Ultimately, this entails integrating our *ecclesiology* with our Christology. Being a Christian, according to Paul, is being in union with the person of Christ *and* being in fellowship with the body of Christ, the church (read Ephesians!). The phrase Paul uses to communicate this reality is "in Christ."[75] It is always and only *in Christ* that we are the called, the chosen, the predestined. Yes, this entails our own personal experience with Christ, but the ultimate goal is corporate, social. Christ wants to bring us together as his body and bride. In fact, through Christ's death and resurrection, God has, in effect, ended fallen humanity and initiated a new humanity—a whole new human race!

We can sum all this up by referring to the "Christ event" and by reflecting on all that has been accomplished through it. Mark Allan Powell helpfully displays these effects by summarizing the findings of Joseph Fitzmeyer—ten different images that depict what God has done for us through Jesus Christ:

1. **Justification**: People stand before God acquitted and righteous (Rom. 3:21–26).
2. **Salvation**: People are rescued from evil and wrath (Rom. 5:9; Phil. 3:20).
3. **Reconciliation**: People are placed in a right relationship with God and each other (Rom. 5:10–11; 2 Cor. 5:18–19).
4. **Expiation**: People have their sins blotted out or wiped away (Rom. 3:25).

---

[74] Hart, *Truth Aflame*, 317.
[75] Elwell and Yarbrough, *Encountering the New Testament*, 266–67.

5. **Redemption**: People are brought out of slavery to sin and death (Rom. 8:18–23; 1 Cor. 7:23).
6. **Freedom**: People are set free from sin, law, and self to live as God intended (Rom. 8:2; Gal. 5:1).
7. **Sanctification**: People are made holy (1 Cor. 1:2, 30; 6:11).
8. **Transformation**: People are being changed into the image of God (Rom. 12:2; 2 Cor. 3:18).
9. **New Creation**: People are given a new life in a new age (2 Cor. 5:17; Gal. 2:20; 6:15).
10. **Glorification**: People share in the glory of God (Rom. 8:18, 21, 30; 1 Thess. 2:12).[76]

We should immediately recognize the predominantly *corporate* dimension of each of these images. Then, we should pause to reflect on the profoundly Christocentric nature of these realities.

For the name of Christ to be found on virtually every page of Paul's letters is absolutely remarkable. Remembering that they were penned so early, we should also ask how such a tectonic shift could have occurred so rapidly. Christ was now a proper name for Jesus: "That in itself is an astonishing fact. For it means that at the time of Paul's writing, the Christian claim that Jesus was Messiah was no longer controversial. No longer was it necessary for Paul to argue the case that Jesus was indeed Israel's long-awaited Davidic Messiah."[77] The devotion Jesus engendered among his original disciples is now intensifying and spreading throughout the Roman world.

As we have already seen, Paul begins his Roman epistle by announcing his apostleship and his calling to the "gospel of God" with these words: "the gospel he promised beforehand through his prophets in the Holy Scriptures regarding his Son, who as to his earthly life was a descendant of David, and who through the Spirit of holiness was appointed the Son of God in power by his resurrection from the dead: Jesus Christ our Lord" (Rom. 1:2–4). "Here is the one certain place in

---

[76] Powell, *Introducing the New Testament*, 249; Joseph Fitzmyer, *Paul and His Theology*, 2nd ed.(Englewood Cliffs, NJ: Prentice Hall, 1989), 59–71.
[77] Dunn, *The Theology of Paul the Apostle*, 197.

Paul's letters where Davidic Son and eternal Son are merged."[78] Later in this epistle as Paul praises the people of Israel, he exults: "Theirs are the patriarchs, and from them is traced the human ancestry of the Messiah, who is God over all, forever praised! Amen" (Rom. 9:5). Paul is claiming in no uncertain terms that Jesus is the Messiah of Jewish hopes, but he says even more here. He avers that Jesus is *God!* Add to this the authoritative tradition he passes on "that Christ died for our sins according to the Scriptures" (1 Cor. 15:3), and you have the ultimate Jewish scandal: a *crucified* Messiah. Furthermore, he is also God's eternal Son, revealed by God himself in Paul (Gal. 1: 14), and he will rule to the end of the age because "God himself" has "put everything under Christ" (1 Cor. 15:27). Then he turns the kingdom over to the Father (1 Cor. 15:23–28/Pss. 110:1; 8:6).

Returning to Romans 1:2–4, we need to make note of Paul's concluding phrase: "Jesus Christ our Lord" (v. 4). This is "the absolute heart of Pauline Christology": *Jesus is Lord!*[79] "Insofar as Christological titles are concerned, and insofar as usage is the measure, the most significant way of speaking about Christ for Paul is indicated by the title *kyrios*, 'Lord.'"[80] The true Messiah of the Jews is also the exalted Lord Jesus Christ! As Paul sought to describe and explain his ministry to the feisty Corinthians, he put Jesus' Lordship at the center (2 Cor. 4:1–6). Paul's was an apostolic ministry bent on communicating "the light of the gospel that displays the glory of Christ, who is the image of God" (v. 4). He explained further: "For what we preach is not ourselves, but Jesus Christ as Lord, and ourselves as your servants for Jesus' sake. For God, who said, 'Let light shine out of darkness,' made his light shine in our hearts to give us the light of the knowledge of God's glory displayed in the face of Christ" (vv. 5–6). It's about Jesus Christ as Lord, not me, Paul argued. It's about a new creation in which God dispels the darkness, revealing his glory in the face

---

[78] Gordon D. Fee, *Pauline Christology: An Exegetical-Theological Study* (Peabody, MA: Hendrickson, 2007), 544. Fee's analysis of Pauline Christology sets the standard in this field of study, and I will rely on it often in this section.
[79] Fee, *Pauline Christology*, 558.
[80] Dunn, *The Theology of Paul the Apostle*, 244.

of Christ. Christ is the very image (*eikōn*) of God (v. 4; cf. Col. 1:15). It is *his* image into which we are being transformed, as we contemplate the Lord's glory (2 Cor. 3:18).

And it all begins, on our side of the equation, with the faith we profess in the risen, exalted Lord:

> If you declare with your mouth, "Jesus is Lord," and believe in your heart that God raised him from the dead, you will be saved. For it is with your heart that you believe and are justified, and it is with your mouth that you profess your faith and are saved (Rom. 10:9–10).

Notice the mouth-heart/heart-mouth arrangement: We confess with our mouth Jesus' Lordship and believe in our heart in his resurrection; with our heart we believe and are justified and with our mouth we profess our faith and are saved.

Paul culminates one of his most important statements on Jesus' Lordship with the assertion that one day every knee will bow before Christ "and every tongue acknowledge [confess] that Jesus Christ is Lord to the glory of God the Father" (Phil. 2:10–11). The entire passage (vv. 6–11), perhaps a preexistent hymn that Paul incorporated into his letter, is a majestic tribute to our Lord:

> Who being in very nature God,
> did not consider equality with God something to be used to his own advantage;
> rather, he made himself to be nothing
> by taking the very nature of a servant,
> being made in human likeness.
> And being found in appearance as a man,
> he humbled himself
> by becoming obedient to death—even death on a cross!
>
> Therefore God exalted him to the highest place
> and gave him the name that is above every name,
> that at the name of Jesus every knee should bow,
> in heaven and on earth and under the earth,

and every tongue acknowledge that Jesus Christ is Lord,
to the glory of God the Father.

This doxological encomium is, as Gordon Fee avers, the "acropolis" among the Pauline Christological passages: It asserts Christ's preexistence, his divinity (and his equality with the Father), his complete humanity, and his superior Name (the Yahweh of Isaiah 45:23!).[81] This is a prime example of what Fee and others refer to as Paul's "Christological monotheism," whereby Christ is included within the definition of God. Ultimately, it would influence the church toward a full-orbed doctrine of the Trinity.

Finally, brief mention must be made of Paul's Adam/Christ analogy or typology (Rom. 5:15–19; 1 Cor. 15:21–22). Here the historical Adam represents fallen humanity in death and Jesus represents redeemed humanity in resurrection life. The Romans 5 passage is especially enlightening in this regard. Here Adam's disobedience and its effects pales in comparison to Christ's obedience and its effects. One thinks of Irenaeus's recapitulation theology! Christ's humanity comes to the fore as "the one man, Jesus Christ" (vv. 15, 17) reverses what the one man, Adam, did. The pattern of the entire chapter is instructive: "if Romans 5:1–11 presents him [Jesus] as the Lord and Son of God, Romans 5:12–21 emphasizes that he is the 'one man' whose righteous act undid the effects of that other man, Adam (Rom. 5:15; cf. 1 Cor. 15:21, 47)."[82]

The drive of the apostle Paul's life was to know Christ and to make him known: "I want to know Christ—yes, to know the power of his resurrection and participation in his sufferings, becoming like him in his death, and so, somehow, attaining to the resurrection from the dead" (Phil. 3:10–11). His writings have contributed greatly to each succeeding generation with the same drive. Paul's life and theology demonstrate that knowing Christ is the heart of Christianity.

---

[81] Fee, *Pauline Christology*, 19–20.
[82] Marshall, *New Testament Theology*, 427.

THE CHRISTOLOGY OF HEBREWS

For people biblically and theologically in the know, Hebrews is a spiritually rich literary masterpiece, though a bit arcane for modern readers. For average folk, the book (if that is what you call it) is about as appealing as most of the Old Testament—the rest of the New Testament has much greater appeal and a lot more "refrigerator verses." There are a lot of modern-day Marcionites out there! But upon careful inspection, the Book of Hebrews has amazing relevance for contemporary Christianity in a global context. There is the perennial Jewish-Christian dialogue. And now, perhaps even more important, we have a resurgent Islam along with cults such as Mormonism, which continue to grow. All these religious movements claim further "revelations" and sacred literature which demote Jesus in stature. The Book of Hebrews addresses this context and conflict explicitly with a strong argument for a high Christology: Jesus as the supreme and final revelation of God and the one who fulfills all the promises of the Hebrew Scriptures. Put every competing religion, philosophy, and worldview on the table beside Jesus, argues Hebrews, and Jesus is simply—better!

As my treasured *NIV Study Bible* says about Hebrews: "From the Old Testament itself, Christ is shown to be superior to the ancient prophets, to angels, to Moses (the mediator of the former covenant) and to Aaron and his priestly descendants."[83] Hebrews argues cogently that Jesus is better than the angels (1:4–5) and better than Moses (3:3). His priesthood is better (4:14–15). His covenant is better (7:22; 8:6). His tabernacle is better (9:11). And his sacrifice is better (9:23–28). As Jesus' followers, we have: "better things…the things that have to do with salvation" (6:9); "a better hope" (7:19); "a better covenant… established on better promises" (7:22; 8:6); "better sacrifices" (9:23); "better and lasting possessions" (10:34); "a better country" (11:16); "an even better resurrection" (11:35); and "a better word [spoken by the blood of Jesus] than the blood of Abel" (12:24). We simply have "something better," something planned for us by God himself

---

83 *NIV Study Bible* (Grand Rapids: Zondervan, 2011), 2065.

(11:40)![84] Karen H. Jobes, in her masterful survey of Hebrews and the general epistles, has entitled Hebrews "The Book of Better Things."[85]

And in Jesus Christ we have the final, definitive revelation.

> In the past God spoke to our ancestors through the prophets at many times and in various ways, but in these last days he has spoken to us by his Son, whom he appointed heir of all things, and through whom also he made the universe. The Son is the radiance of God's glory and the exact representation of his being, sustaining all things by his powerful word. After he had provided purifications for sins, he sat down at the right hand of the Majesty in heaven (Heb. 1:1–3).

No room for new means to salvation, such as in Islam, where Jesus is demoted to one of the many prophets of the past and Mohammed and the Koran displace Jesus and the Bible: False spiritualities, old and new, are exploded by Hebrews' portrait of Jesus and the life of faith to which he has called us. "In other words, the opening verses of Hebrews make a bold claim that Jesus Christ, Son of God, is the full and final way in which God has spoken to humankind."[86]

Interestingly, impressed as we may be by a carefully study of this polished rhetorical masterpiece, we do not know for certain who wrote it or what precisely we should call it. On the latter question, perhaps we could simply call Hebrews a sermon/exhortation/epistle. It is what it is, as they say. And who wrote it? Many have argued for Paul. Certainly Paul's writings reflect a similar perspective on the faith, but Hebrews' style and emphases work against this hypothesis. What about Apollos, Timothy, Luke, Barnabas, or even Priscilla? I like all these possibilities, especially Priscilla, in a day when too often women's ministries in the church are given such short shrift. My best guess is Barnabas, the "son of encouragement" (Acts 4:36), who could have certainly written this "message of encouragement"

---

[84] Cf. Powell, *Introducing the New Testament*, 433.
[85] Karen H. Jobes, *Letters to the Church: A Survey of Hebrews and the General Epistles* (Grand Rapids: Zondervan, 2011), 21.
[86] Jobes, *Letters to the Church*, 60.

(Hebrews 13:22 NAB, CEB), as Tertullian, one of my favorite church fathers, said he did. For our purposes, we will posit that Hebrews was written primarily to Jewish Christians in Rome, around A.D. 67–70, in a time of persecution and perhaps temptation to return to Judaism or paganism. In a day of ever-increasing apostasy, it is again easy to perceive Hebrews' relevance.

And how can we best encapsulate Hebrews' Christology? Hebrews presents Christ as: (1) the *Son of God* who is the supreme revelation of God, the creator and sustainer of the universe; (2) our great *High Priest*, who is *both* the priest and the once-and-for-all sacrifice for our sins; and (3) the Son and High Priest who has *ascended*![87] Hebrews argues throughout for a divine-human Son and High Priest, Jesus' humanity being just as essential as his divinity. We will look first at the witness of Hebrews to the deity of Christ, then to his humanity.

The opening verses, as we have already seen, introduce God's exalted Son as the supreme revelation of God, through whom God has spoken definitively "in these last days" (v. 2). Jesus is the "radiance of God's glory and the exact representation of his being" (v. 3). Patristic theology often utilizes this passage to point to the *consubstantiality* of the Father and the Son ("radiance of God's glory") and the *distinction* between the Father and the Son ("exact representation of his being").[88] It was through the Son that God "made the universe" (v. 2), and the Son sustains "all things through his powerful word" (v. 3). Seated at God's right hand, Jesus rules with God in supreme authority (v. 3). Jesus is superior to the angels and worshiped by them (vv. 4, 6). He is sinless (4:15). And he is coming again (9:28; 10:37)![89]

In terms of Jesus' humanity, Hebrews is quite straightforward and emphatic. "Since the children have flesh and blood, he too shared in their humanity" in order to redeem them by his death, defeating both the devil and death itself (2:14–15). Jesus was "fully human in every way, in order that he might become a merciful and faithful high

---

[87] I am guided in part here by Jobes, *Letters to the Churches*, 80–111.
[88] Philip Edgcumbe Hughes, *A Commentary on the Epistle to the Hebrews* (Grand Rapids: Eerdmans, 1997), 43–45.
[89] Powell, *Introducing the New Testament*, 435.

priest in service to God, and that he might make atonement for the sins of the people" (v. 17). He also suffered temptation and is able, therefore, to help us when we are being tempted (2:18). In fact, he is able to empathize with us in our weakness since he was "tempted in every way, just as we are" (4:15). "During the days of Jesus' life on earth he offered up prayers and petitions with fervent cries and tears" and "learned obedience from what he suffered" (5:7). (Think of Gethsemane.) And Jesus set the pattern of persevering faith for us as "pioneer and perfecter" (12:1–3).[90] As the Incarnate Son, he completed his work on earth and returned to the Father: Therefore, he has been "appointed heir of all things" (1:2).

But we have divided what Hebrews has conjoined: We have separated Christ's humanity and divinity when it was the Son of God, *as both God and man*, who did all the above for us (cf. especially 1:1–4). In that regard, he became the one who could simultaneously be Messiah, High Priest, *and* the sacrifice for our sins. His priesthood was unique: As the Son of God his was a Melchizedekian Priesthood (5:11–10:39), superseding the Levitical priesthood. The writer of Hebrews asks: "If perfection could have been attained through the Levitical priesthood—and indeed the law given to the people established that priesthood—why was there still need for another priest to come, one in the order of Melchizedek, not in the order of Aaron?" (7:11). The question being raised relates to a very important psalm for Jesus and the early church: Psalm 110 (cf. Heb. 7:17). Jesus was that High Priest who through his once-and-for-all sacrifice brought a new and better covenant; the argument of chapters 5:11–10:39 is coherent and cogent.[91]

The culmination of Hebrews' portrait of Jesus is the *ascension*, where Jesus enters "heaven itself, now to appear for us in God's presence" (9:24). The Son of God, our High Priest, enters the true, eternal Holy of Holies (9:11–10:18). It is a finished work where "sacrifice for sin is no longer needed" (10:18). The book concludes in celebration of "our Lord Jesus, that great Shepherd of the sheep" (13:20)—and so should we!

---

90 Powell, *Introducing the New Testament*, 435.
91 See the *NIV Zondervan Study Bible* (Grand Rapids: Zondervan, 2015), 2492.

Lesson Five

The Witness of the Church

THE PERSON OF CHRIST IN HISTORICAL THEOLOGY

No responsible exploration of Christology would neglect mining the riches of the church's reflections on Christ down through her history. The patristic period is of particular interest since the major Christological issues emerged during those centuries and were dealt with substantively. In addition, there are no new heresies; thus, contemporary aberrations are better analyzed in the light of the lessons of historical theology. Obviously, an exhaustive treatment would entail another volume altogether. Thus, what is provided here will in effect be a presentation of highlights and turning points in the history of Christian thought related to Christ. First, we must journey back in time to explore the Christological challenges of the ensuing centuries after the establishment of the church in the apostolic period. As one might expect, the times were often tumultuous!

Immediately, one is struck with the interrelation between trinitarian and Christological issues. I often tell my students that exploration of Christology inevitably leads to the doctrine of the Trinity and vice versa. It is as simple as this: Jews and Christians are monotheists. If the Father is God and Jesus is God—we all know what one-plus-one is! Then the Holy Spirit is added and Christians are immediately accused of being polytheists. The further question as to how Jesus could be both God and a man simultaneously also presented a puzzle. And these questions are perennial! Thus, we may find the need to be kinder to the heretics—or at least sympathetic. After all, at least a half dozen heresies are blurted out in the average Sunday school class or home group every week:

> The church owes a great debt to the heretics. Quite often they have been the ones who have forced us to do our theological homework, to get our act straight. Sometimes contemporary heretics help remind us that the ones we read about in our history texts were flesh and blood folk as well. More often than not, these misled religionists had a legitimate concern, but simply came up with the wrong answers.[1]

There will always be a scandal to our message: A crucified Messiah? A bodily resurrection? A divine-human Savior? A triune God? A salvation solely by grace? Christ as the only way to the Father? The list could go on.

We have already seen in previous chapters the challenges of New Testament times as the apostles and their congregations dealt with false teachers and teachings usually influenced by the surrounding Hellenistic culture. Also, as we surveyed the various quests for the historical Jesus, we noticed the same tendencies as attempts were made to deconstruct and reconstruct the historical portrait of Jesus according to the "acceptable" methodologies of the time (for example, Enlightenment rationalism). In the church of the patristic period (the first five centuries), the overall response to heresies was fourfold: creeds, canon, church (bishops and councils), and Christology. In actuality, it may be that the heresies themselves were *responses* to the developing orthodoxy as the gospel spread across the globe. There will always be a scandal to our message: A crucified Messiah? A bodily resurrection? A divine-human Savior? A triune God? A salvation solely by grace? Christ as the only way to the

---

1 Larry Hart, *For God So Loved the World: The Biblical Doctrine of Grace* (Tulsa: Truth Aflame Press, 2015), 27. Harold O. J. Brown masterfully develops this thesis in-depth in: *Heresies: The Image of Christ in the Mirror of Heresy and Orthodoxy from the Apostles to the Present* (New York: Doubleday, 1984).

Father? The list could go on. We will begin with what we might call the Founding Fathers of historical theology.

FAITH OF OUR FATHERS: THE CHURCH OF THE FIRST FIVE CENTURIES

Though an era of incessant conflict, controversy, and persecution, the patristic period was also one of the most formative and productive periods in the church's history. "The period is also of importance for theological reasons. Every mainstream Christian body—including the Anglican, Eastern Orthodox, Lutheran, Reformed, and Roman Catholic churches—regards the patristic period as a definitive landmark in the development of Christian doctrine."[2] My temptation would be to take the reader on a historical tour, pointing up great stalwarts of faith who remained faithful to the gospel and the faith once for all delivered to the saints (cf. Jude 3). Unfortunately, that enterprise would require a separate volume or two. Rather, our focus will be on six key Christological conflicts that helped form the doctrinal guidelines in this arena of thought for all the centuries to follow. In other words, we will be dealing with heresies.

"The history of Christian theology is in large part a history of heresies because Jesus and the claims he made, as well as the claims his disciples made about him, seemed to be incredible."[3] Christianity began as a messianic sect within Judaism. The first converts were in large measure Jewish. Therefore, one would expect that one immediate struggle coming out of the strongly monotheistic ethos of Judaism would be that of fully embracing Christ's divinity. Early on, Paul encountered the Judaizers, who wanted to impose certain Old Testament practices on the Gentiles, including especially circumcision. Paul perceived immediately that this was a direct threat to the gospel of grace itself, and he strongly opposed it. He even confronted Peter who was tempted to cower before this circumcision group in his

---

2 Alister E. McGrath, *Historical Theology: An Introduction to the History of Christian Thought*, 2nd ed. (Malden, MA.: Wiley-Blackwell, 2013), 17.
3 Brown, *Heresies*, xxiii.

relations with the Gentiles (Gal. 2:11–21). These Judaizers were the precursors of a widely variegated movement which came to be known as *Ebionism*.

The origin of the name Ebionism is uncertain, but its Christological aberration, in its broad parameters, is quite clear: Adoptionism. Jesus was seen as having a normal birth through the marital union of Joseph and Mary, not through a miraculous virginal conception.[4] At some point—usually believed to be at either his birth or his baptism—the Christ descended upon Jesus and he became God's Son. It was also believed that Christ left toward the end of Jesus' life. Obviously, Ebionism espoused a "low Christology" which denied the deity of Christ, even though he was believed to be a wise and virtuous person. Adoptionistic and functional Christologies persist to this day among liberal theologians who stumble at the miracle of Incarnation.

Another challenge to incarnational Christology was the trend, emanating from the surrounding Neoplatonic Hellenistic culture, commonly identified as *Docetism*. Actually, both Paul and John had to deal with this gnostic tendency in their churches. The central idea of this Neoplatonic worldview was a dualism that viewed the material world as innately evil and ephemeral. Only in the eternal realm of ideas and ideals, of mind and spirit, was there actual reality. False apostles, prophets, and teachers spread their gnostic version of the gospel—which was no gospel at all—attempting to combine Christianity with this prevalent worldview. Jesus could not have been incarnate deity for that would taint him with the innate evil of a material existence. He was rather seen as a teacher of a secret, saving *gnosis* (knowledge) that gave one some control of his or her destiny.

In Paul's churches traveling charismatic prophets evidently would stand forth and prophesy, "Jesus anathema" or "Jesus be damned." They were rejecting the earthly Jesus for a heavenly Christ (1 Cor. 12:1–3). Later John would also need to warn against false prophets who denied "that Jesus Christ has come in the flesh," calling the spirit

---

4 According to Eusebius there was one group of Ebionites that accepted the virgin birth but rejected the preexistence of Jesus as God's Son.

by which they prophesied "the spirit of antichrist" (1 John 4:1–4). The movement continued and developed further in the post-apostolic period. Salvation for these second and third century docetic deceivers was *escape*. The Fall, according to Gnosticism, was a descent from the eternal realm into an earthly, physical body—*soma sema*, a body-tomb. Secret, revelatory "knowledge" could extricate a person from such captivity in fleshly existence. The first great heretic of the church, Marcion, who died around 160, became one of the most successful purveyors of this message.

Had Marcion held to orthodoxy, he would have been the John Wesley of his day. His was a spiritual movement, a rival church, with its own canon of Scripture (ten of Paul's letters and an edited version of Luke's gospel—no Old Testament Scriptures) and its own prophets and teachers. Jesus, according to Marcion, simply appeared one day as a full-grown man, in the synagogue at Capernaum, in an angelic sort of body. Weird—but are not all super-spiritual teachings plagued with this atmosphere? It is a false spirit and a false spirituality. It always leads to being spiritually puffed up. Conservatives and charismatics (and I am both) are vulnerable to this error. Conservatives, in reacting to liberalism's denial of Christ's full deity, may fall into the trap of Docetism, not fully affirming Christ's humanity. Charismatics may falsely see themselves as having an advanced spiritual revelation and therefore as being superior to those outside their movement—another deadly trap, another instance of Gnosticism. So the study of Christology even provides practical guidance for the contemporary church! Again, there are no new heresies—just old ones in new garb.

During the first two centuries of the church's life, John's Logos Christology set the pattern for orthodoxy.[5] However, the inevitable question as to the *relation* between Jesus and the Father was inescapable. This was really a trinitarian question: If God is one and Jesus is God and Jesus is other than the Father, then how can there actually be one God? One could anticipate that controversy

---

5 The following comments on Arianism, Apollinarianism, and Nestorianism have been adapted from my previous publication: Larry D. Hart, *Truth Aflame: Theology for the Church in Renewal* (Grand Rapids: Zondervan, 2005), 322–24.

would soon emerge concerning these puzzling implications of Logos Christology. As we have already seen, a new path for this conundrum has been charted by contemporary New Testament scholars who argue that the New Testament writers employed what might be called a "Christological monotheism," which simply includes Jesus in the very definition of God. But predictably in this early developmental phase no such argument was available. The so-called *Alogi* or *Alogoi* were the first to voice opposition to Logos Christology, as the name implies. It was Monarchianism, however, that would present the strongest challenge.

Monarchianism sought to guard the oneness of God in favor of a strict monotheism. One form, Dynamic Monarchianism (Adoptionism), maintained that Jesus was a man endowed with divine power, adopted by God at his birth or baptism to be our Savior. This was Ebionism revisited. The other form, Modalistic Monarchianism, denied that Jesus was other than the Father. Also named Sabellianism, after one Sabellius (a third-century heretic), this teaching depicts God as having three names or roles. Father, Son, and Spirit are really three ways of referring to one person. First God manifests himself in the mode (*prosopon*) of Father, Creator, and Lawgiver. Then he comes to us as Son, the Redeemer. Finally, he returns as Spirit, Lifegiver. God is one person manifesting himself in three ways. Both approaches eased the intellectual tension of the doctrine of the Trinity, but also compromised its saving truth. All these debates formed the backdrop for the heresy that perhaps more than any other threatened to destroy the Church: *Arianism*.

Arius (c. 256–336), a presbyter of the church in Alexandria, developed a nuanced and sophisticated—albeit heretical!—theology that threatened to win the day, had it not been for one of the truly heroic theologians in the history of the Christian Church: Athanasius (c. 296–373). Arius saw the uniqueness and transcendence of the Father in the starkest terms. Nothing and no one could share his essence and attributes, including the Son, Jesus. God created Jesus first and then through him the rest of the universe. Jesus shared the essence of neither God nor humankind. He was a sort of *tertium quid* ("a third something") through whom God created and redeemed us.

Because Arius could be persuasive in his appeal to the Scriptures—texts noting the limitations of Christ through the incarnation and the like—and because he could speak of Jesus in such exalted terms and in such a worshipful tone, still maintaining that Jesus is our Savior, many were tolerant of his view or even embraced it. Athanasius, however, saw the devastating implications of Arius's heresy. Not only did it contradict the scriptural witness to Christ, but it also vitiated the church's message of salvation. At times Athanasius stood virtually alone in his defense of the faith, but in the end the church—guided by the Holy Spirit, no doubt—held true to the gospel. The Council of Nicea in 325, the first ecumenical council, and later the Council of Constantinople in 381 categorically rejected Arianism.

Arius had said that Christ was of a completely different essence from the Father (*heterousios*). The church fathers maintained that Jesus was "of one substance [*homoousios*] with the Father" (compare the Nicene Creed). Perhaps Arius is best known for the heretical statement: "There was a time when he [Christ] was not." The Church officially *condemned* this doctrine and numerous other related teachings. This was one of the most dramatic periods in the history of the church, but in the end the truth of God prevailed!

The Christological battles were not over, however. The next question raised was with regard to the relation of the divine and human natures of Christ. Nicea had authoritatively established that Jesus was fully God and fully human. For the next several *centuries* the church would debate the precise character of the relation of the divine and human in the person of Christ. As both God and human, how could Jesus Christ still be *one* person? Apollinarius (c. 310–390) was the first church leader to deal decisively with this question. Unfortunately, he took an errant path, which we know as *Apollinarianism* today.

Apollinarius (sometimes spelled Apollinaris), a presbyter and teacher of the church at Laodicea, was an ardent supporter of Athanasius. Wanting to end Arianism once and for all, Apollinarius devised an explanation of the union of the divine and human in Christ that combined the traditional Greek trichotomy of human nature with the Logos Christology that had served the church so well. In Greek thought a human being was composed of flesh (a physical body), an animal (animating or human) soul, and a rational soul (spirit, reason, or mind). According to Apollinarius, Jesus had a human body and soul, but not a human spirit or reason (or mind). Since reason was considered by many as a source of sin in humankind, Apollinarius suggested that the divine Logos replaced Jesus' mind (or spirit). The human and divine were merged in an organic union into one nature.

This schema was an ingenious way of arguing for both the deity of Christ and the unity of his person. Unfortunately, Apollinarius made the same mistake as Arius. Jesus becomes a *tertium quid* with this understanding of his humanity and divinity. Whereas Arianism "made Jesus more than human, but less than fully God, or in other words a demigod,"[6] Apollinarianism made Jesus less than human. The Council of Constantinople (381) rightly condemned both.

Students of patristics are often shocked to discover how much ecclesiastical politics came into play in these early controversies. This was never more so the case than in the heretical controversy known as *Nestorianism*. The often confusing mixture of ecclesial and doctrinal concerns was as vexing in those early centuries as it is for us in the twenty-first century. Bitter rivalry and political maneuvering were clearly more dominant in the contention surrounding Nestorius (c. 380–451) than any theological precision. Ironically, Nestorius, an ardent heresy-hunter in his own right, was condemned—almost certainly unjustly—as a heretic himself!

From a purely theological perspective we are dealing simply with the inability of the finite human intellect to comprehend fully the mysteries and paradoxes of the faith. For example, Western Christianity, as we have already seen, has always had the tendency to begin with the oneness of God and move to his threeness. Eastern Christianity, on the other hand, has tended to begin with the threeness of God and move to his oneness. Both approaches are clearly within the parameters of orthodoxy, although the West has often been

---

6 Millard J. Erickson, *The Word Became Flesh* (Grand Rapids: Baker, 1991), 58.

caricatured as modalistic and the East as tritheistic. The same is true in relation to the mystery of the two natures of Christ.

During the late patristic period (the fourth and fifth centuries), two major schools of thought emerged—one centered in Alexandria and the other in Antioch—whose theological approaches sharply differed. Under the influence of Platonic thought, Alexandria was noted for a sharp differentiation between God and creation, allegorical interpretation of Scripture, and a "high Christology" that stressed the deity of Christ in what has been called a Word-flesh concept. According to this orientation the human soul of Christ recedes into the background, and the Logos is seen as the primary actor in the Incarnation. The unity of the person of Christ was thus guarded. At the same time, the heretical tendencies of Arianism and Appollinarianism emerged from this conceptualization. Athanasius provided the orthodox expression of the person of Christ from this vantage point.

In contrast, Antioch was known for its grammatical/historical interpretation of Scripture from an Aristotelian perspective and for a stress upon the full humanity of Christ. A Word-man Christology typified this school of thought. The importance of the complete human psychological makeup of Christ was highlighted. Theodore of Mopsuestia (c. 350–428; affectionately known as "Teddy the Mop" by many a seminarian!) provided an excellent, though somewhat incomplete, expression of Christology from this perspective. Nestorius, who was perhaps one of Theodore's students, got himself into trouble when, as the newly appointed patriarch of Constantinople (in 428), he questioned the unqualified use of the popular description of Mary as *theotokos*, "the God-bearer." Troubled by the obvious connotation of Mary's being God's mother, Nestorius suggested accompanying the term with the additional description *anthrōpotokos*, "the man-bearer," or even better to refer to Mary as simply *Christokos*, "the Christ-bearer." In addition, Nestorius's Christology put such a stress on the complete humanity, understood as being in "conjunction" with the divine nature, that many thought he was describing "two sons."

Ultimately, Nestorianism—understanding Jesus as two distinct persons, the Son of God indwelling the man, Jesus of Nazareth—was condemned by the Council of Ephesus (431). Nestorius was exiled for espousing a heresy named after him, but which he never personally believed. His manner of expression at times seemed to imply two persons in Christ, but there is reason to believe that Nestorius was actually orthodox in his Christology—perhaps more so than his opponent, Cyril of Alexandria, who politically maneuvered him into exile!

Finally, *Eutychianism* emerged on the scene as a distortion of understanding of the divine and human natures and their relationship. This heresy, named for Eutyches (c. 375–454), is again an instance of our having difficulty ascertaining the person's precise views as such. Nevertheless, the heresy itself seemed to aver either a sort of *hybrid* relation of the divine and human in Jesus or the eclipsing of the human by the divine. Monophysitism would later perpetuate this view as well, while Monothelitism would mistakenly argue for Jesus' having but one will, whereas the church would conclude that two natures require two wills (with the human being in entire submission to the divine).

> The Creed (or Definition) of Chalcedon was an attempt to set the parameters of Christology in a manner consistent with the Scriptures and supportive of the church's primary message, the gospel.

Six heresies, six distortions of the real Christ: Ebionisim flatly denied his deity; Docetism compromised his humanity; Arianism demoted Jesus to the level of being a creature of God; Apollinarianism diminished Jesus' complete humanity; Nestorianism made Jesus into a monster comprised of the conjoining of two independently existing persons; and Eutychianism "homogenized" Jesus into one (basically divine) nature. The church's definitive response to these heresies would come to be known as the Definition of Chalcedon (451).

The Creed (or Definition) of Chalcedon was an attempt to set the *parameters* of Christology in a manner consistent with the Scriptures and supportive of the church's primary message, the gospel. It was not an attempt to be creative or even communicative in terms of effective preaching: It was *prescriptive*. It largely became normative for orthodox Christology for its own century and for all ensuing centuries. It reads as follows:

> Therefore, following the holy Fathers, we all with one accord teach men to acknowledge one and the same Son, our Lord Jesus Christ, at once complete in Godhead and complete in manhood, truly God and truly man, consisting also of a reasonable soul and body; of one substance [*homoousios*] with the Father as regards his Godhead, and at the same time of one substance with us as regards his manhood; like us in all respects, apart from sin; as regards his Godhead, begotten of the Father before the ages, but yet as regards his manhood begotten, for us men and for our salvation, of Mary the Virgin, the God-bearer [*theotokos*]; one and the same Christ, Son, Lord, Only-begotten, recognized IN TWO NATURES, WITHOUT CONFUSION, WITHOUT CHANGE, WITHOUT DIVISION, WITHOUT SEPARATION; the distinction of natures being in no way annulled by the union, but rather the characteristics of each nature being preserved and coming together to form one person and subsistence [*hupostasis*], not as parted or separated into two persons, but one and the same Son and Only-begotten God the Word, Lord Jesus Christ; even as the prophets from earliest times spoke of him, and our Lord Jesus Christ himself taught us, and the creed of the Fathers has handed down to us.[7]

One immediately notes that the Christological formula presented here answers the *what* rather than the *how*. It provides boundaries. It

---

7   See Henry Bettenson (ed.), *Documents of the Christian Church* (New York: Oxford University Press, 1963), 51–52.

corrects erroneous attempts such as Nestorianism and Eutychianism. In guarding the gospel, it provides a foundation for conceptualizing how the divine-human Son alone could be our Redeemer. "One could perhaps say that, on the one hand, Chalcedon functioned as a signpost pointing in the right direction, and on the other hand, it was a fence separating orthodoxy and heresy."[8]

THEN AND NOW

The ensuing centuries would see theology wrestling more with the *work* of Christ, which we will deal with in chapter eight. And the modern period witnessed, as we saw in chapter two, a radical departure from Chalcedon with largely deleterious results. What should we conclude? In large measure this is an ecclesiological question. If one has concluded theologically that the Holy Spirit has continued to guide the mission of the church and that the Holy Scriptures remain the touchstone doctrinally, then Chalcedon/Orthodoxy/the Great Tradition remain central and indispensable. We have been able to observe experiments with other theological paths for more than two centuries now and the results are obvious—an enervated, debilitated, sometimes even apostate church. I for one choose to remain on the old, proven path of biblical orthodoxy.

---

[8] Veli-Matti Kärkkäinen, *Christology: A Global Introduction* (Grand Rapids: Baker Academic, 2003), 78.

Lesson Six

A Contemporary Christology

A SUMMARY CHRISTOLOGICAL STATEMENT

> But you are not in the flesh; you are in the Spirit, since the Spirit of God dwells in you. Anyone who does not have the Spirit of Christ does not belong to him. But if Christ is in you, though the body is dead because of sin, the Spirit is life because of righteousness. If the Spirit of him who raised Jesus from the dead dwells in you, he who raised Christ from the dead will give life to your mortal bodies also through his Spirit that dwells in you (Rom. 8:9–11 NRSV).

In a day in which Incarnational Christologies and Spirit Christologies are too often pitted against one another—the former conceived in ontological categories and the latter in functional terms—I would like to propose a Christology which synthesizes the two and more fully integrates with both Trinitarian theology and pneumatology. In fact, I hope it will become increasingly evident as we move through our explorations that Christology is central to *every* essential Christian doctrine:

1. **Revelation:** The greatest revelation of God is Jesus Christ, who is God Incarnate.
2. **God:** To see Jesus truly is to see the Father (in all his attributes) and to discern Jesus' unique triune union with the Father (John 14:9–11).
3. **Creation:** Creation is through Christ and for Christ, who both sustains and redeems his creation.

4. **Humanity:** Jesus is the supreme example of humanity— the only complete human being, reflecting perfectly the divine image.
5. **Sin:** The reason Jesus came was to be the sin bearer and the victor over sin, death, and the devil.
6. **Christology:** It is through the person and work of Christ that we are saved.
7. **Pneumatology:** The Holy Spirit—referred to variously in the New Testament as the Spirit of Christ, the Spirit of Jesus, the Spirit of God's Son—applies Christ's saving work in our lives.
8. **Soteriology:** God saves us in and through Christ.
9. **Ecclesiology:** The church is the Body of Christ and the Bride of Christ.
10. **Eschatology:** Jesus is coming again![1]

My mentor, Dale Moody, defined Christian theology as follows: "A Christian theology is an effort to think coherently about the basic beliefs that create a community of faith around the person of Jesus Christ."[2] Indeed, Christ is central! He is the center of the Bible. He is the center of history. He is the meaning of time and eternity. He is the one we follow in Christian discipleship. In order to fully appropriate all that Christ is and all that he has done, we need the help of the Holy Spirit.

The Spirit mediates Christ to us, makes him present. In the days of his flesh, Christ was determined by the Spirit. The ascended Christ now determines the Spirit. The Spirit's primary role is that of making Christ known, which, of course, infinitely aids our Christological enterprise! The opening passage of Scripture beautifully communicates these realities. It is a trinitarian passage in which reference is made to the Spirit, Christ, and the Father as the one "who raised Jesus from the dead." It gets to the core or essence of Christian experience. And that essence has to do with having the Spirit of Christ

> *The Spirit mediates Christ to us, makes him present.*

---

1 Larry Hart, *Christianity in 3D* (Tulsa: Truth Aflame Press, 2014), 44.
2 Dale Moody, *The Word of Truth* (Grand Rapids: Eerdmans, 1981), 1.

(Rom. 8:9). An older translation (*The New English Bible*) renders this verse: "If a man does not possess the Spirit of Christ, he is no Christian." Obviously, Paul is asserting that union with Christ is the crux of Christianity, and the Spirit himself mediates that union.

It is important to note the *progression* of nomenclature in this passage:

- Spirit
- Spirit of God
- Spirit of Christ
- Christ
- Spirit of him who raised Jesus from the dead (the Father)

This is striking! A Christian is someone who is "in the Spirit, since the Spirit of God dwells in you." Belonging to Christ means having "the Spirit of Christ." It is having "Christ in you." Having *Christ* in you means having the Spirit/Spirit of God/Spirit of Christ. One could add that this also means having the Spirit of the *Father* (="he who raised Jesus from the dead") dwelling in you (v. 11): a trinitarian/pneumatological Christology! And what was true for Paul's day is also true for our day. "The integral linking of Jesus to the Spirit means a necessary linking with his Father—if trinitarian canons are not to be compromised. The focus on Spirit Christology also helps make the necessary connection of the Jesus of the 'past' and the Jesus of the 'present'—who of course is one and the same person."[3]

Further, as Paul will argue in Ephesians, true knowledge of Christ entails engagement with the Body of Christ "until we all reach unity in the faith and in the knowledge of the Son of God" (Eph. 4:13). This growth together in maturity results in progress in ethical behavior (vv. 17–24). In this parenetic section Paul depicts the behavior of the pagan Gentiles and then exhorts his readers: "That is not the way you learned Christ! For surely you have heard about him and were taught in him, as truth is in Jesus" (vv. 20–21 NRSV). Of course, our performance in this regard is too often spotty,

---
3 Veli-Matti Kärkkäinen, *Christ and Reconciliation*, Vol. 1: A Constructive Christian Theology for the Pluralistic World (Grand Rapids: Eerdmans, 2013), 49.

which may cause others to stumble. Craig Keener, in his important study of *The Historical Jesus of the Gospels*, shares his personal pilgrimage out of atheism into faith. He too was scandalized by the lack of evidence of transformed lives until he had his own personal encounter with Christ.

> When I later encountered the risen Christ in an unsolicited and unexpected personal experience, hence came to the conviction that he (not to mention the God with whom he was associated) was in fact alive, I understood that the reality of Jesus rises or falls not on how successfully his professed followers have followed his teachings, but on Jesus himself.[4]

Perhaps *the* classic on this dimension of true knowledge of Christ is Luke Timothy Johnson's *Living Jesus: Learning the Heart of the Gospel*. Johnson argues that the way we come to knowledge of a dead person is categorically different from the way we know a living person. Because of the resurrection and the possibility of Christ's presence through the Spirit new vistas open up for us:

> If he is alive, however, everything changes. It is no longer a matter of our questioning a historical record, but a matter of our being put in question by one who has broken every rule of ordinary human existence. If Jesus lives, then it must be as life-giver. Jesus is not simply a figure of the past, but a person of the present, not merely a memory that we can analyze and manipulate, but an agent who can confront and instruct us. What we learn *about* him must therefore include what we continue to learn *from* him.
>
> To be a Christian means to assert that Jesus is alive, is indeed life-giving Spirit (1 Cor. 15:45). To consider Jesus simply as a figure of the past means to consider Jesus not from the perspective of a Christian but from that of one who stands outside Christian conviction....

---

4 Craig S. Keener, *The Historical Jesus of the Gospels* (Grand Rapids: Eerdmans, 2009), 385.

This seems to be one of those very few choices that allow no equivocation. There is no middle ground between dead and alive. It Jesus is dead, then his story is completed. If he is alive, then his story continues.[5]

Similar to Keener, Johnson shares personally how this process of true knowledge of Christ works. He poignantly depicts his relationship with his wife as illustrative of personal knowledge, then goes on to explore the significantly more complex process of knowing Christ personally.[6] Johnson's moving words prompt me to utilize a similar model: my own marital relationship of some forty-three years with Thea Jane Hamrick Hart.[7]

The whole process began when friends in seminary began to tell me about Thea. They were convinced that we should meet. The more they described her, the more interested I became. We came from similar Baptist backgrounds, were vitally involved in evangelism (her days with Campus Crusade on the Marshall University campus were life-transforming). We both had been touched by the charismatic movement, which was booming at the time. When my friends showed me a picture of Thea and asked "Are you interested?" I responded "Is the Pope Catholic?" Thea lived four hours to the east of Louisville, so they invited her to visit them and introduced us. What followed was months of long distance romance through many letters (handwritten communication on actual paper, for millennials unfamiliar with this archaic practice) and occasional visits.

What followed our marriage was years of ecstasy, agony, and normality—my PhD pilgrimage, planting and pastoring churches, three children, seminary teaching, and the like. We suffered a miscarriage in our first pregnancy. The pressures of completing my PhD while planting a church were sometimes intense. We pastored two very troubled churches, which truly was an agony at points, but

---

5 Luke Timothy Johnson, *Living Jesus: Learning the Heart of the Gospel* (San Francisco: HarperSanFranciso, 1999). 4–5.
6 Johnson, *Living Jesus*, 62–73.
7 For readers who prize precision, Thea and I were married at Highlawn Baptist Church in Huntington, West Virginia, on August 4, 1973.

our church planting work (two different congregations) was generally an ecstasy—along with a lot of hard work. In addition to expertly raising our children, Thea later would enter the business world. We suffered the exigencies of life that are common to us all. And in the process we have really come to know one another. It has been a wonderful relationship involving *heart* (sharing our dreams and deepest feelings), *head* (growing intellectually in our knowledge of God, life, and ourselves), *hands* (doing work together), and *hips* (I have no idea what that could be referring to).

Thea is always embarrassed when my seminary students come up to her and tell her how much her husband talks about her. She is truly the love of my life, my best friend, the wisest and most discerning person I know.

Our knowledge of the *contemporary* Christ, our risen and reigning Lord, is similarly multifaceted—in fact, infinitely more so. We know Christ through…

- The Spirit
- The Scriptures
- The Saints
- The Sacraments
- The Suffering Ones

We have already seen how the Spirit mediates Christ to us. And we have already explored the Scriptures in relation to Christ. We will examine more later how the church (the saints) further enables our knowledge of Jesus as well as how we encounter him in the sacraments or ordinances of the church. Jesus also taught us that we encounter him in the suffering ones to whom we reach out in the love of Christ (cf., e.g., Matt. 25:31–46).[8] As I have already done in a previous publication,[9] I would like to further explore Jesus in relation to the gospel, the church, the kingdom, the Spirit, and the Father.

---

8 See Johnson, *Living Jesus*, 22 for more on how Jesus is "embodied."
9 Larry D. Hart, *Truth Aflame: Theology for the Church in Renewal* (Grand Rapids: Zondervan, 2005), 282–97.

JESUS AND THE GOSPEL

The gospels *are* the gospel. James D. G. Dunn is probably correct to credit Mark with creating this new genre of literature. And the gospels communicate the *Jesus tradition*, the complete story of his life and mission.[10] N. T. Wright provides the following helpful definition of the gospel:

> The gospel is the royal announcement that the crucified and risen Jesus, who died for our sins and rose again according to the Scriptures, has been enthroned as the true Lord of the world. When this gospel is preached, God calls people to salvation, out of sheer grace, leading them to repentance and faith in Jesus Christ as the risen Lord.[11]

So in a very real sense Jesus himself *is* the gospel. Paul put it down in bullet points (1 Cor. 15:3–8):

- Christ died for our sins according to the Scriptures.
- He was buried.
- He was raised on the third day according to the Scriptures.
- He appeared to many (Peter, the Twelve, a gathering of more than five hundred, James, and Paul himself).

I often ask people in my seminary classes, or at various preaching venues, to define the gospel, and I am amazed at how many Christians I encounter simply cannot articulate what it is. But even if we are able to tick off the above bullet points, we may not get the message that this is a royal announcement of Jesus' Lordship and it is something to be *lived* as well![12]

Jesus is the gospel. It is the "gospel of Christ" (Rom. 15:19; 1 Cor. 9:12; 2 Cor. 2:12; 9:13; 10:14; Gal. 1:7; Phil. 1:27; 1 Thess. 3:2) that

---

[10] James D. G. Dunn, *Jesus, Paul, and the Gospels* (Grand Rapids: Eerdmans, 2011), 53.
[11] Cited in Trevin Wax, "The Justification Debate: A Primer," *Christianity Today* 53.6 (2009): 34–35, which I accessed through Michael F. Bird's masterful *Evangelical Theology: A Biblical and Systematic Introduction* (Grand Rapids: Zondervan, 2013), 47.
[12] See Scot McKnight's excellent *The King Jesus Gospel: The Original Good News Revisited* (Grand Rapids: Zondervan, 2011).

we herald. It results in the great Christian confession, "Jesus is Lord" (Rom. 10:9). And hopefully it results in our lives and our world being transformed. It entails our preaching, teaching, and living of the entirety of the Scriptures. Peter's preaching of the gospel at Cornelius's house exemplifies how we should present the message of Christ today:

> You know the message he [God] sent to the people of Israel, preaching peace by Jesus Christ—he is Lord of all. That message spread throughout Judea, beginning in Galilee after the baptism that John announced: how God anointed Jesus of Nazareth with the Holy Spirit and with power; how he went about doing good and healing all who were oppressed by the devil, for God was with him. We are witnesses to all that he did both in Judea and in Jerusalem. They put him to death by hanging him on a tree; but God raised him on the third day and allowed him to appear, not to all the people but to us who were chosen by God as witnesses, and who ate and drank with him after he rose from the dead. He commanded us to preach to the people and to testify that he is the one ordained by God as judge of the living and the dead. All the prophets testify about him that everyone who believes in him receives forgiveness of sins through his name (Act. 10:36–43 NRSV).

True gospel preaching is apostolic preaching. It is the world's only good news. It is glad tidings, joyful news that prompts repentance, faith, then singing and perhaps even dancing! This is the message of the "real" Jesus that the church has the responsibility of guarding and disseminating.[13] We as the church are his body and his bride.

JESUS AND THE CHURCH

This may be the most difficult section of this entire volume for the reader to swallow. I am arguing that we need the entire church of Jesus Christ to truly know him and make him known. We are

---

13 See my further remarks in *Truth Aflame*, 282–86.

his Plan A and he has no Plan B. "Now you are the body of Christ," wrote Paul to the Corinthians, "and each one of you is a part of it" (1 Cor. 12:27). "For in one Spirit we were all baptized into one body—Jews or Greeks, slaves or free—and all were made to drink of one Spirit" (v. 13 ESV). We could apply these words today by saying, "In one Spirit we have all been baptized into one body—Jews or Gentiles, Baptists or Methodists, Pentecostals or Catholics, Charismatics or Evangelicals." "Just as a body, though one, has many parts, but all its many parts form one body, so it is with Christ" (1 Cor. 12:12). Notice Paul does not say "so it is with the *church*," as we might anticipate; he says, "so it is with *Christ*." That is how closely Christ identifies himself with us! And he goes on to say: "The eye cannot say to the hand, 'I don't need you!' And the head cannot say to the feet, 'I don't need you!'" (v. 27).

> We need the entire church of Jesus Christ to truly know him and make him known.

It is complete hypocrisy to say we belong to Christ yet shun another follower of Christ. The charismatic actually *needs* the fundamentalist and vice versa. The Baptist actually *needs* the Catholic and vice versa. There is no such thing as full knowledge of Christ without receiving from those with whom we most disagree. I often tell my students that I learn more from those who disagree with me than from those who agree. Those who agree simply reinforce my blind spots. I went to a seminary that at the time was known as being liberal (at least by Southern Baptist standards). I could love almost anyone but a liberal. But being forced to rub shoulders with them daily, I began to encounter Christ in many of them whom I befriended. When a tornado crashed through our city, the liberals immediately mobilized to help those in need. We conservatives prayed for them. It was the liberals in the main who marched with Dr. King. We conservatives kept our distance and only praised him after he was dead.

Years ago the university where I serve planned an international conference promoting the "Spirit-empowered movement." We had wonderful scholars' conversations across the country in preparation for this event. And the event itself attracted over 10,000 participants. Our scholarly dialogue followed along the lines of how we could hand the torch of Spirit-empowered living to the next generation. I kept interjecting the theme of "what the Spirit is saying to the churches," but to no avail. Every part of the body of Christ needs something from every other part. Too often the church in America is dysfunctional precisely because we do not believe and practice this biblical truth. God help us to repent! We too often shun one another while the fields of harvest lie abandoned. And the Christ we profess to know, love, and follow is grieved.

JESUS AND THE KINGDOM

Christianity is about *learning Christ*. And "Jesus is most fully and consistently learned within the context of the believing community of the church, because the risen Lord identifies himself with this community."[14] But the church serves an even greater reality. We belong to a *kingdom*, headed by Christ himself, a kingdom which is spreading across the globe. It is the gospel of the *kingdom* that we preach. We have the keys into that kingdom which is the gospel itself. This kingdom actually creates the church. Wherever God's Spirit is moving, bringing the rule of God into the world and into our individual lives, that is the kingdom. Miracles attest the reality of this kingdom. And at the center of this kingdom message, and at the head of the kingdom itself, is King Jesus!

Jesus himself seemed to be obsessed with the kingdom. "After John was put in prison, Jesus went into Galilee, proclaiming the good news of God. 'The time has come,' he said. 'The kingdom of God has come near. Repent and believe the good news!'" (Mark 1:14–15). Jesus taught and preached much about the kingdom. His parables poignantly depicted it. He called one and all into his kingdom, even those that the religionists of his day thought were not eligible. Jesus performed miraculous works of power as signs of the reality of the inbreaking kingdom. It was a radical message that called for radical response. Craig Keener provides these fine summary remarks:

14 Johnson, *Living Jesus*, 23.

Jesus taught about God's impending kingdom, and demanded that people get their lives in order to be ready for it, even as signs of the kingdom were breaking in around them. In view of the coming kingdom, his followers needed to be ready to relinquish family ties, possessions, and even their very lives for the greater prize of the kingdom.[15]

Jesus' model prayer for his disciples reads in part as follows:

> Our Father in heaven,
> Your name be honored as holy.
> Your kingdom come.
> Your will be done
> on earth as it is in heaven (Matt. 6:9–10 HCSB).

Our passion for the kingdom—the rule of God—should be the same as that of our Lord himself. It truly is about him and not about us. We are simply following Jesus around, inviting others to join his traveling band. We have joined *his* mission and it literally costs us our lives. It is a marvelous kingdom. It is a festival and we cry out, "Come and dine!" But it is also a serious and costly mission and we cry out, "Come and die!" We pray for the kingdom and work for the kingdom—daily. Mark in his gospel introduces Jesus' call to discipleship with these words:

> Then he called the crowd to him along with his disciples and said: "Whoever wants to be my disciple must deny themselves and take up their cross and follow me. For whoever wants to save their life will lose it, but whoever loses their life for me and for the gospel will save it. What good is it for someone to gain the whole world, yet forfeit their soul? Or what can anyone give in exchange for their soul? If anyone is ashamed of me and my words in this adulterous and sinful generation, the Son of Man will be ashamed of them when he comes in his Father's glory with the holy angels (Mark 8:34–38).

---

15 Keener, *The Historical Jesus of the Gospels*, 213.

N. T. Wright provides the comprehensive perspective on precisely how this kingdom calling is fleshed out in our present day. It is all predicated on what Jesus has *already* achieved:

> It is because he inaugurated the kingdom that we can live the kingdom. It is because he brought the story of God and Israel, and hence of God and the cosmos, to its designed climax that we can now implement that work today. And we will best develop that kingdom vocation if we understand the foundation upon which we are building. If we are to follow Jesus Christ we need to know more about the Jesus Christ we are following.[16]

Closely related to this kingdom leitmotif is the role of the Spirit.

JESUS AND THE SPIRIT

Jesus once healed a blind and mute demon-possessed man (Matt. 12:22–37). The people were amazed, but the Pharisees were enraged, claiming Jesus did this by the power of the devil. Jesus responded: "But if it is by the Spirit of God that I drive out demons, then the kingdom of God has come upon you" (v. 28). Notice the contiguity of Spirit and kingdom. Wherever the Spirit is moving, there is the kingdom. Therefore, after Pentecost we see the accent on the Spirit in the preaching of the early church, whereas Jesus emphasized the kingdom in his teaching. Both were referring to the same reality, and both the kingdom and the Spirit are mentioned by both Jesus and the apostles. In this account Jesus himself is explaining his healing/delivering work in terms of the power of the Spirit at work through him, the Anointed One, the Spirit-bearer, the Messiah, who is bringing the kingdom. The Spirit is key to our understanding of Jesus.

We have already noted the major role the Spirit plays in Luke's Christology. Luke sets the agenda for a Spirit Christology which in no way conflicts with John's Logos Christology. Rather they are

---

[16] N. T. Wright, *The Challenge of Jesus: Rediscovering Who Jesus Was and Is* (Downers Grove, IL: InterVarsity Press, 1999), 53.

complementary. Jürgen Moltmann helpfully interprets Jesus' entire life and ministry in terms of the Spirit's activity.[17] And Veli-Matti Kärkkäinen beautifully integrates Spirit Christology and Logos (incarnational) Christology, with priority given to the latter in his systematics project.[18] This seems to me to be the most promising way forward, leading ultimately to a Trinitarian theology.[19] Recall the words of Peter's apostolic preaching: "how God anointed Jesus of Nazareth with the Holy Spirit and power" (Acts 2:38). These words further explain how the "Word became flesh and made his dwelling among us" (John 1:14).

In Luke's portrait especially we see Jesus setting the pattern for his followers of a life of prayer and humble dependence on the Holy Spirit. It is a pattern of great relevance for our own day. I often ask my students, "How did Jesus do his miracles?" Most often their instant response is, "Well, he is God Incarnate; he can do anything!" Unfortunately, that is not the New Testament answer. Jesus did his mighty works *through the power of the Holy Spirit!* He accepted the same limitations we face as his finite creatures and functioned charismatically in the same way he expects us to do. In fact, our Lord went a step further and offered his followers the same kind of intimacy with the Father that he himself enjoyed. In his extensive teaching on this in John 14–16 Jesus explained in-depth how such intimacy was possible. In nuce, his answer was the Paraclete, the Holy Spirit.

JESUS AND THE FATHER

Mark lifts the veil on Jesus' intimacy with the Father in his account of Gethsemane. Jesus agonized in prayer in preparation for Calvary: "'*Abba*, Father,' he said, 'everything is possible for you. Take this cup from me. Yet not what I will, but what you will'" (Mark 14:36). His address to God, as Mark records it here, contains a transliteration of an

---

17 Jürgen Moltmann, *The Way of Jesus Christ* (Minneapolis: Fortress Press, 1993), 73–94.
18 Kärkkäinen, *Christ and Reconciliation*, 196–209.
19 Hart, *Truth Aflame*, 289–93.

Aramaic term (*Abba*) and its translation into Greek (Father). *Abba* was a term of endearment, of intimacy.

Had you grown up in Nazareth, you might have heard young Jesus calling out to his parents: *Imma! Abba!*—Mommy! Daddy! These would be the first names a little child would learn in addressing his parents.[20] No one would even think of addressing God with *Abba!* This would be blasphemy. Jesus' claim to such intimacy prompted his Jewish opponents to want to kill him for his "calling God his own Father, making himself equal with God" (John 5:19). Perhaps Joachim Jeremias has done more than any other New Testament scholar to more fully appreciate this uniqueness of Jesus:

> The complete novelty and uniqueness of *Abba* as an address to God in the prayers of Jesus shows that it expresses the heart of Jesus' relationship to God. He spoke to God as a child to its father: confidently and securely, and yet at the same time reverently and obediently.[21]

Paul takes us the next step in this Christological pilgrimage by announcing that the Father also makes possible our *own* sonship through his sending the Son and the Spirit (Gal. 4:4–7):

> But when the set time had fully come, God sent his Son, born of a woman, born under the law, to redeem those under the law, that we might receive adoption to sonship. Because you are his sons, God sent the Spirit of his Son into our hearts, the Spirit who calls out, "*Abba,* Father." So you are no longer a slave, but God's child; and since you are his child, God has made you also an heir.

The whole issue in this passage is *sonship*. God sent his Son, Jesus, that we might become God's sons and daughters! The phrase, "adoption to sonship," translates one Greek term (*huiothesia*), a legal term which refers to an adopted male heir with the full legal standing

---

[20] George T. Montague, *The Holy Spirit: Growth of a Biblical Tradition* (New York: Paulist Press, 1976), 197.

[21] Joachim Jeremias, *New Testament Theology: The Proclamation of Jesus* (New York: Charles Scribner's Sons, 1971), 67.

in Roman culture as that of a natural son. The term itself contains the Greek term for "son" (*huios*). In other words, our sonship is derivative of Jesus' Sonship.

Paul brilliantly sets up parallel statements here, which can be displayed as follows:

1. God sent his Son (v. 4).
2. God sent the Spirit of his Son (v. 6).

The sentences are identical in the Greek except for the insertion of the phrase, "the Spirit of." First, God sent his Son into *history* to redeem us. Then he sent the Spirit of his Son, the Holy Spirit, into our *hearts*. That is the full circuit achieved by our Triune God: first, the objective achievement of redemption through his sending his Son into history; then, the subjective application of that redemption through his sending the Spirit of his Son into our hearts. But there is more! The Spirit "calls out" (a strong, passionate term), "*Abba*, Father." The Spirit of God's Son enables us to join in the filial cry, "*Abba*, Father"! Now he is *our* Father—our *Abba*—an address expressing a relationship of confidence, security, reverence, and obedience, to borrow Jeremias's above words.

Jesus' filial consciousness was evident throughout his life. As a twelve-year-old boy, Jesus stayed behind in Jerusalem after the celebration of the Passover Festival, and his parents returned, frantically searching for him. Mary said to him, "Son, why have you treated us like this? Your father and I have been anxiously searching for you" (Luke 2:48). Jesus replied, "Why were you searching for me? Didn't you know I had to be in my Father's house?" (v. 49). Mary mentions Jesus' earthly father and Jesus refers to his heavenly Father. Jesus explained his whole life and ministry in terms of his union with the Father (John 5). And his last words on the cross were a prayer: "Father, into your hands I commit my spirit" (Luke 23:46). His sonship was unique. He was the one and only Son. But he offers to us in our discipleship the same privileged relationship with God as our Father.

I had a godly earthly father. He worked in the oil fields for over fifty years, supervising some pretty rough workers. But he also served for many years as the chairman of the deacons in our very large Southern Baptist Church. Someone called my dad, "the gentle giant." He was that to me. As a seven-year-old, I became aware of the conviction of the Holy Spirit and my need of salvation. One Sunday at the invitation time, my mother turned to me and asked, "Son, are you alright?" I turned to her in tears and said, "O, Momma, I want to become a Christian!" My parents took me to the pastor, and we all sat down together in his study, where I was gently led into a saving encounter with Jesus Christ. The next Sunday, as I stood before the congregation and people filed by to shake my hand, my father leaned over and hugged me. As his sport coat engulfed me and his strong arms embraced me, I felt that my heavenly father was hugging me too. It was a vivid experience I will never forget. This filial consciousness is the true culmination of Christology as it is presented in the New Testament, and it also the beginning of it. The supreme revelation and knowledge of Christ is yet to come—when every knee will bow and every tongue confess (Phil. 2:10–11). In the meantime, the Christian pilgrimage is intended to be a continual experience of learning Christ, something in reality we will be doing both now and throughout eternity.

JESUS AND THE TRINITY

Throughout this chapter and especially in the previous two sections, we have become increasingly aware of the integral relation between Christology and the doctrine of the Trinity. Each doctrine entails the other, as the creeds and the councils of the church also reflect. As we move through the New Testament, the picture emerges of a preexistent divine being—the eternal Logos, the Son of God—being sent from the Father in heaven for the redemption of humanity. This sent-one returns to heaven and pours out his Spirit. This indwelling Spirit prompts two charismatic utterances from the mouth of every believer: (1) *"Abba,* Father" (Rom. 8:15; Gal. 4:6) and (2) "Jesus is Lord" (Rom. 10:9). It is a dynamic *movement.*

British theologian Thomas A. Smail has observed that we often refer to the *Jesus Movement* of the sixties, seventies, and eighties, and to the ongoing worldwide *Holy Spirit movement* of Pentecostalism and charismatic renewal. But according to the Bible, Smail observes, Christianity is ultimately a *Father movement*. He is too often the forgotten member of the Godhead.[22] The movement is: (1) in the Spirit, (2) through the Son, (3) to the Father (Eph. 2:18). Smail provides the following helpful summary:

> What [God] does through his Son on earth reveals what he is like from eternity to eternity. His revelation in the gospel tells us the ultimate truth about God's being and nature.... The love of the Father sending, empowering, guiding, finally vindicating his Son, the love of the Son, coming, obeying, suffering, dying, are particular historical expressions of the love that eternally flows between Father and Son at the heart of the life of God. The complex of relationships between Father, Son and Spirit are not just the *means* by which God communicates with us, they are an essential part of the content of that communication. They are not just *how* he speaks, but part of *what* he says.[23]

From this Trinitarian perspective, the church has perennially confessed Jesus as the Son of God or even God the Son. Saying "God the Son" is accurate but perhaps potentially misleading to those who might hear us as referring to three Gods: God the Father, God the Son, and God the Holy Spirit. The biblical title, however, never misleads us.

Among the Christological titles we have encountered in this study, the Son of God remains the most useful theologically. Historically, this proved true as well. As the church through several centuries corrected heresies and hammered out the parameters of orthodoxy, she ultimately would turn to "Son of God" as the key creedal identity for Christ:

---

22 See Thomas A. Smail, *The Forgotten Father* (Grand Rapids: Eerdmans, 1980).
23 Smail, *The Forgotten Father*, 23 (Smail's italics).

So much so that it is generally taken for granted, axiomatic, part of the basic definition of what Christianity is, that to confess Jesus as "the Son of God" is to confess his deity, and very easily assumed that to say "Jesus is the Son of God" means and always has meant that Jesus is the pre-existent, second person of the Trinity, who "for us men and our salvation became incarnate."[24]

THE DEITY AND HUMANITY OF CHRIST

As we surveyed the various heresies the church combatted, we became aware of four doctrinal rubrics:

1. The deity of Christ
2. The humanity of Christ
3. The unity of his person
4. The distinction of his divine and human natures[25]

In this section I would like to say a little more about the deity and humanity of Christ. One of the first challenges the church faced was that of denying Christ's humanity (the docetic and gnostic distortions coming out of the prevailing neo-Platonic perspective of Hellenism). At the grassroots level one still encounters this tendency, generally in an overreaction to the liberal denial of Christ's deity. In scholarly circles, the besetting sin is more often than not the inability to embrace Christ's full divinity. We in the West are still suffering from an Enlightenment hangover with our rational and empirical strictures. Categories of transcendence and ontology too often make us uncomfortable.

I have vivid memories of being required to read functional Christologies in seminary. Norman Pittenger, a process theologian,

---

[24] James D. G. Dunn, *Christology in the Making: A New Testament Inquiry into the Origins of the Doctrine of the Incarnation* (Philadelphia: Westminster, 1980), 12–13. Unfortunately, Dunn himself is unable to see what is obvious to most other students of the New Testament: that "Son of God" in Scripture is incarnational in connotation and even denotation.

[25] See Millard J. Erickson, *Introducing Christian Doctrine*, 3rd ed., ed. Arnold Hustad (Grand Rapids: Baker Academic, 2015), 266 for a helpful chart.

explained Jesus' divinity in terms of his unparalleled love union with God. John A. T. Robinson viewed Jesus as the man (and only a man) whom God had selected as his representative to the rest of humanity. G. W. H. Lampe depicted Jesus as the man most filled with God as Spirit—no Trinity needed here.[26] In many respects, these theologians were on to something. Jesus *was* the one man among us more in a love union with God than any other man. He *was* God's representative— so determined by God that when he spoke it was God speaking and when he acted it was God acting, as Robinson would argue. (Robinson surely wins the prize for best title for a Christology text: *The Human Face of God!*) And Lampe was correct in portraying Jesus as the most God-filled or Spirit-filled man ever. At least among these three, Lampe was honest enough to acknowledge that his unitarian view was not taught in the Scriptures or the creeds of Christendom. (He had expertise in both New Testament and patristic studies.) He simply felt it was more palatable to the modern mind to conceptualize God and Jesus in this manner.

In a postmodern, and perhaps post-postmodern, world it is somewhat easier to affirm mystery, paradox, and transcendence. Both the Bible and the church for most of the past two millennia have testified to Jesus as someone who was *both* divine and human.[27] But even in our own day, scholars such as James D. G. Dunn balk at a full-orbed Incarnational, Trinitarian Christology.[28] Jesus' divine sonship is more than a metaphor. It reveals an eternal reality and relationship. Scripture requires of us the full embrace of Christ in all his divine-human splendor. This is the true scandal of Christianity.[29] The person and work of Christ—that he was God Incarnate and that through his death and bodily resurrection he offers the only means of salvation to humankind—is the scandal of the ages.

---

26 See, e.g.: Norman Pittenger, *Christology Reconsidered* (London, SCM Press, 1970); John A. T. Robinson, *The Human Face of God* (Philadelphia: Westminster, 1973); G. W. H. Lampe, *God as Spirit* (Oxford: Clarendon Press, 1977).
27 See Russell F. Aldwinckle, *More Than Man: A Study in Christology* (Grand Rapids: Eerdmans, 1976).
28 Dunn, *Christology in the Making* (1980).
29 The following comments on the deity of Christ have been adapted from: Hart, *Truth Aflame*, 297–313.

One of the oldest extra-biblical descriptions of the early Christians (c. 112) comes to us from a letter written by Pliny the Younger, newly appointed governor of Bithynia in northern Turkey, to the Emperor Trajan. Pliny had already executed a number of Christians, but was having second thoughts. He describes their exemplary lifestyles, and faults only their refusal to worship images of the emperor or of other gods. Pliny says that "on an appointed day [Sunday] they had been accustomed to meet before daybreak, and to recite a hymn antiphonally to Christ, as to a god."[30] In those days believers were often faced with the choice of saying either "Lord Caesar" or "Lord Jesus," often with their very lives on the line. Larry Hurtado has argued cogently that this sort of devotion to Christ actually existed during the days of his public ministry.[31]

One trend in current New Testament scholarship is to interpret the high Christology in Paul and John, for example, in terms of a "Christological monotheism" in which Christ is simply factored into the definition of God. Obviously, to show a devotion to Jesus comparable to that shown to God would be to risk the accusation of polytheism. And yet there is no evidence in the New Testament that the early believers were concerned about this. It would take centuries for a full-fledged doctrine of the Trinity to emerge. How were these tricky waters navigated? It is a tantalizing question, and it remains a cutting-edge issue. One could go a step further, however, and note that there is an implicit Christology in Jesus' very words and deeds that would point one in this direction. What was Jesus' own self-understanding? Did Jesus have a Christology?[32]

David Wells makes a helpful distinction between self-consciousness and self-understanding. Self-consciousness is a psychological concept.

---

[30] Henry Bettenson (ed.), *Documents of the Christian Church*, (2nd ed.; New York: Oxford University Press, 1963), 3–4.
[31] See, e.g., Larry W. Hurtado, *Lord Jesus Christ: Devotion to Jesus in Earliest Christianity* (Grand Rapids: Eerdmans, 2003) and Larry W. Hurtado, *How on Earth Did Jesus Become a God? Historical Questions about Earliest Devotion to Jesus* (Grand Rapids: Eerdmans, 2005).
[32] I will be utilizing loosely in this section the pioneering work by I. Howard Marshall, *The Origins of New Testament Christology* (Downers Grove, IL: InterVarsity Press, 1976), 43–58.

As applied to Jesus, it is an impossible goal to attain. Certainly, the Scriptures do not provide such an analysis, and the temptation for wild speculation is great. But self-understanding is another matter. There is much material that is revelatory of who Jesus understood himself to be, that is, how Jesus interpreted the meaning of his life and ministry.[33] David Wells cites a classic quote of John Knox that illustrates well the approach of more liberal scholarship to the portraits of Jesus in the New Testament: "I for one, simply cannot imagine a sane human being, of any historical period or culture, entertaining the thoughts about himself which the Gospels, as they stand, often attribute to him."[34] In fact, Knox in his volume, *The Humanity and Divinity of Christ*, denies the possibility altogether of accepting the biblical testimony of Christ's preexistence as a divine being along with his incarnation in full humanity: "We are restricted to adoptionism and docetism. We can have the humanity without the pre-existence and we can have the pre-existence without the humanity. There is absolutely no way of having both."[35]

This same bias is often found among more liberal scholars utilizing the literary and historical methods to analyze the New Testament. It is a mindset that *begins* with an anti-supernatural proclivity and a basic skepticism toward the reliability of the Scriptures. Reginald H. Fuller's assumptions concerning the sayings of Jesus are illustrative:

> As regards the sayings of Jesus, tradition-historical criticism eliminates from the authentic sayings of Jesus those which are paralleled in the Jewish tradition on the one hand (apocalyptic and Rabbinic) and those which reflect the faith, practice and situations of the post-Easter church as we know them from outside the gospels.[36]

---

33 David F. Wells, *The Person of Christ: A Biblical and Historical Analysis of the Incarnation* (Westchester, IL: Crossway Books, 1984), 36–37.
34 John Knox, *The Death of Jesus* (1959), 58; cited in Marshall, *The Origins of New Testament Christology*, 43.
35 John Knox, *The Humanity and Divinity of Christ: A Study of Pattern in Christology* (London: Cambridge University Press, 1967),106.
36 Reginald H. Fuller, *The Foundations of New Testament Christology* (New York: Charles Scribner's Sons, 1965), 18.

Upon reflection, these assumptions are preposterous. Jesus came from the heart of Israel and later focused his ministry on her. We should be shocked if his sayings did *not* reflect that heritage! And if Jesus himself is the founder of the church through his apostles, then surely we should expect their teachings and practices to parallel his. This is classically flawed reasoning. More recent mainline scholarship has been able to accept much more of the biblical witness to Christ, discovering surprising insights previously overlooked.

For example, there is a rich storehouse of enacted or implicit Christology in the gospels. We have already examined Jeremias's Christological insights into Jesus' use of *Abba*. Jesus' intimacy with the Father sets him apart as unique. It mirrors both his complete humanity and his eternal relation with the Father. James Dunn summarizes well Jesus' own self-understanding in this regard:

> Jesus thought of himself as God's son and as anointed by the eschatological Spirit, because in prayer he experienced God as Father and in ministry he experienced a power to heal which he could only understand as the power of the end-time and an inspiration to proclaim a message which he could only understand as the gospel of the end-time.[37]

Dunn himself is accenting the humanity of Jesus here, his religious experience. Ironically, however, these words could also characterize both Jesus' divine/eternal union with the Father as well as his finite human experience.

Another enacted Christological insight Jeremias points up is Jesus' unique use of the term "Amen." Whenever Jesus wanted to emphasize something important, he would preface what he was saying with these words: "Amen, Amen, I say to you…." (sometimes just one Amen; usually translated in modern versions as "truly, truly"; KJV: "verily, verily"). Of course, in the Jewish worship of Jesus' time, amen was used as a congregational response to public prayer, meaning "so be it," "true," "this is also our prayer" (an affirmation). By doing this, Jesus

---

[37] James D. G. Dunn, *Jesus and the Spirit* (London: SCM Press, 1975), 67 (statement is italicized in the original).

was in effect saying: What I am about to say to you is very important. It is absolutely true. And it is so because *I am saying it to you!* H. Schlier, in his article on *amen* in volume 1 of Kittel's *Theological Dictionary of the New Testament'* comments: "Thus in the Amen preceeding the 'I say to you' of Jesus we have the whole of Christology *in nuce*.[38] Jesus was claiming a unique, absolute authority, a divine prerogative.

Then there are the so-called six antitheses in the Sermon on the Mount (Matt. 5:17–48). Six times Jesus says, "You have heard that it was said…But I tell you." Ernst Käsemann lucidly depicts the dynamic here:

> But anyone who claims an authority rivalling and challenging Moses has *ipso facto* set himself above Moses; he has ceased to be a rabbi, for a rabbi's authority only comes to him as derived from Moses…To this there are no Jewish parallels, nor indeed can there be. For the Jew who does what is done here has cut himself off from the community of Judaism—or else he brings the Messianic Torah and is therefore the Messiah.[39]

Marshall observes: "He [Jesus] claimed the right to give the authoritative interpretation of the law, and he did so in a way that went beyond that of the prophets. He thus spoke as if he were God."[40]

Jesus wielded an authority that was nonpareil. He demonstrated an authority to cast out demons (Mark 1:27; 3:15; 6:7), to heal (Matt. 8:5–13; Luke 7:1–10), to teach (Mark 1:22; 11:28–33), and to forgive sins (Mark 2:5; Luke 7:48). Jesus as a *man* demonstrated that he was also more than a man. Käsemann summarizes it well:

> An examination of Jesus' words—his proclamation of the Reign of God, and his call for decision, his enunciation of God's demand—and his teaching about the nearness of

---

[38] H. Schlier, "Amen," *Theological Dictionary of the New Testament*, vol. 1, 338.
[39] Ernst Käsemann, *Essays on New Testament Themes* (London: SCM Press, 1964), 37.
[40] Marshall, *Origins of New Testament Christology*, 50.

God—and of his conduct—his calling men to follow him and his healings, his eating with publicans and sinners—forces upon us the conclusion that underlying his word and work is an implicit Christology. In Jesus as he understood himself, there is an immediate confrontation with "God's presence and his very self," offering judgment and salvation.[41]

Thus, we encounter a fully developed Christology in the words and deeds of Jesus himself. Jesus the man evinced a self-understanding that communicated a divine identity as well. Richard Bauckham maintains that this Christology was no primitive beginning that would be further developed in the future. "The earliest Christology was already the highest Christology.... This Christology of divine identity is not a mere stage on the way to the patristic development of ontological Christology in the context of a Trinitarian theology. It is already a fully divine Christology, maintaining that Jesus Christ is intrinsic to the unique and eternal identity of God. The Fathers did not develop it so much as transpose it into a conceptual framework more concerned with the Greek philosophical categories of essence and nature."[42]

In addition to all that has been said thus far on the deity of Christ, there are even *direct statements* in the New Testament announcing his deity (cf., e.g., John 1:1: 20:28; Rom. 9:5; 10:9–10; Heb. 1:8–9).[43] And last but not least is his *resurrection*. J. I. Packer masterfully express the Christological import of Christ's resurrection:

> The Easter event…demonstrated Jesus' deity; validated his teaching; attested the completion of his work of atonement for sin; confirms his present cosmic dominion and his coming reappearance as Judge; assures us that his personal pardon, presence, and power in people's lives today is fact; and guarantees each believer's own

---

[41] Fuller, *The Foundations of New Testament Christology*, 106.

[42] Richard Bauckham, *Jesus and the God of Israel* (Grand Rapids: Eerdmans, 2008), x.

[43] The most satisfying and complete book-length treatment of the resurrection that I have found is: Robert M. Bowman Jr. and J. Ed Komoszewski, *Putting Jesus in His Place: The Case for the Deity of Christ* (Grand Rapids: Kregel Publications, 2007). See also Michael F. Bird's useful précis of this work in: *Evangelical Theology: A Biblical and Systematic Introduction* (Grand Rapids: Zondervan, 2013), 470–73.

reembodiment by Resurrection in the world to come. Such is the significance of Jesus' bodily Resurrection in the eyes of Christians.[44]

Also, more could be said from the New Testament concerning Christ's humanity.[45] Often one's instinct in exploring the divinity of Christ is to turn to John's writings. But the humanity of Jesus is also vividly highlighted therein. He showed true human emotion (John 11:33-38). He got thirsty and tired (4:6-7; 19:28). This was a complete enfleshment of the Word—someone who could be seen, heard, and touched (1 John 1:1). His agonizing death was real (John 19:34). Jesus' own self-description was in part as "a man who has told you the truth that I heard from God" (John 8:40). This was no god of the Greek Pantheon or the gnostic heretics.

The Jesus of the New Testament was born like any other child. He had a lineage as does everyone else (Matt. 1:1–17; Luke 3:23–38; compare Rom. 1:3). He grew and developed as a child (Luke 2:40, 52). He experienced physical hunger (Matt. 4:2; 21:18). He had an authentic religious life of prayer, worship, and trust. He had limited knowledge as does any human being (Mark 9:21; 13:32). At the same time, through the power of the Holy Spirit—with words of wisdom and knowledge and with discernment like those gifts distributed by the Holy Spirit to the church (1 Cor. 12:8–10)—Jesus demonstrated amazing knowledge and insight (Luke 6:8; 9:47; John 1:47, 48; 2:25; 4:18, 29).

Paul puts ribbons on the gift of New Testament Christology with hymnic passages useful in our worship today:

> Christ was truly God.
> But he did not try to remain
>   equal with God.
> He gave up everything
>   and became a slave,

---

[44] Gary R. Habermas and Anthony G. N. Flew, *Did Jesus Rise from the Dead? The Resurrection Debate,* ed. Terry L. Miethe (San Francisco: Harper & Row, 1987), 143 (Packer was also a respondent in this debate.)

[45] The following is adapted from: Hart, *Truth Aflame,* 314.

when he became
   like one of us.

Christ was humble.
He obeyed God and even died
   on a cross.
Then God gave Christ
   the highest place
and honored his name
   above all others.

So at the name of Jesus
   everyone will bow down,
those in heaven, on earth,
   and under the earth.
And to the glory
   of God the Father
everyone will openly agree,
   "Jesus Christ is Lord!"
         (Phil. 2:6–11 CEV)

There is one God
   and one mediator between God and humankind,
the man Christ Jesus,
   who gave himself a ransom for all
         (1 Tim. 2:5, author's translation).

He was manifested in the flesh [earth],
vindicated in the Spirit [heaven],
   seen by angels [heaven],
preached among the nations [earth],
believed on in the world [earth],
   taken up in glory [heaven] (1 Tim. 3:16 RSV).

Lesson Seven

The Work of Christ

THE DOCTRINE OF THE ATONEMENT IN CONTEMPORARY PERSPECTIVE

CUR DEUS HOMO

Anselm asked the ultimate question: Why? Why the God-Man? Why did God become man? And why was it *necessary* for the Incarnate Christ to go to that *cross* for our salvation? These are the questions of the ages. Anselm wrote at the turn of the first millennium, but the apologetic he wrote for Jews, Muslims, pagans, and Christians alike has an uncanny ring of relevance at the beginning of the third millennium. We will need to examine his thoughts later.

But why precisely did the Incarnation and the Crucifixion happen? Two major concepts come instinctively to mind: Revelation and Salvation. As we will see, this is a sound instinct. There is, however, an even simpler and more profound explanation—love! We celebrate nationally Christmas and Easter primarily because of the divine love given to us in Jesus Christ. The best known and most memorized verse in the Bible expresses it well:

> For God loved the world so much that he gave his only Son so that whoever believes in him may not perish but have eternal life—John 3:16 (author's rendering).

The Incarnation and Crucifixion reveal the *intensity* of God's love for humanity and *immensity* of his gift to us: He gave his only (*monogenēs* = unique, only, one and only, one-of-a-kind) Son in a sacrificial, saving death so that we would never be lost or destroyed, but rather have eternal life. We memorize this verse as children, but theologians still labor to mine its riches. It is to that sacrificial death that we now turn our attention.

INTRODUCTION

Fleming Rutledge has spent a lifetime studying and preaching the meaning of the death of Christ. She observes:

> Christianity is unique. The world's religions have certain traits in common, but until the gospel of Jesus Christ burst upon the Mediterranean world, no one in the history of human imagination had conceived of such a thing as the worship of a crucified man. The early Christian preaching announced the entrance of God upon the stage of history in the person of an itinerant Jewish teacher who had been ingloriously pinned up alongside two of society's castoffs to die horribly, rejected and condemned by religious and secular authorities alike, discarded onto the garbage heap of humanity, scornfully forsaken by both elites and common folk, leaving behind only a discredited, demoralized handful of scruffy disciples who had no status whatsoever in the eyes of anyone. The peculiarity of this beginning for a world-transforming faith is not sufficiently acknowledged.[1]

Citing Bonhoeffer's example, Rutledge differentiates categorically between Christian faith and all religion. Religion is a human creation, whereas "the cross of Jesus is an unrepeatable event that calls all religion into question and establishes an altogether new foundation for faith, life, and a human future."[2]

---

[1] Fleming Rutledge, *The Crucifixion: Understanding the Death of Jesus Christ* (Grand Rapids: Eerdmans, 2015), 1. It is hard to conceive of a more satisfying and moving presentation of the meaning of the cross than what Rutledge provides here.

[2] Rutledge, *The Crucifixion*, 2.

Down the centuries the cross has stood as a devastating censure of all human religion, including a culturally captive Christianity. Too often Christians prove unfaithful to the very cruciform message and lifestyle which characterizes authentic Christian faith. We cravenly cling to a psychologically comforting, self-help religion rather than identify with the scandal of the cross. The Judaizers of Paul's day feared "being persecuted for the cross of Christ" (Gal. 6:12). A crucified Messiah will always be scandalous to Jews and moronic to Gentiles (1 Cor. 1:23). American Christians are too often enamored with political and military power. But Paul penned an epistle to the Christians living at the seat of such power—Rome—announcing, "I am not ashamed of the gospel, because it is the power of God that brings salvation to everyone who believes" (Rom. 1:16). True disciples of Jesus will always stand with Paul, who wrote: "For the message of the cross is foolishness to those who are perishing, but to us who are being saved it is the power of God" (1 Cor. 1:18). In America we are too often beguiled by political sway and material comforts. We may even boast in these false gods (money, sex, and power). Contrast the apostle Paul: "May I never boast except in the cross of our Lord Jesus Christ, through which the world has been crucified to me, and I to the world" (Gal. 6:14). Thus, perhaps the greatest need of our day is to return to the cross and meditate afresh on its meaning and message, which is the purpose of this chapter.

> *Down the centuries the cross has stood as a devastating censure of all human religion, including a culturally captive Christianity.*

THE FIRST THOUSAND YEARS: THE VICTORY OF CHRIST

Interestingly, the Holy Spirit never led the church to develop a normative statement of the doctrine of atonement comparable to the Chalcedonian Formula (451). It was as if he were saying that the church should mine the riches of the cross anew in each generation and for every cultural setting. It is, therefore, very instructive to move through history and observe how the cross was understood, preached, and lived in previous generations.

Years ago my wife and I had the privilege of traveling to Sweden, where I taught ministry students for a few days. We were won over by the beautiful land and people, and we cherish our memories of that visit. Universities in that country pre-date ours in America by centuries, evincing a rich heritage. Fittingly, it was a Swedish theologian, a professor of systematic theology in the University of Lund, who would largely set the agenda for the study of the atonement in modern Europe and America. And he would do so by calling us back to our roots. Lecturing at the University of Uppsala in March and April of 1930, Gustaf Aulén reminded us afresh that the classic presentation of the meaning of Christ's cross, found in the New Testament and predominant in Christian teaching for the church's first millennium, was simply a vivid portrayal of the *victory* of Christ over all the forces threatening to crush humanity.

The publication of Aulén's lectures became a landmark in atonement studies.[3] Aulén set the parameters for the study of the atonement in terms of three basic categories: (1) the classic view; (2) the objective view (Anselm); (3) the subjective view (Abelard). Aulén's title for the first view, the classic view, was *Christus Victor*, which ultimately became the technical theological term for this view in the decades to follow. We will be following Aulén's sage advice in what is presented here.

For the first thousand years of the church, Aulén argues, the prevailing view—what he calls the "classic view," the "dramatic view," or simply *Christus Victor*—was the simple, striking story of Jesus' victory over sin, death, and the devil. It was not so much a theory as it was a narrative of redemption. This dominant atonement theme was often presented as a ransom paid to the devil, so it has been called the "ransom theory." It was widely held by the early fathers, so it is often called the "patristic theory." It is more widely held in the East,

---

3 Gustaf Aulén, *Christus Victor: An Historical Study of the Three Main Types of the Idea of Atonement*, trans. A. G. Hebert with foreword by Jaroslav Pelikan (New York: Macmillan, 1969). (The original Swedish version was published in 1930).

so it is also termed the "Eastern" or "Greek" view, as opposed to the "Western" or "Latin" view (more fully developed by Anselm).[4]

Irenaeus of Lyons (c. 130–200) was perhaps the first theologian to derive a full-blown theory of atonement.[5] He actually set the pace for the theology of atonement which followed. Irenaeus beautifully blended together the Incarnation and Atonement, showing how Christ assumed human nature and through a "recapitulation" (i.e., living righteously through every phase of human life and *reversing* at every point where the first Adam failed) and a "ransom" justly paid to the devil, delivered mankind from bondage to sin, death, and the devil.

> The Lord therefore ransomed us by his own blood, and gave his life for our life, his flesh for our flesh; and he poured out the Spirit of the Father to bring about the union and fellowship of God and humanity, bringing God down to humanity through the Spirit while raising humanity to God through his incarnation, and in his coming surely and truly giving us incorruption through the fellowship which we have with him.[6]

Summarizing Irenaeus' atonement view, Aulén comments: "The work of Christ is first and foremost a victory over the powers which hold mankind in bondage—sin, death, and the devil."[7] Again, only God Incarnate could win such a victory for humanity. Helpless humanity is rescued by God himself from the dominion of these very real powers. I am tempted to devote the next hundred pages to Irenaeus! He was my favorite theologian during my patristic studies in seminary. He has been too often neglected or given superficial treatment. His wise leadership as bishop of the

---

4 Robert H. Culpepper, *Interpreting the Atonement* (Grand Rapids: Eerdmans, 1966), 73–74. In what follows I will be drawing upon Culpepper's useful presentation.
5 Robert S. Paul, *The Atonement and the Sacraments* (New York: Abingdon Press, 1960), 47.
6 Alister McGrath's rendering of an excellent passage from Irenaeus' *Against Heresies* in: Alister E. McGrath (ed.), *The Christian Theology Reader*, 2nd ed. (Oxford: Blackwell Publishing, 2001), 328.
7 Aulén, *Christus Victor*, 20.

church in Gaul (south France today) for the last twenty years of his life—protecting against heresies and promoting spiritual vibrancy—is exemplary.

Other theological giants would follow suit with similar ransom theories. Origen (c. 185–254) also taught a ransom paid to the devil to deliver a humanity held captive, providing victory over death and the devil. Gregory of Nyssa (c. 335–395) used a colorful "fishhook" analogy in which God catches the devil with the bait of the flesh of Christ. The devil was rightly owed a ransom, but ended up swallowing the Godhead like a fishhook, God justly deceiving the deceiver for our salvation. Augustine (354–430) in his writings and sermons presented a God of infinite grace, who delivered us from the power of the devil. Christ paid the price of our redemption by setting forth his cross as a mousetrap, baited with Christ's own blood to capture and defeat our captor. Obviously, these giants often utilized literary and homiletical license to communicate their views. And Scripture nowhere teaches a ransom paid to the devil as such. But it does teach that a ransom or price was paid by Christ himself for our redemption (cf., e.g., Mark 10:45). And it was a real victory! Why don't we hear more preaching like this in our own day? It is a sorely neglected and extremely needful gospel theme in these difficult and dangerous times.

In our own day, Gregory A. Boyd has sought to revive the victory model as the controlling motif of his theory of atonement.[8] His argument is generally good as far as it goes, but it does not go far enough. Ultimately, the church found the need to provide more objective reasons for Christ's death in terms of our *forgiveness* and *justification*. In other words, God dealt with the devil, but how did he deal with our own sin and guilt? This brings us to the next major historical theory of the atonement and another theological cathedral in the history of Christian thought: the writings of Anselm (1033–1109), the Archbishop of Canterbury from 1093 to 1109.

---

[8] See his contributions in the excellent volume: James Beilby and Paul R. Eddy (eds.), *The Nature of the Atonement: Four Views* (Downers Grove, IL: IVP Academic, 2006).

THE NEXT 800 YEARS: ANSELM'S SATISFACTION THEORY

Justo L. González says that Anselm was "without doubt the greatest theologian of his time" and that with Anselm "a new era began in the history of Christian thought."[9] Anselm stood as a transition figure in historical theology, preparing the way for the full bloom of scholasticism as well as recasting the doctrine of the atonement in an entirely new mold. In this regard, Anselm set the agenda for the next eight hundred years. His basic theological method was: "I believe in order that I may understand" (*Proslogion 1*). Anselm was a believer who put his great intellect in the service of faith. He argued that unbelief was sin and provided an appropriate apologetic for the Christian faith by *challenging* that unbelief. His ontological argument for the existence of God is still being used in new forms today. He sought to convince Jew, Muslim, and pagan alike and to consolidate the faith of the Christian. It was in this vein of thinking that Anselm set about to give a rationale for the atonement. He shifted the setting from the battlefield (ransom theory) to the law court (satisfaction theory), and faced head-on the question of the *necessity* of the death of Christ for our redemption. In providing a solidly argued *objective* theory of the atonement he made a lasting contribution to Christian theology.

Anselm lived in the medieval times of lords and vassals. (I don't know why a cable television series hasn't been produced on his life, given the popularity of this period in current culture!) This feudal system would serve as the backdrop for his theory of atonement. *Cur Deus Homo,* his classic work on the subject, beautifully correlates Incarnation and Atonement, similar in this regard to what Irenaeus did for his day. Anselm addresses the questions: Why did God become man? Why was it necessary for our redemption that Christ should have to take on human existence and die for us? Anselm formulated his response in terms of a juridical model.

---

[9] Justo L. González, *A History of Christian Thought*, vol. 2 (Nashville: Abingdon Press, 1971), 166.

According to feudal law, whenever a vassal defrauded his lord, the honor of the lord could only be maintained by restoring what was taken *and* adding an additional amount known as the "satisfaction." In the atonement instead of a ransom being paid to the devil, a ransom or satisfaction was required by God for our redemption. Only God could pay such a debt, but only man should: thus, the rationale for the God-Man, who did pay our satisfaction! The nature of our sin is the problem: It is infinite because committed against an infinite God. ("You have yet to consider what a heavy weight sin is," says Anselm to his mythical opponent Boso, who poses all the challenging questions.) What could we offer for our satisfaction, when we already owe him a fully dedicated life? We are literally helpless. Christ did live such a sinless life, then went further by providing satisfaction though his sacrificial death. Christ's "excess merit" should be rewarded, but he already owns everything. So the Father gives salvation for mankind as the reward.

It seems a quaint argument in our day, but the juridical principle at its core is central to the biblical doctrine of the atonement, as we shall see. Anselm was communicating for his day how God could be both just and the justifier, as Paul would phrase it (Rom. 3:26). It is instinctive to human nature that there be justice, whatever law system we devise. It is often difficult for us to forgive those who have sinned against us. We want justice. We think, "There needs to be a hell for a Hitler." But what about us? If sin against our Holy God is infinite, then we too deserve hell. In effect, Anselm is saying that God pays the debt and endures the just punishment for us himself in the person of his suffering Son. He is thereby able to forgive us our sins while maintaining his perfect righteousness.

At the same time, it must be admitted that this theory could easily be misapprehended as God's being more concerned with solving his own problem of maintaining his righteousness—that is, atonement is more about him than us. If the ransom theory could be misconstrued as making the devil a god, the satisfaction theory could be distorted into making God into a devil who demands the torture of his Son for justice. Anselm knocked this objection to the ground by pointing out that it was God himself who was providing the satisfaction. Still more needed to be said to complete the atonement picture. More needed to be said about God's *love*.[10]

ABELARD: THE MORAL INFLUENCE THEORY

Peter Abelard (1079–1142), a near contemporary of Anselm, stepped forward in his widely popular lectures at the University of Paris, and in his publications, to address this issue of the neglect of divine love at the heart of the doctrine of atonement and many other theological concerns. Four of his publications tell the whole story. His autobiography, *The Story of My Misfortunes,* relates the dramatic and tragic events of his life. *Sic et Non (Yes and No)* and *Christian Theology* display his whole theological program, the former by raising concerns and controversies in traditional philosophy and theology, and the latter by addressing these issues systematically. Finally, in his *Exposition of the Epistle to the Romans* we find our most reliable and complete account of Abelard's moral influence theory.

Seeming to love controversy or debate, Abelard rejected out of hand the ransom theory and Anselm's satisfaction theory. He particularly challenged Anselm's theory. In Abelard's view, a treatment of the love of God was sorely lacking in the satisfaction theory. At its core, according to Abelard, the atonement was not about a ransom paid to the devil or a satisfaction paid to God. It was about the conquering love of God. The cross was not a legal transaction but a sublime revelation of the love of God which inspires our repentance, faith, and Christian living. It was a *subjective* theory in which Christ's *example* of love was the key saving dynamic. Abelard's answer to *cur deus homo* was simple: love.

Abelard's approach differed significantly from that of Anselm. Abelard did not assume an Augustinian understanding of the sinful plight of humanity as did Anselm and his focus was almost

---
[10] I am in debt to the following for the general parameters of this presentation of Anselm: Culpepper, *Interpreting the Atonement*, 81–87; Paul, *The Atonement and the Sacraments*, 65–80.

solely on the subjective impact of the cross. And he could be quite persuasive:

> Indeed, how cruel and wicked it seems that anyone should demand the blood of an innocent person as the price for anything, or that it should in any way please him that an innocent man should be slain—still less that God should consider the death of his Son so agreeable that by it he should be reconciled to the whole world![11]

Indeed! And if one completely omits Anselm's Trinitarian perspective in which *God* is the principle actor in the redemptive drama, then what we have is a grotesque example of divine child abuse. Unfortunately, this was Abelard's fatal mistake. The ultimate question to Abelard is: How exactly is Christ's death on the cross the supreme revelation of God's love? Abelard seemed oblivious to this fundamental issue.

In my seminary classes I enjoy conjuring up a personal illustrative parable to demonstrate the fatal flaw of Abelard's theory. Suppose on my honeymoon I walk my new bride out to the end of a long pier over the deep Atlantic waters. I am telling her how my heart is so filled with love for her. But words seem to fail. I cannot swim. But to give the ultimate demonstration of my love for my wife, I jump off the pier and drown. That would be more of an indication of a severe mental condition than of a deep and abiding love, would it not! But let us consider a different honeymoon scenario. Instead of a trip to the ocean, let us say that we decide to shop at a quaint little town nearby. As my wife steps out into the street to cross over to a cute little antique store, I notice a Mack truck barreling down on her. My loving instinct is to leap out and shove her out of the truck's path, but tragically at the cost of my own life. Now that would be the supreme example of my love for her. Why? Because it was *necessary* for me to die that she might live. (Admittedly, both stories are a little depressing: The truth is my wife and I had a wonderful—

---

11 From Abelard's Romans commentary; quoted in Paul, *The Atonement and the Sacraments*, 81.

safe!—honeymoon on Boone Mountain, North Carolina.) Abelard's subjective theory lacks the *objective* ingredient we find in Anselm. Unless it was *necessary* for Christ to die for our sins, then the cross cannot be the supreme revelation of God's love. In fact, the genius of Anselm is precisely at this point: Only the objective transaction of the atonement can provide the appropriate foundation for our salvation. Calvary was not just an inspiring story. It was the ultimate, objective saving event of history, wrought by God himself.

Nevertheless, we can thank Abelard for moving divine love to the fore: For God so loved the world! And God did certainly intend for the cross to impact us subjectively and to inspire discipleship. We immediately see that the core insights of these three classic theories need to be combined. The cross was victorious, objective, and subjective. It was God doing it all—and all for us!

LUTHER: THE BEST OF THE PAST, THE WAY OF THE FUTURE

Beyond the foundational theories presented above, I would like finally to draw attention to that giant of the Reformation, Martin Luther (1483–1546), as someone who represents the best of the past and points the way toward the future. Then we shall attempt to draw together all the threads of biblical evidence we have come across in our learning of Christ thus far into a comprehensive biblical/systematic statement of the meaning of the cross.

Luther's story and status are well known. Less known is his comprehensive theology of the cross, because Luther did not provide us with his systematic theology. I will begin by following the lead of Gustaf Aulén, who also singles Luther out as instructive of the way forward. I will need, however, to move beyond Aulén to accent Luther's classic penal theory of the atonement.

Luther's entire theology he himself would characterize as a *theology of the cross*. His thought is a powerful antidote to speculative theology untethered from Scripture, what Luther would call a theology of glory.

And it was not as if Luther neglected the resurrection. Luther was a Bible teacher, and he stuck to biblical categories. To move beyond them was a fatal mistake, in Luther's view—*Sola Scriptura!* The debt we owe Aulén is his pointing out the obvious, but too often ignored, dramatic character of Luther's theology: Luther's theological writings, catechisms, and hymns are rife with victory images. Aulén provides an example among many that could be cited of Luther's communicating the cross in the classic categories of the defeat of sin, death, and the devil. Using a fishhook analogy similar to that of Gregory of Nyssa, Luther depicts God's fishing for the devil with his incarnate Son, taking the devil captive, and liberating us from death and hell. And Luther utilizes these images in his most careful doctrinal statements in his catechisms and as a unifying leitmotif in his total theological program.[12]

What Aulén fails to perceive, however, is that Luther seamlessly integrates this language with an objective, penal concept of the atonement. Luther had a love relationship with Galatians and his theological exposition of Galatians 3:13 was the centerpiece of his understanding of the cross. "Christ redeemed us from the curse of the law," writes Paul, "by becoming a curse for us—for it is written: Cursed be everyone who is hanged on a tree" (Gal. 3:13 NRSV). Christ was the sin-bearer, the substitute. And true saving faith perceives that he did it for *me* individually. This was an objective transaction. Christ became a curse for us. As Moltmann expresses it in powerful paradoxical language: He died the God-forsaken death we all deserve to die. He endured the precise punishment we all deserve.

What I see in Luther is an exquisite weaving together of all three classic theories of atonement. And he accomplished this, I believe, because he stayed close to the Scriptures. To be sure, Luther had a proclivity toward brusqueness and crudeness in expression at times. Aulén observes: "Luther loves violent expressions, strong colours, realistic images, and in innumerable passages he describes Christ's conflict with the tyrants in this way. For him no colours are too strong, no images too concrete; even the most grotesque analogies

---

12 Aulén, *Christus Victor*, 103–04,

from the Fathers come back again."[13] And yet, in many ways, what he says needs to be heard afresh in our own day. We need as it were another Reformation, another return to the Christ of the cross as communicated to us in the Scriptures. Luther's crucicentered theology points the way.[14]

We turn now to a synthesis statement. In one sense, what follows is the culmination not only of this chapter, but also of all that has been said thus far. It is intended as a broad stroke depiction of Christ's saving work on our behalf with a view toward greater personal knowledge of Christ and a more fully devoted discipleship. I want to use five simple words to summarize Christ's saving work: love, judgment, deliverance, sacrifice, and substitution.[15]

LOVE

The cross of Christ is the supreme revelation of the amazing depths of the love of God for sinful humanity.

This insight into the atonement is ultimate, not penultimate. It is the bottom line, to use business nomenclature. Too often divine love is mentioned almost as an afterthought. If any concept of the atonement cannot be integrated with God's love, it is an inappropriate concept to be discarded. Only God's love would go to such lengths for our redemption. Only a God of love would give us the aid of his Spirit to receive the benefits of the atonement. Only a God of infinite love and wisdom could deal justly with his own divine wrath toward sin and evil and take our place in judgment. The cross reveals a loving God absorbing back into himself his own wrath and judgment in self-substitution. The atonement is a Trinitarian event. In fact, it could be argued that the greatest revelation of the triunity of God is in the cross:

---

[13] Aulén, *Christus Victor*, 103.
[14] For a satisfying and insightful presentation of Luther's doctrine of atonement see the following: Timothy George, "The Atonement in Martin Luther's Theology," in Charles E. Hill and Frank A. James III (eds.), *The Glory of the Atonement* (Downers Grove, IL: InterVarsity Press, 2004), 263–78.
[15] In what follows, I have adopted and substantially adapted the very helpful constructive statement found in the following: Culpepper, *Interpreting the Atonement*, 131–57.

> It is not too much to say, then, that *the proper understanding of God as Father, Son, and Holy Spirit takes place only within the movement of atoning propitiation whereby God draws near to us and draws us near to himself in believing response and brings us into union with himself through the gift of his Spirit,* for it is only within that two-way movement of reconciling love that God's self-revelation to mankind attains its end. Through Christ and his awful self-sacrifice on the cross alone may we sinful and alienated human beings have access by one Spirit to the Father.[16]

The Bible communicates this most astounding of all truths in myriad ways and through a variety of images. God's love pervades the Scriptures from beginning to end. God *is* love and this is how we know it: he "sent his Son as an atoning sacrifice for our sins" (1 John 4:10; see the entire context: vv. 7–21). This is not a sentimental, insipid love which merely winks at sin and evil, but rather a fierce, jealous love that will go to any lengths to rescue us, to reconcile us. "When we see man for what he is, the wrath of God for what it is, and the cross for what it is, then and only then do we see love for what it is."[17]

This kind of love is unfathomable. It shatters all convention. "Indeed, rarely will anyone die for a righteous person—though perhaps for a good person someone might actually dare to die. But God proves his love for us in that while we still were sinners Christ died for us" (Rom. 5:7–8 NRSV). "No one has greater love than this: to lay down one's life for one's friends" (John 15:13 NRSV). Perhaps the best known verse in the Bible, John 3:16, sums it all up: "For God so loved the world that he gave his only Son, so that everyone who believes in him may not perish but may have eternal life" (NRSV). God *gave* his only Son to be the atoning sacrifice: "For our sake he made him to be sin who knew no sin, so that in him we might become the righteousness of God" (2 Cor. 5:21 NRSV). "Christ suffered for you," Peter writes. And his suffering is beyond our comprehension.

---

[16] Thomas F. Torrance, *The Mediation of Christ* (Colorado Springs: Helmers and Howard, 1992), 110 (author's italics).

[17] Leon Morris, *Testaments of Love: A Study of Love in the Bible* (Grand Rapids: Eerdmans, 1991), 131.

In actuality, Christ suffered throughout his life. He was the one sinless man, immersed in a sea of sinners. The pressures and persecutions must have been enormous. But he never compromised. He only loved. Even his own family misunderstood him. He was rejected by both Jews and Gentiles. Then to undergo the tortures of scourging and crucifixion—unspeakable suffering. But we see his worst suffering expressed in his cry of dereliction: "My God, my God, why have you forsaken me?" (Matt. 27:46; Mark 15:34). For the first time in his earthly life he, as the cursed one, experienced alienation from his Father. Again, this mystery transcends our understanding. What a price was paid for our redemption! Isaiah wrote about this Suffering Servant some seven centuries earlier (Isa. 52:14–53:12 NLT) and his words read like a newspaper account of the event:

> But many were amazed when they saw him.
>> His face was so disfigured he seemed hardly human,
>> and from his appearance, one would scarcely know he was
> a man.
> [15] And he will startle many nations.
>> Kings will stand speechless in his presence.
> For they will see what they had not been told;
>> they will understand what they had not heard about.
>
> 53 Who has believed our message?
>> To whom has the Lord revealed his powerful arm?
> [2] My servant grew up in the Lord's presence like a tender green shoot,
>> like a root in dry ground.
> There was nothing beautiful or majestic about his appearance,
>> nothing to attract us to him.
> [3] He was despised and rejected—
>> a man of sorrows, acquainted with deepest grief.
> We turned our backs on him and looked the other way.
>> He was despised, and we did not care.
>
> [4] Yet it was our weaknesses he carried;
>> it was our sorrows that weighed him down.

And we thought his troubles were a punishment from God,
    a punishment for his own sins!
⁵ But he was pierced for our rebellion,
    crushed for our sins.
He was beaten so we could be whole.
    He was whipped so we could be healed.
⁶ All of us, like sheep, have strayed away.
    We have left God's paths to follow our own.
Yet the Lord laid on him
    the sins of us all.

⁷ He was oppressed and treated harshly,
    yet he never said a word.
He was led like a lamb to the slaughter.
    And as a sheep is silent before the shearers,
    he did not open his mouth.
⁸ Unjustly condemned,
    he was led away.
No one cared that he died without descendants,
    that his life was cut short in midstream.
But he was struck down
    for the rebellion of my people.
⁹ He had done no wrong
    and had never deceived anyone.
But he was buried like a criminal;
    he was put in a rich man's grave.

¹⁰ But it was the Lord's good plan to crush him
    and cause him grief.
Yet when his life is made an offering for sin,
    he will have many descendants.
He will enjoy a long life,
    and the Lord's good plan will prosper in his hands.
¹¹ When he sees all that is accomplished by his anguish,
    he will be satisfied.
And because of his experience,
    my righteous servant will make it possible

> for many to be counted righteous,
>   for he will bear all their sins.
> ¹² I will give him the honors of a victorious soldier,
>   because he exposed himself to death.
> He was counted among the rebels.
>   He bore the sins of many and interceded for rebels.

Could there be any more moving words in all literature? This is the amazing love of God: "For God was in Christ, reconciling the world to himself, no longer counting people's sins against them" (2 Cor. 5:19 NLT). "For if, while we were God's enemies, we were reconciled to him through the death of his Son, how much more, having been reconciled, shall we be saved through his life!" (Rom. 5:10). And this divine love is a *covenant love:* "This cup is the new covenant in my blood" (1 Cor. 11:25). In truth, Jesus "is the mediator of a better covenant" (Heb. 8:6 NRSV)!

JUDGMENT

The cross of Christ is God's judgment upon the sins of humanity.

Jesus himself interpreted his cross as both the divine judgment on the sins of humanity and the means of salvation for humanity: "And just as Moses lifted up the serpent in the wilderness, so must the Son of Man be lifted up, that whoever believes in him may have eternal life" (John 3:14–15 NRSV). He was referring, of course, to the wilderness story in which God's murmuring, rebellious people were judged by God through his sending venomous snakes among them. Moses interceded and was instructed by the Lord to make a bronze serpent and put it on a pole. Those who had been bitten could look at the bronze snake and live (Num. 21:4–9). So the serpent represented both judgment and salvation. Jesus was saying that the same is true of the cross. His being lifted up on that cross would be the occasion of God's judgment on our sins as well as the means of salvation from our sins.

The apostle Paul also highlights this theme: "There is therefore now no condemnation for those who are in Christ Jesus" (Rom. 8:1 NRSV).

Condemnation (*katakrima*) here signifies punishment, judgment, death penalty. Paul further explains: "For God has done what the law, weakened by the flesh, could not do: by sending his own Son in the likeness of sinful flesh, and to deal with sin [or 'and as a sin offering'], he condemned [*katakrinō*; the verb form of the noun in verse 1] sin in the flesh" (v. 3). The good news is that God judged both our sins and our sin nature in the death of Jesus, bringing forgiveness of sins and the power to live holy lives! The entire passage (vv. 1–17) deserves serious study.

Earlier in this epistle Paul provides a précis of his entire presentation in one sentence—that is, in the Greek it is one sentence; translators are forced to break it up into several sentences (Rom. 3:21–26). In the middle of this passage we read: "God presented Him [Jesus] as a propitiation through faith in his blood" (v. 25 HCSB). Propitiation (*hilastērion*) refers to the mercy-seat, the cover on the ark of the covenant, where atonement, in terms of a sacrifice which turns away God's wrathful judgment, is made. The apostle John uses similar judgment language: "Love consists in this: not that we loved God, but that He loved us and sent His Son to be the propitiation for our sins" (1 John 4:10 HCSB). Propitiation here (*hilasmos*) refers again to the atoning sacrifice that averts God's wrath. Note that this turning away of God's wrathful judgment is provided by God himself, as the supreme expression of his *love!* Because of Christ's atonement we no longer face the judgment of our sins and the eternal consequences. They have already been judged at Calvary—therefore…no condemnation!

DELIVERANCE

The Christ-event is God's decisive action by which we are delivered from all the evil powers which hold us in bondage: sin, the condemnation of the law, death, and the devil.

This is the victory theme of the classic view of the atonement that predominated for the first thousand years of the church—we need to bring it back! "God wiped out the charges that were against us for disobeying the Law of Moses. He took them away and nailed them to the cross. There Christ defeated all powers and forces. He let the whole world see them being led away as prisoners when he celebrated his victory" (Col. 2: 14–15 cev). Through Christ we are no longer under the condemnation of the Law, and through Christ's victory over the devil and his demons we also have victory! Our foe is defeated. Further, Jesus has decisively delivered us from the devil and our fear of death: "We are people of flesh and blood. That is why Jesus became one of us. He died to destroy the devil, who had power over death. But he also died to rescue all of us who live each day in fear of dying" (Heb. 2:14–15 cev). "Death has been swallowed up in victory" (1 Cor. 15:54)! Finally, "We know that our old sinful selves were crucified with Christ so that sin might lose its power in our lives. We are no longer slaves to sin" (Rom. 6:6 nlt). Now that is deliverance! And it is solely the work of Christ. His cross made all of this possible.

Too many people today are unaware of the victory Christ has won for them. Still living in bondage and fear to seemingly capricious forces beyond their control, they long for deliverance. Christ literally died that they might have that freedom and healing. Salvation is deliverance. It is rescue. And it was made possible by the atoning death of Jesus.

SACRIFICE

Christ as our high priest makes the perfect representative sacrifice for sin so that we can come to God.

We owe the writer of Hebrews a great debt for developing this theme. We are defiled and defeated in our sin. "But Christ offered himself as a sacrifice that is good forever. Now he is sitting at God's right side, and he will stay there until his enemies are put under his power. By his one sacrifice he has forever set free from sin the people he brings to God" (Heb. 10:12–14 cev). This is an ongoing ministry as well: "Because Jesus lives forever, he has a permanent priesthood. Therefore he is able to save completely those who come to God through him, because he always lives to intercede for them" (Heb. 7:24–25). "We have an advocate with the Father," John reminds us,

"Jesus Christ, the Righteous One. He is the atoning sacrifice for our sins, and not only for ours but also for the sins of the whole world" (1 John 2:1–2). Undoubtedly, this is the most neglected aspect of the atonement in our day. We are so preoccupied with this world that we tend to be oblivious to what Christ has done and continues to do for us (intercession) in heaven.

Sacrifice as a concept is easily misunderstood. We associate it with the Law and therefore as obsolete. We certainly do not link the concept with grace! Too often we picture a pagan animist, cowering under a tree during a terrifying lightning storm, who runs out from under the tree (good move) and slaughters an animal to assuage the wrath of the god of the storm, then runs back under the tree (bad move). Sacrifice is the polar opposite of this: God gave the Passover sacrifice (Ex. 12), the sacrificial system of gift, communion, and expiatory offerings (Lev. 1–7), and the Day of Atonement (Lev. 16) as gifts of grace to his people, providing a covering for their sins and means of humble approach to his holy presence. But that was only the shadow. The fulfillment came with the once-for-all sacrifice of Christ, who also serves as our High Priest.

SUBSTITUTION

Christ as our substitute endures the just penalty of our sin, thus providing acquittal and forgiveness.

This is the truth of the atonement that the Reformers helped to restore to prominence. And it is controversial. But it should not be. When we rightfully view the atonement from a Trinitarian perspective, we discover a divine self-substitution transpiring: "The LORD has laid on him the iniquity of us all" (Isa. 53:6). "'He himself bore our sins' in his body on the cross," Peter tells us. Christ is the great sin-bearer at Calvary.

Fleming Rutledge, a retired Episcopal priest and widely known preacher and lecturer, has spent her entire life studying the atoning death of our Lord. Her published findings received immediate attention.[18]

---
18 Fleming, *The Crucifixion* (2015).

When it came to the concept of substitution in the atonement, she too struggled. Now she can easily enumerate the objections.[19] It was Karl Barth's writings on the subject that tipped the scale for her. Barth, who always interacts meticulously with the Scriptures, provided Rutledge with the overarching perspective of a narrative theology of the death of Christ. Placing the atonement in a Trinitarian context, Barth argues strongly for substitution: "Man's reconciliation with God takes place through God putting Himself in man's place and man's being put in God's place, as a sheer act of grace. It is this inconceivable miracle which is our reconciliation."[20] Substitution in the atonement is a divine *self-substitution*. It is God as judge, stepping down from the bench, removing his righteous robes, putting his arms around us, and assuming the judgment in our place. Here are Barth's words on the subject:

> *The message of the atonement becomes very personal. In the cross Jesus says to us, "I died for you."*

> The passion of Jesus Christ is the judgment of God in which the Judge Himself was the judged. And as such it is at its heart and center the victory which has been won for us, in our place, in the battle against sin. By this time it should be clear why it is so important to understand this passion as from the very first the divine action…the radical divine action which attacks and destroys at its very root the primary evil in the world; the activity of the second Adam who took the place of the first, who reversed and overthrew the activity of the first in this world, and in so doing brought in a new man, founded a new world and inaugurated a new aeon.[21]

The message of the atonement becomes very personal. In the cross Jesus says to us, "I died for you." As a seven-year-old boy I heard our Southern Baptist pastor say time and again, if you were the only person God ever made, Jesus Christ would have died for you. And

---
19 Fleming, *The Crucifixion*, 489–506.
20 Karl Barth, *Church Dogmatics in Outline* (New York: Harper Torchbooks, 1959), 115; cited in Rutledge, *The Crucifixion*, 508.
21 Karl Barth, *Church Dogmatics*, IV/1, 253–54; cited in Rutledge, *The Crucifixion*, 523.

he did!" Luther would have said a hearty *Amen!* Charles Wesley captured the wonder in his timeless hymn, "And Can It Be That I Should Gain?"

> Amazing love!
> How can it be
> That thou, my God,
> Shouldst die for me!

Lesson Eight

Christ and the Future

FUTURE PROSPECTS IN THE STUDY OF CHRISTOLOGY

We have come to the end—yet only the beginning. When it comes to Christology, the past is prologue to the future. The Bible is a future-oriented book. The Christian pilgrimage is as well: We are "looking forward to the city with foundations, whose architect and builder is God" (Heb. 11:10). We are running "with perseverance the race marked out for us, fixing our eyes on Jesus, the pioneer and perfecter of faith. For the joy set before him he endured the cross, scorning its shame, and sat down at the right hand of God" (Heb. 12:1–2). "From first to last, and not merely in the epilogue, Christianity is eschatology, is hope, forward looking and forward moving, and therefore also revolutionizing and transforming the present."[1] "With the arrival of Jesus Christ we have the ultimate eschatological event."[2] And he is coming again!

> When it comes to Christology, the past is prologue to the future.

---

[1] Jürgen Moltmann, *Theology of Hope*, trans. James W. Leitch (London: SCM, 1967), 16.

[2] Larry D. Hart, *Truth Aflame: Theology for the Church in Renewal* (Grand Rapids: Zondervan, 2005), 469. See also: Donald G. Bloesch, *The Last Things: Resurrection, Judgment, Glory*, Christian Foundations series (Downers Grove, IL: InterVarsity Press, 2004), 28, 32.

> "Look, he is coming with the clouds,
>   and every eye will see him,
> even those who have pierced him";
>   and all peoples on earth "will mourn
>   because of him."
>   So shall it be! Amen.
>
> "I am the Alpha and the Omega, says the Lord God,
> "who is, and who was, and who is to come, the Almighty"
> (Rev. 1:7–8).

We have endeavored in this book to present the living Jesus, the contemporary Jesus. He is the supernatural Jesus—naturally supernatural and supernaturally natural, complete in Godhead and complete in manhood. "He has forced open a door that has been locked since the death of the first man. He has met, fought, and beaten the King of Death. Everything is different because He has done so. This is the beginning of the New Creation: a new chapter in cosmic history has opened."[3] "Therefore, if anyone is in Christ, the new creation has come: The old has gone, the new is here!" (2 Cor. 5:17). All this—because of Good Friday, Easter, the Ascension, the Second Coming…but supremely because of Christmas!

The Incarnation is the Grand Miracle, the Central Miracle: "Every other miracle prepares for this, or exhibits this, or results from this."[4] It is a mystery beyond our ken. "Here are two mysteries for the price of one—the plurality of persons within the unity of God, and the union of Godhead and manhood in the person of Jesus."[5] The supernatural Jesus is the only Jesus there is. He is man, but also more than man, as the creeds and confessions of Christendom have always averred.[6] Martin Luther was transfixed by the Incarnation:

> He [Jesus Christ] condescends to assume my flesh and blood, my body and soul. He does not become an angel or

---

[3] C. S. Lewis, *Miracles: A Preliminary Study* (New York: Macmillan, 1947), 150.
[4] Lewis, *Miracles*, 112.
[5] J. I. Packer, *Knowing God* (Downers Grove, IL: InterVarsity Press, 1973), 46.
[6] See Russell F. Aldwinckle, *More Than Man: A Study in Christology* (Grand Rapids: Eerdmans, 1976).

another magnificent creature; He becomes a man. This is a token of God's mercy to wretched human beings; the human heart cannot grasp or understand, let alone express it.[7]

Mystery though it will always be, there is a logic here as well. The basic formulation is clear: (1) Christ was divine; (2) Christ was human; (3) Christ was one person. The creeds profess two natures not to be confused and one person not to be divided. But there are common misperceptions. One is to conceive of human nature as a self-contained entity, which is *deism*. Another is to attempt to define human nature apart from divine image and origin, which is *naturalism, secularism*. Human nature can only be understood in relation to God. Human nature is utterly dependent upon God. "For in him we live and move and have our being" (Acts 17:28). God's immanent presence alone enables human existence.

Moving one step further, we contemplate Christian experience of God's presence. That presence does not destroy or subvert humanity, but rather actualizes, fulfills, and completes our humanity. We are our true selves only in relation to God. Keeping these two dimensions of God's immanence in view prepares us for the next step: Incarnation.

In the Incarnation God moves from his general immanence in human nature to his special immanence in the believer, to his personal incarnation in a human life. It was precisely *because* of his divinity, his perfect and eternal union with the Father, that Jesus' humanity could be perfect and complete. In that regard, we are at present actually *less than* human because of our sin. If you want God's definition of what a human being is, simply look at Jesus. If you want to know what God looks like, look at Jesus. "Whoever has seen me has seen the Father," Jesus said (John 14:9). The purpose of the Incarnation was *remedial revelation*, according to John 1: (1) to show us the Father (vv. 1–18) and (2) to save us from our sins (vv. 29–34).

---

[7] Martin Luther, "Sermon on the Gospel of St. John 6:47," in *Luther's Works*, 55 vols., ed. Jaroslav Pelikan and Helmut T. Lehmann (St. Louis: Concordia; Philadelphia: Fortress, 1955-), 22:102–3; cited in John C. Clark and Marcus Peter Johnson, *The Incarnation of God* (Wheaton: Crossway, 2015), 19.

It will always be a great mystery—but it is a mystery, not of darkness, but of excess light![8]

CHRISTOLOGY AND THE CHURCH

For some strange reason, the church has never been able fully to discover her identity in Jesus. This sounds unkind, but it is demonstrably true. If every Christian fully embraced our corporate identity in Christ, there would be only one church, not more than 22,000 churches. And there is only one explanation for this failure: sin. Pope Francis has been humbly spreading this message. He is controversial, but his message of loving all persons, and especially the poor and disadvantaged, is obviously biblical and relevant. Christians are known for almost everything except loving each other. But Jesus taught: "By this everyone will know that you are my disciples, if you love one another" (John 13:35). Somehow we think that we are greater than our Master for we simply *refuse* to wash one another's feet (John 13:1–17).

I suspect that ecclesial divides will persist until his return. On the other hand, there is evidence and hope that *spiritually* God's people can come together in prayer and worship, in mission and ministry, respecting our differences, in myriad ways as we move into the future. Only as we keep our eyes on him can we do so. Looking at each other, or ourselves in the mirror of God's Word, can be depressing at times. But the vision of Jesus, which can only come through our *doing* Christology daily, can liberate us. Learning Christ together can be an exciting enterprise!

CHRISTOLOGY AND THE THEOLOGY OF RELIGIONS

But there is another daunting challenge in our day. The globe is shrinking rapidly and the religions of the world are now on our

---

[8] I owe these insights to a Southern Baptist theological patriarch, W. T. Conner: Walter Thomas Connor, *Revelation and God: An Introduction to Christian Doctrine* (Nashville: Broadman, 1936), 190–91.

doorstep. It is easy to write off these religious adherents as simply deceived, but they are people too, people for whom Christ died. Yes, sometimes religious extremists persecute us and even kill us, but that does not exempt us from loving them. We are called to take the message of Christ to the world, which in part means taking the gospel to every person's world. Sometimes the best way we can honor the *imago dei* in every person is simply to *listen* to them. A cutting edge discipline, therefore, has emerged in recent years called the theology of religions.

A theology of religions is not merely a study of comparative religions. It is a theological enterprise which views religious beliefs through, in the case of Christianity, Christological lenses. One lesson learned from studying the patristic fathers is that distortions of the gospel and false so-called revelations can be discerned in terms of what they say about Christ. Thus, Christology plays a central role in developing a theology of religions. Neither is the challenge here a call to pluralism or relativism. In simplest terms that would be a denial of Christ. The cross of Christ stands in judgment on all religions, including the Christian religion. Defining religion as the practice of beliefs enables us to subject Christianity itself to Christological critique. But the beliefs themselves, rooted in Christ and his cross—the gospel—are nonnegotiable.[9]

At the outset, the church was faced with the Jewish-Christian question. Historically, the answer is simple: The two religions went their separate ways. Theologically, however, the Christian testimony is that Christ is the fulfillment of Jewish hopes. He *is* the Messiah. Further complicating the religious scene is the phenomenon of Messianic Judaism, forming somewhat of a *tertium quid*. Messianic Jews in New Testament times formed the embryonic church. The evangelistic tactic of present day Messianic Jews is often to distance themselves from the church and portray themselves as completed Jews under a new rabbinic leadership. The Jewish community generally seems to view them as a hoax, a cheap counterfeit. And often even the

---

[9] A helpful treatment of this subject is found in: Daniel Strange, *Their Rock Is Not Like Our Rock: A Theology of Religions* (Grand Rapids: Zondervan, 2014).

church itself feels an awkwardness in terms of how to relate properly to these "Jews for Jesus."

Jewish-Christian relations continue on at least two tracks. One track is simply the numerous attempts at dialogue without what the Jewish community is fond to call *proselytizing*. Much good can be accomplished from these efforts. Another track is self-evident: attempts at converting each other. I have fond memories of significant conversations as a seminary student with my eye doctor, who was Jewish. I gave him a copy of the Bible in a contemporary translation and other literature. We talked at length about Jesus. We also shared autobiographically. One day he said to me: "For you to proselytize me, all I have to do is something positive: add faith in Jesus to what I already have. But for me to proselytize to you, you would have to do something negative: abandon your belief in Jesus as the Messiah and Savior." I asked him, "Doctor, what are you trusting in for your salvation? Are you trusting in your ability to obey God's Law, or are you trusting in the grace and mercy and love of God?" He said without hesitation, "I am trusting in the grace and mercy and forgiveness of God." These were cordial conversations with much mutual affection.

The elephant in the room, of course, is antisemitism. Christians have a spotty history in this regard which must be humbly acknowledged. It was certainly one of the topics that came up in my conversations with my eye doctor. He had been treated horribly a few times in the military because of his Jewishness by so-called Christians. He did not, however, harbor bitterness and was more than eager to dialogue with me. There were times when I felt he understood the grace of God better than some of my Christian friends. It is probably impossible for Christians to comprehend the sufferings of God's people, the Jews, through the centuries. But part of our conversation will surely entail processing the impact of these sufferings. Presently, Christians are now experiencing similar suffering at the hands of radical Islam.

I grew up with a Jewish friend back in Bible-belt West Texas. We made model planes together in our younger days and generally enjoyed a great friendship. At our twenty-year high school class reunion, I was asked to give some remarks, having been class president. I reflected on the past twenty years in America and snuck in a little paragraph on Jesus, being an inveterate Southern Baptist "evangelist." Later I received a long, single-spaced typed letter from my friend. He told me he was tired of having Jesus "stuffed down his throat" by Christian prayers at football games and rodeos and the parochial attitudes of Christians. I replied in a letter, arguing that freedom of religious belief and expression was the genius of the American experiment and that a part of my having authentic Christian faith entailed sharing it! He replied by offering an olive branch which I enthusiastically welcomed. He is a brilliant, likeable human being, who now is somewhat alienated from all religions, viewing them as basically the root of all the present ills of the world.

My personal conviction is that Jesus must be kept at the center of the dialogue. Once in such a dialogue session on the campus of the university at which I teach, a Jewish lady stood and said, "If you Christians want to proselytize [there's that word again] us Jews, make us jealous." I wanted to stand and say, "Why aren't you already jealous? We've blanketed the globe with the gospel, building great hospitals and universities along the way!" (But I didn't.) When Paul explicated his faith in the Romans epistle, "God's gospel concerning his Son," he basically entitled his message (Rom. 1:1–3), he argued strongly that both Jew and Gentile had the same need for the gospel (1:18–3:20). And this glorious gospel he characterized as offering a righteousness "given through faith in Jesus Christ to all who believe. There is no difference between Jew and Gentile, for all have sinned and fall short of the glory of God" (3:22–23). Thus, Christology must remain at the heart of our discussions.

In recent decades Jewish scholars have shown renewed interest in the historical Jesus, and Christian scholars have rediscovered more fully the Jewishness of Jesus. This is another avenue of possible scholarly crosspollination which could enhance the conversation. I often remark to my students that Jews and Christians have an awkward relationship, but we pray to the same God that Jesus prayed to—we are at least *cousins!* We're stuck with each other, like it or not!

As a Christian, my prayer is that my Jewish friends will come to know God as "the God and Father of our Lord Jesus Christ" in the filial consciousness that Jesus offers. From my travels in the Middle East, I have sensed at times an "antichrist spirit" with animus toward both Christians and Jews. This may be another way in which we may be drawn together in mutual support in the potentially dark days ahead. This obviously less than scientific observation leads to a consideration of Christian-Muslim relations.

Because Jews, Christians, and Muslims share a common Abrahamic heritage, there is much on which to build meaningful dialogue. Many Christians are shocked to discover that Muslims actually believe in Jesus. Of course, this belief differs categorically from Christian beliefs concerning Jesus. It is not the trust in Christ for salvation that Christianity preaches. But Muslims accept the virginal conception of Jesus and the special role of Mary. They embrace Jesus' status as the Messiah of Israel. They acknowledge the miracles of Christ. But they stop short of the Christian profession of Christ as the crucified and risen Savior of mankind. Jesus was only a prophet, special though he was, in the succession of prophets leading to *the* prophet, Muhammad. In fact, according to the Qur'an, Jesus was not crucified at all—certainly there was no atoning sacrifice for the sins of humanity. Jesus simply was not the divine Son of God. The Christian-Muslim conversation will probably have two foci in terms of evaluating Christian claims. (Christians in turn would be expected to give a hearing concerning the Qur'an and Muhammed.) The two core issues would be differing concepts of monotheism and, of course, Christology.[10]

These two dialogues are illustrative of the challenges we face in doing theology in a global context. Veli-Matti Kärkkäinen has pioneered in addressing these issues and provides this helpful assessment:

---

10 See the following for sage counsel in this arena of scholarship: Paul Louis Metzger, *Connecting Christ: How to Discuss Jesus in a World of Diverse Paths* (Nashville: Thomas Nelson, 2012); Veli-Matti Kärkkäinen, *Christ and Reconciliation*, A Constructive Theology for the Pluralistic World, vol. 1 (Grand Rapids: Eerdmans, 2013), 236–90.

Indeed, of all the turns in Christian theology in general and the study of Christology in particular, the 'turn to other religions' will be the most scary but at the same time potentially the most fruitful with regard to the continual mission of the Christian church.[11]

CHRISTOLOGY AND RELIGIOUS EXPERIENCE

We come full circle now to the themes with which we began our explorations of Christology. The future of Christology lies with those who have a vital experience with the living Christ. In my opinion, that is the primary explanation for the shift of the growth of Christianity to Asia, Africa, and Latin America and toward a Pentecostal/charismatic spirituality. It is humbling for the churches in Europe and America to watch their own precipitous decline. Their theological enterprise has continued to flourish, but too often without an accompanying spiritual vitality. In missionary endeavors one of the significant developments has been the efforts to provide essential biblical, theological, and practical training for the leaders of the explosive spiritual movements in the developing nations. The obverse side of these efforts is the spiritual impact that often occurs with these encounters. Viable Christianity in every era has perennially entailed an integration of heart and head.

> *In order for our Christology to be sound, our experience of Christ must be vital. In order for our experience of Christ to be vital, our Christology must be biblically and theologically grounded.*

In order for our Christology to be sound, our experience of Christ must be vital. In order for our experience of Christ to be vital, our Christology must be biblically and theologically grounded. Christology is penultimate. The worship and mission of the church is ultimate,

---

11 Veli-Matti Kärkkäinen, *Christology: A Global Introduction* (Grand Rapids: Baker Academic, 2003), 288.

and Christology exists to serve those biblical purposes. To rip the theological enterprise from the context of the worshipping, witnessing, and serving church is to innervate it. Jesus Christ is alive and moving across the globe. That is the most important reality of which to be aware. The study of Christology is profoundly dependent upon this vital reality and exists to serve it.

Conclusion

Now the eleven disciples went to Galilee, to the mountain to which Jesus had directed them. When they saw him, they worshiped him; but some doubted. And Jesus came and said to them, "All authority in heaven and on earth has been given to me. Go therefore and make disciples of all nations, baptizing them in the name of the Father and of the Son and of the Holy Spirit, and teaching them to obey everything that I have commanded you. And remember, I am with you always, to the end of the age (Matt. 28:16–20 NRSV).

We began our journey with Mark's account of the crucifixion and Jesus' cry of dereliction (Mark 15:25–34). We end with the Great Commission from the risen Jesus. The deity of our Lord is now in full view. And the Son of God now returns to the glory he has had with the Father and the Holy Spirit from all eternity. He reminds us that he has all authority and sends us on a mission of making disciples of all the people groups of the world. And most importantly, he assures us that he will be with us to the end of the age.

This is a fitting ending to our journey through his life and ministry. Each generation must discover the wonders of Jesus for themselves. If we are faithful to his Great Commission and live by his Great Commandment, we will see a Great Church ready and waiting for him when he returns. Actually, we will no matter what—because he is with us to the end of the age! Our Vicar became our Victim to emerge as Victor and to share with us his victory.

ALL GLORY AND PRAISE TO OUR RISEN KING!

About Larry Hart

An ordained Southern Baptist minister, Dr. Larry Hart received his B.A. in psychology from ORU and his M.Div. and Ph.D. from the Southern Baptist Theological Seminary in Louisville, Kentucky.

Dr. Hart has pastored churches in Indiana, Kentucky, Oklahoma, Texas, and Florida and served as Chaplain of the University at ORU from 1981 to 1984. He has had the privilege of planting two churches—one in Kentucky and one in Oklahoma. Presently he serves as Professor of Theology in the Oral Roberts University Graduate School of Theology and Ministry, where he has taught for more than thirty years.

From time to time, Dr. Hart picks up his guitar and croons a tune. His claim to fame is that while a junior high student in his hometown of Odessa, Texas, he sang in a quartet with Larry Gatlin. The group named themselves the Silvertones (after Dr. Hart's Sears Silvertone guitar). Dr. Hart played for ORU's basketball team during student days and can still be found on the basketball court at Life Time Fitness center today. He loves to travel and to preach—and gladly accepts invitations to do both!

Other Books by Larry Hart

Truth Aflame

Christianity in 3D: A Three-Dimensional Perspective on the Most Powerful Force on Earth

For God So Loved the World: The Biblical Doctrine of Grace

www.ingramcontent.com/pod-product-compliance
Lightning Source LLC
Chambersburg PA
CBHW050635300426
44112CB00012B/1809